Life without Principles

Life without Principles

Reconciling Theory and Practice

JOSEPH MARGOLIS

BLACKWELL
Publishers

First published 1996
2 4 6 8 10 9 7 5 3 1

Blackwell Publishers Inc.
238 Main Street
Cambridge, Massachusetts 02142, USA

Blackwell Publishers Ltd
108 Cowley Road
Oxford OX4 1JF
UK

Library of Congress Cataloging-in-Publication Data
Margolis, Joseph, 1924–
Life without Principles: reconciling theory and practice / by
Joseph Margolis.
p. cm.
Includes bibliographical references and index.
ISBN 0–631–17462–1 (alk. paper). – ISBN 0–631–19502–5 (pbk. alk. paper)
1. Ethics. 2. Theory (Philosophy) 3. Practice (Philosophy)
I. Title.
BJ1031.M312 1996
170–ac20   95-36405
                                                                          CIP

British Library Cataloguing in Publication Data

A CIP catalogue record for this book is available from the British Library.

Typeset in 10 on 12 pt Sabon by CentraCet Ltd, Cambridge
Printed in Great Britain by Hartnolls Ltd, Bodmin, Cornwall

This book is printed on acid-free paper

Contents

Wisdom in moral matters?

    – certainly, utter failure in first principles
    – certainly, irreconcilable intuitions
    – certainly, blindness within ideology and history

Preface

To me, it seems very natural, ten years after having completed *Pragmatism without Foundations*, that this account of moral questions and the relationship between theory and practice should form the fourth volume of what was originally planned as a trilogy. I suppose I did not see at the start that it would be needed or how it would play itself out. Looking back on the entire effort, I find it difficult to suppose that its main argument was not already forming in my mind in working through the trilogy. But I have no memory of having dwelt on it. It now makes more than good sense in terms of my own grander dreams of reclaiming pragmatism in our late age.

I have tried my hand several times at moral theory, never, however, without misgivings wherever I presumed to speak about how people should live. Philosophy has never seemed to me to be a proper training for any such presumption. And yet, I feel that I have, here, succeeded in some measure in joining the point of that uneasiness with an equally serious commitment on the substantive matter. I hope so. Because, ultimately, the inability of professional philosophers to bring their skills to bear in a fresh and convincing way to the question of how we should live is, to my thinking, the supreme mark of philosophy's self-delusion. It is very hard, in speaking of moral matters, to hide the obvious nonsense of what one utters – it is much harder to hide nonesense there than in what may be said in musing abstractly about Truth and Reality and Meaning and Knowledge. Yet, in a pragmatist vision, theory is itself a form of practice; and so, in a sense, our answers to the largest questions of metaphysics and epistemology are rightly instructed (at least in part) by what we may have discovered about moral matters.

I see that now, well after the fact. I believed it before but hadn't worked out the required connections. For me, the thread of the entire undertaking lies with the idea and process of history. In a strange way, it was always hidden by the original pragmatists. It appears as evolution in Peirce (and Dewey), as the rejection of fixed dualisms in Dewey, as flux in James, and as social constitution in Mead. But it almost never appears in its own name. My trilogy, I suppose, has been my labyrinth for that discovery. Having now exited into the light once again, I confess I see almost no philosophies about me that are committed to the postulate that thinking *is* history – is historicized. The idea is Hegel's, of coure, although Hegel was no pragmatist. It doesn't matter. We have the benefit of two hundred years of honing the idea, of freeing it from its florid sources. I call that recovery pragmatism also – that is, the marriage of the themes of flux and historicity. But its career is largely not American and even not English-language. You cannot make it out without Marx, Nietzsche, Dilthey, Heidegger, Adorno, Gadamer, or Foucault. But you cannot hold on to it in its strongest form without the work of the older pragmatists. The reason, I believe, is that the great tradition of twentieth-century analytic philosophy, which has deliberately opposed both classical pragmatism and continental philosophy, has itself been increasingly infected (if that's the right word) by the conceptual disorders it has opposed – apart from the curious fact that both the late pragmatists and the late continental philosophers have themselves noticeably estranged the idea of history. I believe these three "crowds" of philosophers are destined to find a common ground in recouping the theme of history. If they come together in this way, they will find the argument of this book waiting for them.

I am convinced that, now, at the turn of the century (and the millennium), philosophy is at the edge of a very large transformation. In fact, the whole of Western society is at a turning point that we cannot yet fully fathom. That prospect invites a long discussion of its own, although I concede that it may be considerably postponed. It is hardly inevitable, though I think it cannot be stopped. It will sweep out the principal canons of English-language philosophy at least. The changes are already dawning in the philosophy of science. When they are collected as well in a plausible way in moral philosophy, the transformation will accelerate. For moral philosophy has a closer link to the motive powers of history than our grander metaphysical speculations, wherever the latter fail to reflect the state of the sciences. In this fourth volume, then, I bring my own inquiries to bear on the point of changing our moral vision in as radical a way as I can support. Doubtless, bolder conceptions will spring up. But I take some oblique satisfaction in observing that there is, now, almost nothing in Western moral and political philosophy that is not reactive and backward-looking on normative matters. We need to be alerted to the needs of conceptual invention. We are now in that sort of intellectual lull that is the sure sign of misperception. Philosophy requires a meteorological instinct.

Much of this book proceeds by polemic. It cannot have been otherwise, since (I am persuaded) most of current moral philosophy is profoundly doubtful in its *philosophical* intuitions. I admit I am bent on clearing the woods. But I am unwilling to offer nothing beyond a destructive critique. In the epiloque, you will find a compendious statement of a reconstruction of how (on the strength of the gathering polemic) to view moral matters in a new way. I leave it to you to judge its merit.

I must add a particular word of thanks to Raeshon Sykes and Nadia Kravchenko for putting a particularly messy manuscript into final form. also, as always, to many dear friends who have given me good advice and the benefit of their judgment. I'm afraid I can no longer single them out or say just how they have helped me. This book, then, is theirs as much as mine.

J.M.

Acknowledgments

Some of the chapters in this book have incorporated, in altered form, materials that have appeared elsewhere. These include: "Moral Realism and the Meaning of Life," *Philosophical Forum*, XXXI, 1, Fall (1990); "A Reckoning of Sorts on the Prospects of Moral Philosophy," *Philosophic Exchange*, Nos 24–5 (1993–4); "Rawls on Justice – Once Again," in J. Ralph Lindgren (ed.) *Horizons of Justice* (New York: Peter Lang, 1995); "Moral Optimism," in G. B. Madison (ed.) *The Ethics of Postmodernity* (Evanston: Northwestern University Press, 1996); "Moral Philosophy in Four Tiers," in Thomas Magnell (ed.) *Explorations of Value* (Amsterdam: Rodopi, 1996).

Prologue

A Sense of the Issue

I

It is a great irony that recent changes in the orientation of the philosophy of science have deliberately favored reversing the canonical relationship between theory and practice. For its part, moral philosophy has tended to construe the problem of practical reason as even more reliably directed by theoretical reason, or some theoretically endorsed consensus, than might otherwise have been supposed convincing. These reversals have been gathering strength in the last third of our century more or less in tandem. The sciences have proved so impressive that theorists hardly fear that the admission of any deep methodological or epistemological informalities – or doubts – will place their achievement at serious risk. By contrast, uncertainty about the objective pretensions of moral claims has noticeably worsened, possibly in part as a result of the perceived dangers of diverse, often opposed, even politically unstable societies that cannot be counted on to converge satisfactorily in support of the moral truisms different pockets of Western theories have usually favored. As a result (or so it seems), moral philosophy has redoubled its efforts to claim the firmest objective grounds it can imagine – somehow reconciled theoretically with the undeniable diversity of global life – in its effort to legitimate its own notions of validity. The best efforts of the philosophy of science now face the question of interpreting the conceptual significance of the stable achievements of the best sciences under conditions that can no longer claim anything like an algorithmic precision or fixity. But conceptual risks in theorizing about the epistemic resources of the physical sciences hardly disturb our confidence in their first-order mapping of the world; whereas uncertainty about the legitimative credentials of moral judgment and moral commitment profoundly threaten our first-order confidence in the supposed norms of practical life. Moral philosophy, it seems, cannot easily risk second-order doubts about the objective norms of politics or law or morality as deep or as candid as what is being increasingly aired in the philosophy of science. One ought not, however, rush to conclusions about the conceptual differences in the relationship between first- and second-order questions affecting the sciences and morality, although there is indeed a puzzle there that demands attention.

The excesses of twentieth-century politics lend a certain urgency to our concern. How, we wonder, can we possibly condemn barbarian politics convincingly if we admit that our own best, most civilized values may be no more than dogmas themselves? Or, if you believe otherwise (one may imagine the challenge taking form), please state clearly (if you can) the objective basis for your claim. The fear is: you cannot answer! And so, philosophers troubled in their responsible souls retreat instinctively to even more inflexible legitimative strategies than were ever trotted out by the positivists or the defenders of the unity of science program.

You will find the irony incipient in the work of such figures as Thomas Kuhn and Paul Feyerabend. Kuhn is almost singlehandedly responsible for entrenching the now-perceived impossibility of disjoining the theoretical assessment of the actual work of the sciences from the assessment of the living practice and history of the societies on which such work depends and gains its meanings.[1] I don't mean by that that Kuhn was the first to grasp the bearing of science's history on the formation of our theorising understanding. Of course not. But Kuhn has had an inordinately large influence on the whole Anglo-American philosophy of science as well as on those currents, chiefly of German and Austrian origin (as in the work of the Berlin and Vienna Circles and within the more informal network that grew up around Karl Popper), that have dominated Western philosophies of science since nearly the beginning of the century.

I am tempted to say that Kuhn managed to accomplish, particularly in the English-language world, what Hegel and Marx could not. I hope you will allow the exaggeration: it points to the remarkable mystery of Kuhn's having been at the right place at the right historical moment, as well as the general irrelevance of his conservatism regarding the process of history and his occasional confusions. For his part, Feyerabend trained himself meticulously to play the role of court jester of philosophy against the same company of philosophers of science that Kuhn addressed. As an avowed philosophical anarchist or Protagorean, Feyerabend willingly endorsed a world of flux and rejected any and all fixed principles of rational thought or of what is real,[2] in doing that, he obliged many, more systematically occupied with the epistemological fortunes of science, to defend their theories in terms of the actual history of social and professional practice. John Earman confirms that Carnap found Kuhn's monograph "congenial"[3] – which flies in the face of the familiar picture of Carnap as a doctrinaire positivist. And I know from personal experience that Herbert Feigl was enormously hospitable to Feyerabend's extravagant attacks on the orthodoxy of the unity of science program – at various meetings Feigl arranged at the University of Minnesota, when his department served as a center for the best American efforts in the philosophy of science. In fact, it would not be far from the truth to discern in Imre Lakatos's risky notion of "research programs" an inadequate (but well-intentioned) compromise between the practice-centered conceptions of Kuhn and Feyerabend (distanced, to be sure, by Lakatos himself, as well as, more archly, by Popper) and the theory-driven visions of the inductivists and the (Popperian) falsificationists.[4]

My purpose, here, is not to review the history of the philosophy of science. I do wish to lay a proper ground for considering the inseparability of the philosophical fortunes of science and morality in cognitive and/or rational terms – and perhaps I have already made something of a start. I introduced the reversal mentioned in order to draw attention in an arresting way to the peculiar, relatively unacknowledged (but certainly worrisome) vulnerability of moral theory at the present time. I don't mean to suggest that the penny contrast I've imputed to the fortunes of science and morality is entirely reliable. I don't believe it is. But it serves to feature the profound uneasiness with which moral philosophy now pursues its usual questions regarding the objective standing of would-be norms and values and the cognitive and practical resources by which we claim to validate our judgments and commitments.

The reversal affecting moral philosophy is, I think, accurately attributed. It represents a retreat from a conception risked on the priorities of history and collective practice – just those themes, as I say, that have begun to claim an initial following in the philosophy of science. Current philosophies of science show a distinct skepticism about the autonomy of epistemological theory: the good news is that such doubts are a sign of strength, not a source of weakness. But if you recall such diverse figures as Dewey, Nietzsche, Hegel, Marx, Gadamer, and Foucault, you cannot fail to notice that recent moral philosophy (chiefly analytic – and Anglo-American) has largely (though not entirely) abandoned the themes of history and *praxis* that are now being taken up (however thinly) by mainstream theories in the philosophy of science. I say it is a fact that the best moral theorists of our day – at least the most visible, the most influential, the most debated – have closed ranks firmly enough to offset the impression that moral philosophy has lost its way in legitimative matters or that those theorists have lost the right to claim that they have not lost their way. To make their case, they bring practical reason under the strict control of theoretical reason, or they elevate practical reason to a status rivaling theoretical reason; but they do so so dubiously – in fact, as blatant partisans – that recent moral theories are seen to have spawned conceptual infelicities that mark their own labors in a pointedly lame way.

I say that all the standard assurances about moral philosophy are quite hollow now. Perhaps they always were. But the perception of the weight of the role of history has changed, and it has deepened our sense of theoretical unease. It might have done so as well in theorizing about the sciences, except for the obvious fact that the sciences have prospered; their success is not altogether immune to legitimative quarrel, but the quarrels that arise are plainly tempered by a steady sense of the robust realism that, in holist terms (that is, in terms that yield nothing in the way of the truth of particular claims), can hardly be denied. That's not the case at all with realist pretensions regarding moral truths. A sneeze in the direction of legitimative doubt produces a spate of first-order moral colds. And yet, I don't believe the prospects of a strong moral theory are actually weak. Far from it. It's only that our leading moral philosophers have little appreciation of the substantive role of history in forming a plausible account of moral objectivity. It's the very contingency of history, of context, of practical judgment that cannot claim theoretical fixities, that frightens the leading theorists. Lacking the easy assurance of the physical sciences, they fall back instinctively (but inappropriately) to strengthening the canon along the strictest ahistorical lines, when all the signs point to the need to abandon what can no longer be thus secured. In the bargain, the needed fixities are confidently affirmed, but their legitimating arguments are hardly to be found. There you have the breeding ground for nervous and insistent ideologies.

I emphasize the central role of moral philosophy of course, but I treat the "moral" as a metonym for all the forms of practical reason – for all the forms of reason applied in judgment and action to the particularities of actual life. I don't pretend that "practical reason" is a settled notion. Far from it. It is surely hardly more than a dummy term, a placeholder for all accounts of a responsible sort regarding how to claim (or whether we can rightly claim) that judgments and commitments made in the name of practical norms *are* demonstrably capable of justifying verdicts of "objectivity," "neutrality," "reasonableness," and the like. Here, the quarrel extends to moral, political, legal, economic, religious, educational, also artistic and critical and interpretive matters – and even to laboratory and theorizing efforts in the sciences as far as they bear on truth and knowledge – although the pertinent similarities in normative respects are not always acknowledged.

Thinkers who are severe about the pretensions of moral claims (but not of science) – John Mackie, for instance[5] – are sometimes oblivious to the fact that the objective standing of normative predicates is just as problematic in the sciences as in the moral sphere. At any rate, they often neglect to explain or justify the putative differences between the two. (I don't deny that there are differences, but they are not – I claim – differences that would justify the familiar disjunction between theory and practice, or between theoretical and practical "reason," or between the supposed epistemic resources of science and morality.) That is what is so instructive about Kuhn and Feyerabend's example – read without prejudice to the strength or weakness of their respective claims.

What I have in mind in urging a reconsideration of the relation between theory and practice rests with the fact that many of our leading moral theorists – again, chiefly American (or Anglo-American) and German – have fallen back to endorsing (uncritically, as far as I can see) the supposed invariances of "practical reason," even within the flux of history. Much of what I undertake in what follows, therefore, is occupied with dismantling (for cause) all those pretensions in the name of practical reason. It may strike you as improbable, but there is a distinct convergence on the *theory* of reason that collects such companions as John Rawls, Alasdair MacIntyre, Karl-Otto Apel, Jürgen Habermas, and Hans-Georg Gadamer. I cannot, at this moment, afford more than a hint of the nature of the "universal" powers of practical reason shared by these philosophers, and I have nothing as yet to say about the relative strengths of their particular theories. But their agreement is more strategic than doctrinaire; and it is their strategies that I call into question. Without legitimative support, their doctrines are hardly more than pious hopes. The danger is that moral zeal is more than merely plentiful and plainly at war with itself.

Gadamer, for instance, although clearly drawn to a bold form of historicity, unaccountably relents, reverses himself, and claims to have found that all the disparate local histories that we can number confirm the enduring presence of a ubiquitous, single, recurrent, relatively unchanging "classical" norm of humane llfe – in spite of the fact that each individual human "I" and "you" is actually *constituted*, socially, *by local histories*. Gadamer offers no argument in support of his confidence; and the idea is completely baffling in the context of his own account.[6] It is even somewhat dangerous in its presumed plausibility: it is, I suggest, much too sanguine and reassuring, given the meager reasons it can muster.

I am persuaded that the German moral and cultural theorists who survived the Nazis feel particularly obligated to give evidence of their bona fides (as humanists or liberals or something of the sort), regardless of what their particular doctrines entail. I cannot imagine what else might explain Gadamer's adherence to the invariance of the "classical." He dare not confess, I think, that the classical is as partisan or as contingent historically and philosophically as the normative pretensions of any other age or school. The German world would be very uneasy *just now* without the assurance of a reliable moral anchor – preferably one drawn from an idealized Hellenic world (that "must" have penetrated Africa and Asia, say) if not one actually drawn from father Kant.[7] (Recall Habermas and Apel, here.) Surely, the American devotion to liberalism, affirmed again and again in the most admired moral philosophies, is made of the same straw.

The point of taking notice of these accommodations is to expose the implied conspiracy of moral theorists who, however generous-minded, betray their discipline for would-be lofty visions. They give up the pretense of laboriously reclaiming the objectivity of moral norms. But which policy is more dangerous, I ask: the frank admission that we cannot defeat the barbarians we fear by merely intoning *our* moral "heritage," or the insistence that our philosophy endorses *our* ideology at all costs? I see no difference in this regard in the labors of Gadamer, Habermas, Apel, Rawls, or MacIntyre – to remind ourselves of a number of the most influential moral theorists of the day. There is also no prospect of improving the tale by adding to this tally others (drawn from the English-language world) such as Alan Gewirth, Alan Donagan, Thomas Nagel, Robert Nozick, Stuart Hampshire, David Wiggins, John McDowell, Sabina Lovibond, David Gauthier, Richard Bernstein, Charles Taylor, John Kekes. They have all missed the essential theorem I find adumbrated (hardly perfected) in Kuhn's and Feyerabend's profound subversion of the supposed invariances of theoretical reason: viz., that *thinking is historied, historicized*, an artifact of one cultural practice or another, largely intelligible in its variant forms across the entire human family, but variable nonetheless – particularly in the choice of normative values. I don't mean by that that the forms of human thought or reason are completely plastic, invented, merely "normalized" in different societies. We must surely concede that the flowering of different cultures is grounded in some way in the biological limitations and dispositions of the species. But we hardly know what that entails; and what we do know assures us (if that is the right term) that what it permits or endorses is already too diverse to support the universalized normative pretensions of the theorists mentioned. Any objective moral philosophy must begin with the patent spread of plural ideologies and strangely diverse traditions. (The philosophy of science *begins* with more agreement about the achievement of the *sciences*.)

Perhaps this is close to what Wittgenstein meant in speaking of the human *Lebensform* (in the singular).[8] But if it is, then, since the *Lebensform* was intended in a holist way and not in any essentialist way, no determinate consequences of a normative sort drawn from it can possibly be brought to bear on actual human behavior. By that logic, humans cannot violate "human nature" or the human *Lebensform*. There may be good reason for opposing this or that particular behavior, but it cannot be derived from a critical reading of the *Lebensform*. Furthermore, if that is so, then much of the movement known as "moral realism," which has recently sought to derive or recover objective moral norms in an oblique way from Wittgenstein's notion, or from analogues drawn from the would-be normative conditions of shared meanings and communicative success in natural languages or of truth in ordinary practical circumstances, cannot possibly succeed.[9] All such maneuvers and countermaneuvers constitute, I suggest, a certain busy work resulting from the enormous inertia of Western moral philosophy anxious about its ideological correctness.

The point at issue is a double one: first, that now, philosophy, like science (and moral philosophy, like the philosophy of science), cannot ignore or deny its own historicized setting; and second that, admitting that, it cannot recover any form of privileged neutrality, objectivity, universality, apodicticity, apriority, or modal necessity. We cannot ensure the human relevance of science or morality without recovering the human subject, and we cannot recover the human subject without recovering its historicized life. Philosophy admits that its findings arise out of the experience of actual societies, but it resists the full import of that admission.

II

I concede that I am arguing for a clean sweep of moral theories. I find most of the going theories preposterous – not that they lack subtlety, humane instinct, structural ingenuity, plausible intuition. But their executive presumptions are all wrong. I am arguing against the grain, therefore. But consider the objections. First of all, all theories that rely on a universal rational consensus regarding norms and values (Rawls's view, for instance) or that assume that what such a consensus would require can be reliably known (Apel's and Habermas's view, for instance), are utterly implausible, utterly suspect. I am not arguing the matter here, merely serving notice of certain obvious targets. Rawls offers no argument whatsoever in his own behalf; and those that Apel and Habermas advance are entirely uncompelling. (I shall turn to the evidence in due time.) Secondly, no theories that admit that reason and cognitive competence are artifacts of historical constitution can possibly demonstrate that such competence can yield a universal consensus on normative matters or a neutral form of rational judgment in either inter- or intrasocietal disputes (contrary to the views of Gadamer and Mac-Intyre). Thirdly, no theories can reconcile universalism with historicism in such a way as to ensure a universal consensus of any kind as a basis of moral objectivity (contrary to the views of Habermas and Apel). Fourthly, there are no known arguments that confirm that moral norms and values can be discerned in nature or reality at large (contrary to the views of the Aristotelian tradition), and there are no known arguments that demonstrate that there must be a universal principle or rule that can determine what, on rational or objective grounds, would count as morally admissible (contrary to the views of the Kantian tradition). The point is that nearly all the strategies favored in the disputes of current moral philosophy are occupied with one or another of the dubious doctrines just mentioned or implied – or others that are even less attractive. A deeper question that all this raises is whether there might not be very different, possibly more promising, options overlooked (or even rejected) by the dominant philosophies of the day. I believe there are, and I believe they are rather easy to identify.

I am not urging a clever form of skepticism or nihilism or irrational-ism. By and large, the moral philosophies of the academy have simply taken a wrong turn. It is that wrong turn – if anything – that nourishes skepticism. What is the right path? you ask. It begins with a genuine sense of just how unlikely it is that we shall ever be able to claim convincingly that we have found once and for all (or are getting closer to finding) the unique, objective, neutral, universal, rationally necessary, invariant, natural, self-evident basis for the moral norms and values we prefer. All the epithets just listed are fatally compromised in the history of philosophical debate. Admitting that, I say, is the beginning of conceptual success!

Here, moral philosophy properly instructs epistemology and methodology; our permanent inability to discern – simply and straightforwardly – the right, the good, the obligatory, the forbidden, the permissible, the virtuous, we may be sure, applies to the counterpart distinctions of all our inquiries: the true, the false, the factual, the real, the actual, the objective, the rational. The world is not transparent enough to ensure such direct findings. They are artifacts of our inquiries. We must construct our sense of what the world is like as well as our sense of our competence to discern what our world is like, and then – at considerable risk – propose within the terms of that construction what to count as objectivity and truth and rational judgment.

As I say, the point is not the destructive skeptic's toy; it is rather that our theories of what is true and good (and the rest) are always *second-best* – in just the sense in which Plato was concerned in the *Statesman* (really, everywhere in the Dialogues), with (a) the cognitive intransparency of the world and our cognitive powers, and (b) the awareness that we can never convincingly claim possession of any cognitive resource (knowledge of the Forms, for instance) by which the world and our powers are made transparent enough to justify claiming more than a "second-best" doctrine. I urge that all moral philosophy is of the "second-best" sort, that we know we cannot escape such limitations, that canonical philosophies refuse (however obscurely) to admit the fact, that as a result they are hardly more than self-congratulatory dogmas.

The admission releases a world of possibilities the academy resists or refuses to examine. There's the benefit of Kuhn's and Feyerabend's subversion. For what they espied was that the philosophy of science was also a second-best conjecture (which Plato had already grasped) – because *theorizinq is itself a form of practice*, of cognizing and rationalising practice. Any (would-be) principled distinction between the epistemic pretensions of "theoretical reason" and "practical reason" – as in endorsing Aristotle's fantastic doctrine of *nous* (or the equally fantastic inductivist's doctrine: that we may approximate, by observational and experimental increments, ever more closely to the essential lawlike invariances of nature) – presupposes some cognitive privilege or other. In short, the denial of privilege is tantamount to what I am calling the "second-best" standing of our would-be cognitive and rational powers.

Nothing so far said is meant to be the least discouraging about science or morality. It serves only to disallow unsupported claims about our objectivity and competence in inquiries of either sort. "Second-best" signifies that whatever objectivity we may plausibly claim for the legitimation of our science or morality is an artifact of conjectures dialectically opposed to those (canonical) conjectures that have proceeded as if we were *not* thus constrained. Now, at the end of the century, we may dare to pursue a "second-best" strategy. I say only that such a strategy is almost unknown in the annals of contemporary philosophy, except where it is meant in a more disruptive or skeptical spirit – as among so-called "postmodernists" (Richard Rorty, most bafflingly).[10] Philosophy is inherently bound to something like the Socratic *elenchus*: it knows no way of escaping the limitations of the second-best. (In my opinion, there is considerable political danger in ignoring the fact.)

I should add – returning to my tally of the lines of resistance against the canons of privilege – that there is no assured sense that we could possibly ever identify what, among the supposed instances of morally admirable behavior, could *never* be plausibly condemned (or vice versa). For instance, on matters that bear on the moral treatment of oneself (suicide, sexual deviance, the development of one's talents and capacities) or that bear on the puzzle cases near or involving the beginning or the end of life (abortion, euthanasia, capital punishment, the sacrifice of innocent lives), there are no reliable disjunctions between what is moral and what is immoral. How is it possible, you may ask, that we can make any progress at all, philosophically, under such circumstances? Well, gains *are* possible. But only, I insist, on the assumption that we are working within the limits of a second-best conceptual space.

I must mention another item for my tally, therefore: namely, that there is no principled disjunction between "objective" moral norms, moral principles, moral rules, moral criteria, moral values, and whatever we imagine is opposed to the pronouncements of practical reason lying within convenient neutral reach just below our breastbone. There is no assured neutrality of that sort! Moral philosophy conducted according to a "second-best" policy no longer enjoys the luxury of dismissing *a priori* any sincerely held convictions that might otherwise invite derogatory charges – as being not "neutral," or "disinterested," or "objective," or "rational," or "natural," or "normal," or "self-evident," or "consensually confirmed," or "humane," or the like. Because, of course, all such dismissals are themselves self-serving and the targets of other forceful ideologies. I view that lesson as a part of Nietzsche's lesson about the self-deceptive nature of conventional morality. The upshot is that much of what I must (and will) undertake in what follows includes an exposé of the general conceptual disorder that obtains among the canonical views. If the charge holds, then (I concede) the specimen doctrines I examine cannot possibly have more than transitory interest.

I'm afraid that verdict is probably correct. It is, for instance, well-nigh impossible to develop a serious account of recent moral philosophy in America or Germany without close attention to Rawls or Habermas.

They are obviously ideologues – of whatever expert competence you may imagine. And yet Rawls and Habermas endure as eminent moral philosophers. They really do endure: because, as I say, there is a widespread unacknowledged fear (terror, almost) that the barbarian "moralities" are pressing at the stockade gates and must be resisted. Liberalism is the philosophical kriptonite of the West meant to keep the barbarian hordes from entering. (Although, of course, they are surely already among us.) And because, more significantly, Rawls's and Habermas's moral visions are recognizably attenuated, pared-down, cleverly diminished versions of the great Kantian doctrine that must be counted among the few that truly dominate the moral imagination of the West. They are pared-down so far that Kant's transcendental excesses never quite afford a reasonable target; and they are so robust in the Kantian spirit that they never quite seem vulnerable in the way of ideology. MacIntyre's Aristotelianism is, I think, very similarly "adjusted" to Aristotle's master vision. The whole tendency to find a new canon for legitimating moral doctrines close to the old canon is a grand retreat to Kant and Aristotle – and lesser figures, Hume for instance.

But that only points to part of the necessary labor. If we are to make a fresh beginning, we cannot fall back to the postmodernists. The postmodernists believe that if there is to be any philosophy, it must be privileged – it must be able to discern conceptual necessity, exceptionless invariance, cognitive certainty, the universal requirements of reason, legitimatize first principles, and the like. Since, as they also believe, such findings never fall within the human ken, philosophy must be at an end.[11] There's the charm of the second-best strategy; it offers a fresh option between the transcendentalists and the postmodernists, between privilege and skepticism. We must ask ourselves whether it is still possible to construct an objective moral philosophy (or a philosophy of science, for that matter) in which (a) cognitive privilege of every sort is refused (b) our rational and cognitive powers are thought to be constructed within a constructed world, and (c) our sense of what may be defended in accord with (a) and (b) is itself historicized. There is no account of this sort in the whole of Anglo-American philosophy. Dewey has perhaps caught a very small part of it; Nietzsche another; and in our own time, Michel Foucault has probably come closest to its nerve.[12] But there is no sustained account that works its way patiently through the principal literature: the literature that shows why the canon fails and why the new option need not fail.

You cannot, however, admit items (a) – (c) without also admitting that the epistemic fortunes of moral and scientific inquiry are inseparable.[13] That is the reason the historicized and fluxive tendencies in Kuhn and

Feyerabend are so instructive. For, by and large, contemporary moral philosophies avoid such concessions, whereas philosophies of science no longer do. It is inquiries that can claim only the weakest credentials that usually make the most strenuous charges. I should add – entirely out of the blue – that I regard any philosophy that subscribes to (a) – (c), now, at the end of the century, as a straightforward form of *pragmatism*. (I say this, knowing full well that the classic pragmatists respected history but had little interest in historicity – the historied structure of sheer thinking.) The best prospects for the philosophy of science and moral philosophy belong, accordingly, in the pragmatist camp – to be deployed along strategic lines frankly incompatible with the general intuitions of Aristotle and Kant and their contemporary enthusiasts.

Nevertheless, no one is entirely clear about what new resources and new limitations will confront us, once we accept the constraints of a second-best strategy. We must proceed with a certain dialectical care. I have no intention of anticipating what moral visions make sense under these altered circumstances. I am certain of one thing, however: if we proceed in the second-best way, there cannot be any exclusively correct or exclusively viable resolution of the question of moral (or scientific) objectivity. You will find, I believe, that that concession leads directly to a form of relativism. The argument is hardly obvious. But what I wish to emphasise is that conditions (a) – (c), mentioned a moment ago, entail admitting the possible validity of objective truth-claims or rational commitments that, on a bivalent logic but not now, would be judged incompatible or contradictory.[14] I mean you to understand that departing from canonical views – rejecting privilege and embracing historicity – will inevitably lead to fundamental changes in our conception of objectivity itself.

III

To put the point in a nutshell: if, for instance, you cannot show that suicide as such is either right or wrong in bivalent terms (whether in terms of truth and falsity or of something like a bivalent reading of what is obligatory and forbidden), in spite of the fact that a moral policy on suicide may be needed, may even be central to one's moral vision, then you have no recourse but to consider a relativistic logic of the sort I am hinting at. But to admit that much is already to concede that the entire canonical approach to moral theory may be replaced by a relativistic and historicized account that refuses to countenance exclusionary options (without yet affirming that "anything goes").

All I need emphasize at this point is that the proposal is plainly coherent, hospitable to competing and conflicting normative intuitions, opposed to privilege of every sort, consistent with the tally (given above) of objections against the principal theorists of our time, and open to substantive proposals that are not yet explicit. More needs to be said of course: otherwise, it would not be clear that the proposal of a second-best strategy would be worth the bother. Fine. You can already see that a moral theory of this sort is bound to be more flexible and more generous than the stricter, more ambitious theories Rawls and Habermas and MacIntyre favor. They, not I, rely on some normative invariance or other, or some cognitive or rational privilege, by means of which they are able to impose an inclusive system on the whole of human life. For my part, I see no reason why morality should be systematic in that way. But these are observations that merely hint at the conceptual flexibility possible under a second-best strategy.

Beyond that I offer two additional observations. Both concern the distinction between theory and practice. The first goes very deep. It's this. The discursive resources common to science and morality, common in fact to all human undertakings, include preeminently the resources of reference and predication; and the successful use of those resources in natural-language contexts already precludes an independent, rule-like, principled, or algorithmic practice – or any competence of reason – that does not accord with my so-called pragmatist conditions (a) – (c). If that is so – the thesis would need to be explained, of course – then the theorizing powers of reason could never rightly be disjoined from the conditions of social *praxis*; meaning, by "praxis," pretty well what Aristotle means by attending to the particular in the context of deliberate action, but (now) also in a sense entirely opposed to Aristotle's sanguine insistence on the autonomy of *theoria*.[15]

Once you give up invariance in world and thought (that is, give up the necessity of invariance, give up "modal" invariance) or treat invariance as an artifact encumbered by whatever rightly encumbers reference and predication,[16] "theoretical reason" becomes no more than a form of "practical reason," itself subject to all the contingencies of enculturing history and collective life. In short, the argument from reference and predication precludes Aristotle's disjunction between the powers of theoretical and practical reason as well as Kant's confidence regarding the autonomy of practical reason. There's a conceptual leap there, it's true, but the idea is entirely plausible and coherent. You can see well enough that Kant, in the *Foundations of the Metaphysics of Morals*, imputes to practical reason a theorizing competence (different, of course, from Aristotle's *nous* but easily as potent).

Between them, Aristotle and Kant champion the principal ways of segregating theoretical and practical reason, all the while each preserves (cleverly, you must admit) our capacity to discern invariance (in the world or in thought) sufficient to confirm the supposed objectivity and neutrality of science or morality or both. You see, therefore, how theories like Rawls's, Habermas's, MacIntyre's, and others' even less influential or less directly keyed to Aristotle's and Kant's doctrines hang by a philosophical thread that no one of them has actually secured – or, for that matter, rightly construed.

As I see the field, it is impossible to mount a convincing defense of any moral philosophy that departs from the canonical view without demonstrating in a reasonable way why the dominant theories *should* now be set aside. There's a thankless labor for you. But the innocent conspiracy of professional exchange that fastens on barely more than a half-dozen or so of the leading theories – among them, prominently, the ones I single out for the first stage of my account – would otherwise never acknowledge a wider run of viable strategies than the ones that seem already to have failed. To be candid, I cannot see how Rawls's or Habermas's theories could ever have become the influential theories they are, without their having been pressed to explain the relationship between reason and history. They have never been strenuously so pressed, however, and they have no answer. They pretty well neglect the question. As a consequence, their own claims unravel: their pedestrian ideologies begin to masquerade as high philosophy. MacIntyre, who cannot claim the same importance, does at least broach the question, although, in my opinion, he falls back too quickly to an ahistorical view of his own. But the pattern was surely already preset by the conventional reception of Aristotle and Kant.

In our time, Kant's transcendental project has been "recovered" (or "improved" by being placed) in the context of human history, as by Apel and Habermas (and Dilthey before them); and Aristotle's noetic direction of practical life has similarly been "strengthened" and "relevantly" attenuated by accommodating the entire variety of the forms of human life (as by MacIntyre and Nussbaum). But none of these champions has yet explained (or can explain) how the contingencies of history yield the exceptionless universalities they require.

I have, therefore, begun to mark out a small corner of a very large space. But I believe that what can be discovered in that corner, both in the way of diagnosis and correction, can be applied with little difficulty to every other sector of philosophical work. That accords with my intention in having drawn a conceptual link between moral philosophy and the philosophy of science. It points to a larger, still unfinished, story.

The second consideration I wish to mention bears on the radical import of interpreting the connection between theory and practice along the lines of historicity. It's not simply a matter of a change in local strategy. It is certainly that. But you may already see that a conceptual turn of such a sort, applicable (on the argument) to every serious inquiry, must also count as a reversal of the essential theme of the whole compendium of Western philosophy. Most of the liveliest work of Western philosophy ("analytic" and post-Kantian) may be read as a continuation of eighteenth-century philosophy distracted somehow by nineteenth-century historicism. There's an extravagance, I admit, that runs through Hegel and Marx and Nietzsche and Heidegger and Gadamer and Foucault. I have no wish to restore all that. But history must surely be recovered. Give up the idea that history must have an objective *telos*, or that history is inherently progressive, or that history is one encompassing process, or that there is a kind of strict necessity in history, or that certain gifted humans discern the laws of history or the unique fate of history. Give up all that, I say, and history – or better, the historied (or historicized) nature of thought – yields a new family of strategies for moral philosophy and, because of that, new exemplars for other sectors of philosophical inquiry.

I see, nevertheless, the possibility of reconciling the rigor of analytic philosophy with the new options of history. It's not a question of imposing new doctrinal loyalties; it's rather a question of conceptual strategies that have hardly ever or have never been tried, that have, in fact, been ruled out of court for most of our century. Now, at the close of our age, it is nearly impossible, in Britain, in the United States, in France, in Germany, to identify a single important program of philosophical work committed to historicity that commands the regular attention of the profession and compares favorably with the salience of any other influential movement. There is, however, no known argument that compellingly demonstrates that there is no serious point to the historicist orientation. You will find the remnants of its beginnings, so to say, in Hegelian, Marxist, pragmatist, hermeneutic, phenomenological, and other such sources. But it has obviously failed to weld itself to the leading currents of the day. And that is extraordinary if, as I shall show, the moral philosophies of our time cannot seriously withstand a critique along historicist lines and would be infinitely more supple if they only reached out to history. If they had, however, they would also have abandoned their firmest claims. Grant that the conceptual fortunes of moral philosophy and the philosophy of science go hand in hand, and you will see the deeper irony of the irony of the role reversal Kuhn's and Feyerabend's forays offer in a brief encounter.[17]

PART I

The Practice of Theory

1

Adequational and Existential Strategies

When John Rawls recounts (with obvious authority) the distinguishing features of "moral intuitionism" (as they appear in the views of such eighteenth-century figures as Richard Price and Samuel Clarke), we cannot ignore the fact that he has surely hit on an important *differentia*, the full significance of which largely eludes him.

I begin with Rawls's observation because it affords a decisive but neglected clue about the main thrust (and weakness) of contemporary analytic moral theory (even analytic epistemology and philosophy of science). It suggests that twentieth-century analytic philosophy (including Rawls's important work and whatever of continental European thought is congruent with it) is hardly more than the continuation of eighteenth-century English-language philosophy occasionally interrupted by the perceived need to exorcise certain nineteenth-century musings (chiefly Hegelian) about the "constructivist" role of history (or historicity). The apparent irrelevance is much more serious than Rawls appreciates: it raises profound doubts about our ability to discern just such sturdy moral principles as Rawls is known to champion. Rawls himself never examines its full threat or subversive power. Hardly any contemporary moral theorist does.

I

Rawls correctly remarks that "rational intuitionism" features no more than a "sparse conception of the person," one that "needs little more than the idea of the self as knower."[1] He contrasts its economy with what he calls "constructivism" – both the "moral constructivism" of Kant and his own "political constructivism" – because, on his reading, "more complex conceptions of person and society [than those the intuitionists offer] are required to provide the form and structure of [the] constructivist procedure."[2] Rawls is prescient here; but what he actually adds leads to very little more than another "sparse conception of the person." He misses the full significance of his own perception, namely, that intuitionism's self-appointed (cognitive) assurance precludes the need to explore precisely *how* moral judgment begins to take form as human agents are themselves socially formed; failing to grasp that, he fails to see that the alternative assurance he assigns his own doctrine (neutral reason applied to natural self-interest) precludes the very same need he saw slighted in the intuitionist's account.

The point is worth emphasising because it confirms that, contrary to the claims of *A Theory of Justice*[3] and now (in summary) those of *Political Liberalism*,[4] Rawls omits (without being aware of doing so) an entire family of theories of rationality and the human person that profoundly dampen the likelihood of a favorable appraisal of what he calls "the original position" – that is, those theories that bear on confirming or legitimating the supposed neutrality, universality, objectivity of the principles of rational justice he promotes.

Rawls misjudges how little distance there is between his own constructivism and the intuitionism he means to retire, because he has his eye on the abstract difference between cognitivist and noncognitivist theories of moral and political judgment; whereas the decisive feature of his doctrine concerns the determinate linkage between the *competence* of such judgment – *any* competence adequate to the deed: reason, let us say, whether intuitive or constructivist – *and* the formative conditions of societal life under which the *agent* (the self or person) actually acquires such competence (if he truly does). Rawls's account is thin ("sparse") because, assuming the validity of the liberal morality he favors, he believes the essential question rests with how to characterize the operative power of reason on which such validity depends rather than to explain how human agents actually live, learn to judge and act, and respond to practical problems, and *thereby* first become competent. He problematizes the conceptual picture of the resources on which moral competence depends: he never seriously problematizes that competence itself or the supposed objectivity of what it ultimately delivers. He falls back (by habit) to what is common to eighteenth-century and twentieth-century analytic philosophy, and he fails to perceive the relevant challenge posed – against all its strategies – by nineteenth-century existentialist, historicist, *praxis*-centered philosophies and *their* continuation.

Effectively, Rawls fails to acknowledge his own equivocation on what he calls "constructivism": between, say, the social or historicized "construction" of actual human persons and the philosophical "construction" of a transcendentally or noetically endowed competence ("reason") fitted to his own prior moral and political convictions. In this, Rawls is the clearest exemplar of late twentieth-century continuations of the great (but failed) tradition that spans Aristotle, Descartes, Kant, and Husserl at least, that attempts to conflate the contingent horizonal powers of human reasoning with a certain separable god-like power of Reason that does not answer merely to human interests (though it may scan them).[5]

I introduce these classificatory epithets in their intuitively obvious sense. I shall come back to them shortly. The confrontation has been nearly erased from late English-language philosophy, perhaps as a zealous consequence of the original anti-Hegelian themes of Bertrand Russell's and G. E. Moore's redirection (very early in the century) of what has been canonized as analytic philosophy.[6] In any case, the upshot is that Rawls nowhere actually vindicates the normative powers of reason he proclaims. That is an extraordinary failing, given his well-deserved prominence and the elegance of his own analytic labors. But the complaint is not intended in the way of a local quarrel. Rawls's neglect marks the conceptual habit of the dominant practice of recent English-language moral philosophy and much of what is congenial in continental European thought.

What misleads Rawls is the exaggerated importance of distinguishing between "cognitivist" and "constructivist" ("noncognitivist") accounts of moral *objectivity*. Rawls rightly remarks that, for the intuitionist, "moral principles and judgments, when correct, are true statements about an independent order of moral values" and that "moral first principles are known by theoretical reason."[7] Certainly, in this sense, Kant is no cognitivist and no moral realist either. Neither is Rawls, of course. But Rawls does not follow the Kant of the *Foundations*. He hardly needs to. He is more sanguine than Kant in supposing that, in a sense favorable to a "sparse" account of person and reason, all human persons appropriately queried (that is, neutrally), would, in the actual world, favor the thesis – his own thesis – "justice as fairness." It's for this reason that Rawls says: "The veil of ignorance, to mention one prominent feature of [the original] position, has *no specific metaphysical implications* concerning the nature of the self."[8] Rawls adds: the "diversity of opposing and irreconcilable religious, philosophical, and moral doctrines [includes some that] are perfectly reasonable [and is itself] the inevitable long-run result of the powers of human reason at work within the background of enduring free institutions." Moving from *A Theory of Justice* to *Political Liberalism*, the "elements [of the original position,]" Rawls assures us, "are still in place, as they were in *Theory*; and so is the basis of the argument for them."[9]

In *A Theory of Justice*, Rawls had offered a thought-experiment by which he claimed to draw on a convincing model of rationality that was at once neutral, universal, effectively unanimous in electing his own moral principle ("justice as fairness"), capable of addressing the human condition in morally relevant terms (even though) detached from all pertinent information about actual contingent differences between one-self and others, and capable of appreciating (in doing that) the validity and relevance of applying that same (first) principle in (all further) real-world encounters in which one *did* possess information about actual differences.

Apart from our testing opposed preferences regarding fundamental conceptions of justice, it is certainly not clear *how* Rawls could ever justify ruling out the possibility: (1) that it might be judged rational for someone constrained by "the veil of ignorance" (in the sense sketched) to conclude that there was, and could be, *no* universally valid (no non-trivial) principle of justice, or (2) that one might be well advised to believe that, *in* real-world situations – viewed from an "interested" and informed stance – one could never construct more than provisional, possibly diverse, general (but *not* consensually universal) maxims meant to accommodate the inevitable discovery of evolving complications resulting from living in the actual world. That is, one *might* well believe it *irrational* to suppose that *anyone* ("behind the veil of ignorance") could formulate *any* universal, changeless, exceptionless, "blind" but still invariably relevant principle of justice *suited* (*a priori*) to serve all the contingencies of *all the possible contexts of real-world life* – or, for *that matter, any reasoned approximation to same.* I cannot find any discussion in Rawls of such a possibility, and I cannot (yet) locate any secure basis on which either my own demurrer or Rawls's insistence may be judged to be more or to be less neutral than the other. (That is what the "Hegelian" deflection already remarked obliges us to reconsider.)

Rawls evidently believes that a universal consensus *can* be counted on. But he must concede that the *prior* condition for entertaining the plausibility of that conjecture entails the conviction: (1) that rationality *is* essentially uniform and constant among human beings of every historically contingent way of life; (2) that such rationality may be confirmed (by the force of his own thought-experiment), no matter what divergences in experience and thought may characterise particular societies; and (3) that such rationality may be counted on to discern what is normatively objective in the way of directing human life – anywhere.

Hence, if Rawls is committed (as he is) to a "sparse conception of the person," then either he relies on a circular argument that (at best) is not essentially different from Kant's (in the *Foundations*) or the intuitionist's, or (at worst) is affirmed by fiat alone. An important premiss is surely missing. That is what I say requires an existential inquiry.

"The veil of ignorance makes possible," Rawls says, "a unanimous choice of a particular conception of justice."[10] How so? "If the original position is to yield agreements that are just," he goes on,

> the parties must be fairly situated and treated equally as moral persons. The arbitrariness of the world must be corrected for by adjusting the circumstances of the initial contractual situation. Moreover, if in choosing principles we required unanimity even when there is full information, only a few rather obvious cases could be decided. A conception of justice based on unanimity in these circumstances would indeed be weak and trivial. But once knowledge is excluded, the requirement of unanimity is not out of place and the fact that it can be satisfied is of great importance. It enables us to say of the preferred conception of justice that it represents a genuine reconciliation of interests.[11]

Yes, of course. But *how* is knowledge "excluded"? And *how* is the consensus of reason secured if knowledge is excluded? How could we ever suppose that rational agents, aware that *they must judge* what is just in real-world terms and that, there, their interests and relative fortunes will be different from others', would be willing to judge *any* would-be *principle* of justice – formulated without regard to such differences but meant to apply categorically to them – as objectively preferable? I cannot see the plausibility of supposing that Rawls's reasoning ensures, or approximates, such unanimity, or that reason is reliably constant.

In short, Rawls's impressive theory is no more than an ideology built without regard (apart from considerations of internal consistency) to the shifting, historically seismic instability of the human terrain – particularly, its "constructed," possibly its historicized, nature. Notice that Rawls relies on two strategic contentions: one, that we probably cannot convincingly secure any wide-ranging principles of justice by cognitivist means, and so we fall back, reasonably, to constructivist resources; the other, that, although the principles of justice are constructed by rational consensus, reason itself is not subject to historical or cultural construction at all. There you have the essential transcendental theme of Kant's moral philosophy as well as the implied resistance (common to Kant and Rawls) to the historicizing of reason. It's the second contention that needs to be secured if Rawls's liberalism is to be vindicated – or, indeed, any comparable noncognitivist moral principle. The decisive point in all this is that Rawls suppresses his own transcendentalism and presents the invariance of "practical reason" as if it were a natural fact. (That is what I mean by "eighteenth-century thinking.") In any case, one might well imagine that if cognitivism fails (in the way Rawls supposes), then it would be difficult to see why any noncognitivism would be said to be in a stronger position. Only a Kantian transcendentalism would seem to be adequate to the task.

Look more closely at the *differentia* Rawls mentions, the one that separates intuitionism from constructivism. Rawls distinguishes three "practical" (moral or political) doctrines: "rational intuitionism, Kantian moral constructivism, and the political constructivism [Rawls's own] of justice as fairness"; "each," he says, "have [*sic*] a conception of objectivity, although they understand objectivity in a different way."[12] Their difference is not unimportant, but neither is it as wide-ranging as Rawls supposes. To guess at the limitation (as well as the precision) of Rawls's catalogue, I offer a distinction that Rawls nowhere considers. I regard it more as a matter of philosophical *strategy* than of *doctrine*; but I admit that, if it is allowed, it defeats Rawls's thesis instantly and utterly. It is more a matter of strategy than of doctrine (I say), because what it marks is the failure of Rawls's presumption to have canvassed the most important counterarguments against his own thesis rather than simply an alternative doctrine that we might conceivably prefer – and merely announce. If conceded, the maneuver would apply with equal force to cognate options in the philosophy of science, epistemology in general, logic, or any cognitively focused aptitudes we may assign ourselves. There's a suggestion there (which I favor) that the objectivity of moral reason cannot be segregated from our general epistemic competence (in both theoretical and practical matters).

For the moment, I see no reason to suppose that a constructivist account of science (or morality) need be conceptually or epistemically inferior to a cognitivist account; and, thinking of the Kant of the first *Critique*, I see no reason to suppose that constructivism and cognitivism (or, more temperately, constructivism and cognitive objectivity) cannot be coherently joined. That much may be inferred from Rawls's catalogue of moral theory, though Rawls himself ventures no opinion about our cognitive competence in science and does not consider the possible union of the two options.

There's more to the matter. For, for one thing, it is entirely possible (I take it to be true) that cognitivist and realist views of cognition make sense (ultimately) only within constructivist (or historicist) terms; for

another, no such constructivist account of rational or cognitive competence need suppose that such competence must be, or must entail, a
particular sort of socially emergent or transcendental aptitude adequate
"in the long run" (Rawls's phrase, recalling Peirce) or invariantly
adequate (in Kant's sense) for its proper cognitive or rational function.
For the moment, it hardly matters whether such conjectures are the right
ones to favor. The point is that Rawls does not address them or anything
like them; that they challenge the presumed consensual universality of
"justice as fairness"; *and* that they are part of the import of the
historicized deflections Rawls so easily ignores in claiming to have
canvassed all relevant alternatives to his own view.

There you have the clue to the subversive meaning of Rawls's
differentia between cognitivism and constructivism. For Rawls rightly
sees that both cognitivism and constructivism can support an objectiv*ist*
thesis about moral claims (Price's and Kant's, for instance), although
Rawls does not also remark that this extends as well to science. What is
important is that Rawls nowhere concedes that constructivist theories
may also provide for moral and scientific objectiv*ity* without being
objectiv*ist* and without insisting on the fixed competence of reason or
any specifically cognitive powers. (The option needs to be explained, of
course.) Rawls fails to see that there may be *no* moral or scientific
principles *to be* validated at all (for the sake of objectivity) in either the
cognitivist or the constructivist way – without our falling prey as a result
to skepticism or epistemic anarchy. We need some additional distinctions
to capture this last possibility: it would clarify the sense in which (as I
have already said) twentieth-century analytic philosophy is little more
than a continuation of Cartesian, Lockeian, Humean, and Kantian
philosophy.

Here is what Rawls says about objectivity:

> A conception of objectivity must specify a concept of a correct judgment
> from its point of view, and hence subject to its norms. It may conceive of
> correct judgment in the familiar way as true of an independent order of
> values, as in rational intuitionism, or, as in political constructivism, it
> may see correct judgments as reasonable; that is, as supported by the
> preponderance of reasons specified by the principles of right and justice
> issuing from a procedure that correctly formulates the principles of
> practical reason in union with appropriate conceptions of society and
> persons.[13]

I have already noted part of how Rawls characterizes intuitionism,
namely, as a form of cognitivism by which it "conceives of truth in a
traditional way by viewing moral judgments as true when they are both

about and accurate to the independent order of moral values." (Moral intuitionists often speak of moral judgments "as self-evident"; Rawls thinks this "is not essential" to the doctrine.[14] Nevertheless, in this sense, we may characterise Aristotle, whom Rawls barely considers, as a moral cognitivist though not an intuitionist.)

Rawls's notion of objectivity is complicated in a way that is local to his own political theory – which I shall touch on in a little while. For the moment, I mean to pursue philosophical "strategies" rather than "doctrines." Bear in mind that all three of Rawls's options regarding practical judgments (moral intuitionism, moral constructivism, political constructivism) afford a form of *objectivity*; although only intuitionism (or alternatives like the Aristotelian) is committed to a *realist* reading of objectivity. (Rawls treats the constructivist options as necessarily excluding realism.) The irony about Kant is that he is a realist (of sorts) about science but not about morality, *in spite of the fact that he is an a priori constructivist about both*. Rawls makes no mention or use of the point, although its admission threatens *both* Kant's *and* Rawls's doctrinal claims. (It does so on what I am calling strategic, rather than doctrinal, grounds.) For, if Kant cannot support (as I suppose he cannot) his objecti*vist* (transcendental) reading of objecti*vity* in science, then he cannot possibly support his objectivist (but noncogniti*vist*) view of objecti*vity* in morality. And if Kant fails in this, then (I say) so must Rawls – both as a kind of diminished Kantian (a moral constructivist) in *A Theory of Justice* and as a political constructivist (explicitly committed to avoiding Kant's supposed resources) in *Political Liberalism*.

What Rawls fails to grasp is this: that (1) his political constructivism presupposes some form of moral constructivism; that (2) although (his) political constructivism is neither cognitivist nor realist, his moral constructivism is (must be) or must implicate a more general realism or cognitivism (as does Kant's own moral constructivism); that (3) as a result, there is and can be no pertinent, no principled, distinction (as far as moral objectivity is concerned) between the three general philosophical strategies Rawls offers; and that (4) there may still be other defensible (unmentioned, possibly even superior, even less encumbered) forms of moral and political (or scientific) constructivism that preserve a viable sense of objectivity but are, or implicate, neither cognitivism (or realism) nor invariant (or universal or necessary) normative principles of any kind. (I take Rawls to be betrayed by his use of the term "correct" in the passage cited just above.)

On the terminological issue, I should add at once that I call a theory of objecti*vity* (regarding judgments or truth-claims) objecti*vist* – whether cognitivist or constructivist or both – if the judgments or claims it would legitimate are taken to be either *true* because (in Rawls's sense) they are "true of an independent order of values" (or, more generally, they are true of a "factual" order, even if it is one that is not altogether independent, as in Kant's account of science), or *right* because (in the constructivist *but* noncognitivist sense) they are confirmed as conforming with relevant constraints drawn from universal or invariant principles of reason binding in practical contexts. For, validity in the constructivist sense (Kantian or Rawlsian) *presupposes certain invariant truths about human reason. That* is a realist presumption.

What I claim, therefore, is that there is no pertinent difference between moral intuitionism and Kantian moral constructivism: because, although the first is explicitly cognitivist where the second is not, the second does still presuppose, implicate, or entail a more general cognitivism (about human reason or understanding) on which (alone) its *a priori* moral principles depend; hence, that Rawls's political constructivism (at an even greater remove) presupposes but does not pretend to validate (as Rawls claims to have done in *A Theory of Justice*) the universal moral principle, "justice as fairness." In that sense, Rawls presupposes objective (objectivist) knowledge of the normative preferences of practical reason. Rawls never justifies that move.

Rawls does not see this – hardly any analytic moral liberal concedes the point – because, as I say, twentieth-century analytic philosophy is the continuance of eighteenth-century philosophy interrupted more or less irrelevantly by historicist theories of persons and reason. That interruption explains the sense in which – as affirmed in item (4) of the tally just given – there *are* forms of constructivism that preserve objectivity but not on objectivist grounds or not on grounds that might be construed as cognitivist. There are hardly any analytic theories of this kind – certainly, Rawls's theory cannot be so characterized; and yet such theories are the only ones that have the least chance of remaining viable *if* it can be shown that the familiar forms of moral realism, moral cognitivism, moral and political constructivism cannot be defended or are arbitrary or committed to some form of unearned cognitive privilege. There is no difference, here, between the epistemic credentials of science and morality, although there is obviously a difference between the kinds of inquiry each pursues. One cannot ignore the economy – but Rawls surely does.

II

The clue regarding the objectivity of moral principles lies with a very small discovery. In *A Theory of Justice*, Rawls never shows us that or how he discerns – "rationally" – the "unanimous choice of a particular conception of justice." He affirms that "justice as fairness" *is* unanimously favored by practical reason, but he manages to show us only that his conception of "the original position" is not incompatible with such a principle. His is hardly a transcendental argument; it is, rather, as he suggests, the result of an "equilibrative" adjustment between the liberal principle he is unwilling to abandon or deform and a conception of the supposedly neutral operations of practical reason attracted to a certain ideology of science and morality.[15] By contrast, Kant's *Foundations of the Metaphysics of Morals* is explicitly grounded in the apriorism of the first *Critique*.[16] Deny that apriorism, and the principled use of the Categorical Imperative becomes completely pointless.

Kant's doctrine, of course, is also an explicit constructivism (in Rawls's sense): to that extent, Rawls is correct to distinguish between cognitivism and constructivism. But Kant's *concept* of the kind of moral principle autonomous reason *must* favor is, first of all, based on a putatively compelling analogy between what would otherwise be an illicit noumenal competence and the *a priori cognition* of how human understanding *constitutes the phenomenal world it knows*; secondly, Kant's concept serves as the paradigm of how to ensure that human reason *is* invariantly (or universally) structured – apt enough to legitimate (if that is indeed possible) even Rawls's presumption of a "unanimous choice of a particular principle of justice."[17] That is part of the reason Rawls's account of moral and political constructivism may be said to presuppose a form of objectivism – in particular, a form of cognitivism – even if it is true that Rawls is unwilling to avail himself of the transcendentalism of Kant's first *Critique*. It hardly matters, for the comparison exposes Rawls's unguarded assumption: namely, that *practical reason is, invariantly, aptly structured for discerning (in noncognitivist terms) the very principle of justice he favors*. How could Rawls possibly know that his principle would, should, or must prevail? For that matter, why, lacking transcendental support, *would* it ever prevail? Clearly, Rawls supposes that reason, though "natural," is invariant. But where is the argument?

I admit Kant's theory of knowledge is problematic: possibly even open to a reading that would deny a literalminded apriorism. (Although Kant could not have supported the particular constructivism he does if he had not also meant it to be apriorist.) The textual issue need not distract us. The dialectical lesson is plain enough: *if* one adheres to the modal universalism of the *Foundations*, one needs the support of an apriorist reading of the first *Critique*; and if one adheres to Rawls's presumption of a "unanimous choice of a particular principle of justice," one will still require Kant's apriorism or something very much like it – which *would be* a form of cognitivism if it were not utterly arbitrary. Rawls nowhere addresses that puzzle; if he had, he would not have been content to distinguish in the casual way he does the "sparse" conception of person and reason offered by intuitionists or what is (now) hardly more than another "sparse" conception (his own). Notice that Rawls believes the unanimity *he* prefers answers in some unexplained way to a real-world survey of rational people that *we* may at least sample. The quick charge against Rawls is this: although he holds that the principles of justice are constructed in accord with the competent powers of practical reason – *not* discovered in any independent world – he nowhere considers that practical reason may itself be a "construction" or artifact of social history. But, of course, on that admission, the objectivity and universality of the supposed principles of justice are put at grave risk.

Let me introduce, therefore, a distinction of art. Let us say that what Rawls adumbrates – in identifying "sparse" theories of persons and reason – are *adequational* theories. The earliest important instance of such a theory that I know of is Aristotle's notion (in *De Anima* and elsewhere) of *nous* ("rational intuition"), the putative native power of directly discerning the essential, changeless forms of particular things.[18] (Adequational theories, I hold, may be either cognitivist or noncognitivist.)

If you revisit Aristotle's account, you will see that the sole rationale for inventing *nous* is to denominate an instant competence in cognizing subjects (persons) to discern whatever is *sui generis* and essential to Aristotle's science (grasping the forms of things).[19] The complexities Aristotle admits regarding *nous* (its relationship to a deductive science, for instance: the relationship between grasping the forms of things and perceiving particular things) are occupied solely with what is internal to that invented competence. Nowhere does Aristotle construe *nous* problematically: for instance, in terms of the testable development of actual human subjects, as by first considering the cultural formation of persons and *then* addressing in *its* terms any empirical evidence we might collect about pertinently developing skills. Aristotle invents the doctrine (nous) whole cloth. We are never invited to test or legitimate the attribution of nous's powers. We have here the exemplar of the cognitivist version of an adequational theory, a theory that (1) presupposes ("objectively" or "neutrally") what is *true* about the world; (2) invents a corresponding competence "adequate" for discerning such truths; and (3) offers nothing more about the human subject that instantiates such competence. Aristotle is hardly a transcendentalist in Kant's sense. Neither is Descartes. Neither is Rawls. But we see how the postulation of a native power of reason or understanding competent to discern what is universal and invariant in the world or in the normative direction of human life anticipates the full thrust of Kant's transcendental constructivism. Here, pre-Kantian and post-Kantian thought leads up to and away from Kant's apriorism but without relinquishing the doubtful power. That explains why mere intuitionism and Rawls's constructivism are, ultimately, not very different from one another: the one is pre-Kantian and the other post-Kantian; the one is cognitivist and the other constructivist. But that is all: both are epistemically privileged.

There is, therefore, no serious difference, in the strategic sense, between Aristotle's *nous* and what Rawls attributes to the moral intuitionist. Furthermore, the intuitionist's view confirms a remarkable similarity between late seventeenth- and eighteenth-century epistemologies and twentieth-century analytic epistemologies. The only difference – and even that is open to dispute – is that twentieth-century theorists tend to be more chary of cognitive certainty, self-evidence, apodicticity than their eighteenth-century counterparts.[20]

Once we have this much in place, it is easy to propose what should count as the constructivist (or noncognitivist) analogue. It would be a theory that (4) presupposes what is ("objectively" or "neutrally") *right* about how we should act in the world; (5) essentially invents, whole cloth, a matching (rational) competence "adequate" for deciding that much; and (6) offers nothing more about the human subject that proves to be rationally competent. I find these parallel formulations very pretty – and an apt analysis of standard views. (I may say I find very little difference between Donald Davidson's cognitivism and Rawls's constructivism, in the regard in question.) But more than that, I cannot see how it can be denied that constructivist versions of the adequational view cannot possibly escape – if they claim to be neutral or universally favored (rationally) or necessarily valid – *some* privileged epistemology. That surely accords with Kant's strategy. I don't deny that one may dispute this picture of Kant's first *Critique* (which happens to be both cognitivist and constructivist). I say only that if one does dispute it, one instantly undermines the grounds on which Kant's moral philosophy could ever claim to be objective and universally binding.[21] I cannot see how Rawls's thesis could possibly fare better.

I shall not pursue the analogy here. But I think it is fair to say that

Alasdair MacIntyre's *After Virtue* is, for instance, meant to be the start of a pared-down (but exemplary) Aristotelian theory of the adequational sort[22] and that Jürgen Habermas's "Discourse Ethics" is meant to be the start of a pared-down (also exemplary) Kantian theory of the adequational sort.[23] Such theories are now suspect (even before they submit to analysis) because they rely on "sparse" accounts of reason and because they implicate, even where they masquerade as constructivist, cognitivist assumptions that cannot be independently confirmed. That is what Rawls fails to grasp.

I must, therefore, venture another distinction of art. Let us say that a theory of persons and reason is *existential* if (1) it essays, without first presuming any cognitive or rational competence matched to what is true or right in science and morality, to analyze the actual nature or cultural formation of, or what it is to exist as, a human person in societal, historical, and practical terms; and (2) it raises, but only in the context of (1), the legitimation of our supposed cognitive and/or rational competence in science and morality. Clearly, existential and adequational theories may and usually will exclude one another. By and large, adequational theories concede nothing to persons and reason beyond what is antecedently needed to match whatever is first said to be true or right regarding some given sector of the world; whereas existential theories expressly subordinate our supposed cognitive and rational competence to the contingent, possibly quite variable, conditions of effective human existence. The exemplars of the existential orientation surely include Kierkegaard, Marx, Nietzsche, Dewey, Heidegger, Sartre, Gadamer, Kuhn, and Foucault at least. I speak here only of philosophical strategies, not of substantive doctrines of any sort. My point is that the "existentialists" are quite capable of recovering objectivity – by way of constructions of one sort or another, blind as far as objectivist presumptions are concerned – *within* the reflexive space of viable societal life. They give up privilege willingly, but they need lose no conceptual scope in doing so. On the existential view, objectivity is itself a variable social construction.

Occasionally, adequationists masquerade as existentialists. Perhaps the most striking recent instance is offered by Karl-Otto Apel, who is of course a bona fide Kantian – a true apriorist. Apel introduces the notion of a "consensual–communicative discursive ethics," an ethics that we are to suppose develops within the discourse of any and every actual society *that is* (or insofar as it is) *rational*. You have here, then, a marriage between what Apel calls the "utopian" aspect of rational ethics (seen in historical circumstances) and its effectiveness in actual historical life. Apel admits that he adopts (here) "the Kantian principle as the formal internalization of the principle [the utopian principle of his own 'consensual–communicative discursive ethics'] of *universal reciprocity* which requires that concrete norms be justified where possible, by an *agreement* ([an] informational and argumentative mediation) upon *the interests of all those concerned.*"[24]

I am not bent on vindicating or defeating Apel. You cannot fail to see, however, the parallel with Rawls's thesis and of course with Habermas's, which Habermas acknowledges is due to Apel's original influence and which, like Rawls's, means to eschew apriorism. Apel's maneuver remains the boldest, most explicit, and most challenging of the three. (For instance, its defeat would entail the unqualified defeat of both Rawls's and Habermas's views; but the reverse would not be true.) I mention the point expressly to draw attention to the fact that an adequational (even an apriorist) theory of the constructivist sort may masquerade as an existential theory; but it would never convince us that it was existential, if only we remembered that the apriorist assumes that (what he treats as) the competence of reason is antecedently known to be operative *in* the existential life of actual societies.

Here is what Apel specifically claims:

> We have reached a dialectically salient point in our discussion of the relationship between *utopia* and *ethics*. For the question now arises as to whether the specified principle of ethics [just mentioned] itself proves to be untenable because of utopianism [that is, because it fails to be grounded in the existential life of actual societies] or whether – independently of the charge of utopia, which of course itself still requires clarification as to its meaning – it can be justified as binding by rational arguments. If the latter were to be the case, then this would mean at the same time that utopia – more precisely, a specific form of the human *utopian intention* – can be justified as being unavoidable and indispensable.[25]

Let it suffice to say that Apel concedes that his moral principle cannot be derived in the manner of a logical or formal proof. He insists only that the very observation that an attempted proof would yield a "logical circle" *presupposes*, by way of "transcendental–pragmatic" grounds – which we discover reflexively govern argument itself – that to fail to subscribe to the principle enunciated would be to fall victim to a "pragmatic" contradiction. There is (Apel thinks) a *"philosophical final justification of principles"* adequate for both rational argument and rational ethics.[26] (You would not be wrong to see in this Apel's "logical socialism," which Apel draws from Charles Sanders Peirce, as does Habermas as well.)[27] But Apel offers no supporting argument at all – only his ukase.

What Apel fails to show is the full relationship between "utopian" rationality and any contingent constraints arising from the seemingly local forms of rationality and effective life (in the existential sense). There's the theme that needs to be considered, the point neglected (in different ways) by Rawls, Habermas, and Apel. For, it is certainly fair to say – in the abstract – that *if* any relevant objection (to an argument or policy or judgment or commitment) were presented to a "rational agent" (construed as generously as you please), then that agent would, preserving rationality, treat the objection seriously. Nevertheless, I cannot see how such a purely formal or abstract consideration (formal consistency or, "intentionally," consistency in practice or policy ranging over all particular cases as they arise) *could ever yield, existentially, the principle of "universalized reciprocity" at any point in actual historical situations.*

Alternatively put, what Apel favors presupposes: (1) that rationality is invariantly structured and known to be such – transhistorically; (2) that, however contingently "constructed" linguistically or culturally informed reasoning may be, every such competence necessarily ("pragmatically") implicates a condition tantamount to what is reported in item (1); and (3) that the denial or "violation" of (1) and (2) *is* "pragmatically" self-contradictory, that is, contradictory in the sense that Apel's "utopian" principle *is* presupposed by every would-be rational act of (such) denial, or in the sense that either the associated practice would be unworkable or could not be construed as workable except arbitrarily.

I don't see the force of (2) or any close alternative to it. The modal necessity Apel insists on – whether formal or pragmatic – is entirely uncompelling. Even "pragmatic consistency" cannot be shown to entail any "rational" agent's acceptance of a "universalized reciprocity" of *actual interests.* There is, and can be, no determinate rule or criterion or criterially operative principle for showing that favoring the "interests" of any local or finite community of agents rightly approximates to anything like Apel's principle. It is not even clear what, in existential terms, the principle would require or forbid, or tolerate or not tolerate. Furthermore, it is certainly coherent (certainly not implausible) to hold that human rationality is itself a changing artifact of diverse cultural formations; and that arguments, concepts, meanings, generalizations, assertions, and the like are inseparably embedded in the contingent practices of one society or another. (Which is not to say, of course, that societies are hermetically sealed or unintelligible to one another.) One way of focusing the essential puzzle is to challenge Apel to make clear the sense in which "successful communication" – identified initially only in terms of the holist fluency of social life – entails or presupposes (at least "pragmatically," if not formally) *any* determinate universal criteria of intelligibility or communicative success. That challenge cannot be successfully met, I suggest, if we cannot (and, of course, we cannot) supply the operative criteria of referential and predicative success in general. More recently, Apel has increasingly distanced himself from the sheer "formalism" of Kant's specific strategy. Apel pretends instead to draw his own transcendental discoveries from the modally necessary "pragmatic" constraints that hold in all contingent forms of argumentation and linguistic communication. (Here, he follows the general thrust of Dilthey's critique of historical reason, the critique of the pragmatists and the hermeneuts. But, like a number of them, he fails to grasp the impossibility of reconciling modal necessity and historicity.)[28]

There are deeper objections that Apel fails to consider: those arising, for instance, from the sheer complexity of the most elementary linguistic acts. There is no setting in which exceptionless principles, universal rules, argument forms, presumptions of invariant rationality, make any sense at all if separated from the actual improvisational practices of one society or another.[29] But to allow the point is to call into question the very idea that "universalized reciprocity" could (as a principle) take a legible form – let alone function as a necessary presupposition, *pragmatically*. It is only because Apel construes social practice and history in the "adequational" sense that he supposes that that principle must be implicated "existentially" as well. For the present, it is enough to grasp that Apel's modal claim fails on internal grounds. That invisible failure explains both Apel's oddly sanguine expectations about ethical "progress" and his dictum about the modal link between the actual and the "ideal" (speech community). So he says:

> Everyone who engages in serious argument – and even before that, who communicates with other people in the sense of a possible redemption of validity claims and who assumes others and themselves to be responsible – must *anticipate* as an *ideal state of affairs* and assume as fulfilled in a certain manner, counterfactually, the condition of an ideal community of communication or an ideal speech situation.[30]

What Apel must suppose – what is either false (as I contend) or at the very least unproved and *not* necessary to assume – is that effective communication under any and all "existential" conditions is impossible if meanings are not or cannot be neutrally (hence universally) grasped. There is no known argument that demonstrates the incoherence of denying that doctrine or any doctrine like it – without jeopardizing the apparent "pragmatic" success of communication itself. One may in fact suspect, hardly unreasonably, that Apel has simply confused the pragmatic (substantive) requirement of "universalized reciprocity" with the (logically trivial) requirement of mere ("universal") consistency of usage. Others *have* confused the two, though it is clear enough that Apel has the stronger thesis in mind.

III

An additional step remains to be taken, a step beyond adequational strategies, a transition to relatively untried conceptual possibilities: the exposé of partisan limitations normalized from our theories of knowledge and rational practice read as the necessary bounds of reason. The clue lies with resisting confusing any merely adequated concept of the cognizing or rationally effective agent with the actual human self emerging as such in a particular historical milieu. On the foregoing argument, I insist (1) that the analysis of the "human subject" (which cognition and rational practice presuppose) cannot rightly be drawn from any merely prior constraints of the adequational sort; (2) that, on the contrary, the cognitional and the practical are themselves hostage to, conceptually dependent on, conditions (whatever they are) of actual human existence; and (3) that, at best, the cognitional and the practical are no more than part (however distinctive and important they may be) of the enabling and effective processes of human life. The best evidence in favor of these caveats is entirely straightforward: surely there are culturally and historically contingent processes (the linguistic, preeminently) that serve to enculture the human infant in the first place, so that one evolves *as* a cognitively and practically apt self under their enabling influence. The adequational (the "sparse") model does not acknowledge this dependency or make provision for its continuing bearing on the human condition.

I have demonstrated the arbitrariness of Rawls's moral constructivism, the complete absence of any effort on Rawls's part to explain why we should suppose practical reason to be invariantly ordered and, being invariant, natively apt for that "consensual unanimity" that favors the liberal principle of justice. (The attempt, in *Political Liberalism*, to detach "political constructivism" from "moral constructivism," to treat the former as "effectively" autonomous – if that, finally, is what Rawls means to defend – would instantly consign the appeal to "justice as fairness" to the status of an ideological postulate nowhere backed by legitimate reason.) Kant is never arbitrary in Rawls's way; nor is Apel. Yet all three are adequationists and open to challenge for much the same reasons. Kant's account fails because it rests on an apriorism that is no longer compelling in cognitive matters. Apel's apriorism is dialectically more inviting than Kant's, because it makes an explicit, testable claim about pragmatic necessities. It too fails (I say), because it does not take the trouble to show (and would not succeed if it did) that the conditions of effective linguistic communication must presuppose some neutral aptitude for understanding meanings (hence, for being able – always – to make moral and political contracts open, under real-world conditions, to the endorsement of universal reason).

You will find the evidence of Apel's failing in his remarkably weak confirmatory examples: for instance, in the analysis of the Cartesian-like speech-act, "I hereby assert that I do not exist," or the Peircean-like speech-act, "I hereby assert as true that I am not obliged *in principle* to recognize all possible members of the unlimited community of argumentation as having equal rights."[31] The first is not unreasonably construed as a "pragmatic" contradiction, but it has nothing (as such) to do with the "rights" (or "equal rights") of "all possible members of the unlimited community of argumentation"; that way of speaking is surely nothing but a *façon de parler*. The Cartesian case is marginal and unique and well-nigh vacuous. Nothing of interest follows from it. The second trades on a fatal equivocation: every party to an argument may be said to "have a right" to lodge an objection, in the trivial sense that rational debaters mean to be consistent and are prepared to respect evidence of inconsistency wherever it arises; but that has nothing to do with the determinate rights or interests of – or the conditions of communication and understanding among – actual human selves or subjects. *In extremis*, it tolerates – it does not presuppose – the possibility of the universal uniformity of reason; it certainly does not entail it. (It is hardly more than a matter of ideological hope.)

Once the viability of the existential thesis is conceded, the adequationist can no longer fall back to the self-evidence of his claim. For one thing, the necessity of linguistic communication's manifesting or entailing a neutral or universal or invariant form of understanding cannot be shown: its denial cannot be shown to disable effective practical life. For another, rationality may be coherently construed as itself an artifact of contingent and diverse forms of enculturation. Neither Kant nor Apel nor Habermas nor Rawls has shown the incoherence of admitting such possibilities – or, indeed, the possibility that actual human life accords with them. But if we admit that much, then even neutrality and consensual agreement may be artifacts of a constructed or interpreted agreement!

Rawls's thesis seems peculiarly bold, because it mounts an argument that implicates a complete indifference to the actual history of moral and political experience (the "original position") or an indifference to the working relevance of different histories on actually being able to confirm the "unanimous consensus" said to be achieved in the "original position." It assures us that we can construct a *rational* principle of justice by way of a thought-experiment detached from actual history but pertinent enough for moral direction in all subsequently encountered real-world situations. (That surely is sheer ideology.) Kant had based his own theory of rational obligation on the *concept* of autonomy originally drawn from and reconciled with the theory of knowledge offered in the first *Critique*. (That theory, too, was ultimately adequational.) Apel overcomes the Kantian dualism by pretending to extract a concept of universal reason from any existential history among actual "communicative communities." But Apel neglects to confirm that such communicative neutrality ever obtains (or might ever be effectively extended in the "utopian" way he favors); and he nowhere shows that human persons and human reason *are* formed (or must be formed) in such a way that communicative neutrality ever, or regularly, or necessarily obtains.

All this is on the Kantian side of the ledger. To many, Aristotelian strategies appear more hospitable to existential options simply because they place moral *praxis* squarely in the context of social history. Or so it seems. Instructively, that very presumption does not (finally) hold true of Alasdair MacIntyre's important effort to historicize Aristotle's strategy (for our own time), for instance, without a loss of objectivity or universal relevance. Here is the evidence:

> The hypothesis which I wish to advance [says MacIntyre] is that in the actual world which we inhabit the language of morality is in [a] state of grave disorder.l . . . What we possess, if this view is true, are the fragments of a conceptual scheme, parts which now lack those contexts from which their significance derived. We possess indeed similacra of morality, we continue to use many of the key expressions. But we have – very largely, if not entirely – lost our comprehension, both theoretical and practical, of morality.[32]

It's the strategy, not MacIntyre's particular doctrine, that needs to be unmasked. Plainly, MacIntyre means that there *is* a true morality that can be discerned in history that is not itself confirmed in the historicized way; that our society is morally out of true, known to be such, and largely unable (as a result) to grasp what true morality requires; that the true norms of morality may yet be recovered and satisfied; and that that morality cannot be made to rely in a principled way on the mere contingencies of history. After all, morality insists (MacIntyre claims) that it is our "disordered" history that must be corrected.

MacIntyre is an adequationist, of course, but also a cognitivist and an Aristotelian. Had he been a constructivist like Rawls, he could never have affirmed the *truth* of the moral "disorder" of our times. Still, the novelty of his account is not entirely obvious. He *is* a cognitivist (in the "Aristotelian–Thomist" sense) regarding the normative import of the human *telos*. But in all else regarding practical reason – particularly, the contingencies of history – he pretends to function as a constructivist. He confines the work of legitimative reason to the determinate resources of one historical tradition or another; he positively avoids involving any explicit ahistorical norms. But he also denies that practical reason is thereby restricted to the norms of any local tradition. There is, as he explains, a dialectical power internal to any tradition to accommodate ("empathetically") the "reason" of "alien" traditions. On the evidence, apparently, the "Aristotelian–Thomist" tradition is competitively better than any other in this regard: it never violates the formal *telos* of the human condition, and yet it shows a superior resilience in resolving the practical *aporiai* of its evolving history. If that argument were sound, MacIntyre's maneuver would afford a stunning reconciliation of the existential and the adequational, the historicist and the essentialist, the constructivist and the cognitivist.

MacIntyre's argument is, frankly, more instructive than Apel's: it engages history more directly. It remains at risk, however, because it never tests the possibility of a historicized metaphysics of persons. Yet it gives us no reason for refusing to cross that line, and it never explains why it is entitled to demur:

> Moral philosophies are, [MacIntyre says] before they are anything else, the explicit articulations of the claims of particular moralities to rational allegiance. And this is why the history of morality and the history of moral philosophy are a single history. It follows that when rival moralities make competing and incompatible claims, there is always an issue at the level of moral philosophy concerning the ability of either to make good a claim to rational superiority over the other.[33]

How so? you ask. MacIntyre admits that "the protagonists of . . . rival moralit[ies] are committed" to rival "rational standards"; but the contest between such moralities is, he also insists, a contest within "a single history." He means to assure us that the "rational superiority" of the one over the other *can* be decisively discerned in spite of that contingency: "The history of morality-and-moral-philosophy is [he says] the history of successive challenges to some pre-existing moral order, a history in which the question of which party defeated the other in rational argument is always to be distinguished from the question of which party retained or gained social and political hegemony."[34]

Just so. And yet, saying that is itself an *aporia*, hardly the resolution of the historicist's *aporia*. Where, for instance, is the demarcation line between "rational" superiority and "hegemonic" power, *if* reason is itself an artifact of different histories? MacIntyre's *strategy* (and doctrine) makes no sense unless several more or less equivalent principles can be counted on to be in place: (1) some form of Aristotelian essentialism regarding the human *telos* – which, however modified, cannot be defeated by appeal to the mere historical contingencies of actual human life or the flux of history;[35] (2) an insistence on the necessity of bivalence in analyzing and assessing truth-claims regarding reality and moral options – ranging, in particular, over shifts in moral paradigms;[36] and (3) the invariance of theoretical and practical reason, however embedded in diverse histories – hence, the invariance and invariant adequacy of rational norms in deciding the validity of "rival moralities."

The *aporia* of MacIntyre's strategy lies with the unavoidability of (his) subscribing to something like Aristotle's *nous* in the midst of competing histories. Otherwise, *if* diverging histories generate rival "rational standards," then there will always be a real threat that the apparent victory of one morality over another is largely the work of ideological hegemonies. The only other possibility requires that, in *all* important contests between "rival moralities," something like a paradigm shift (from one form of practical reason to another) – in a sense more or less in accord with T. S. Kuhn's well-known contention – will be so completely compelling in the face of a given *aporia* that the shift will be irresistible. The trouble is that, even in the context of the physical sciences, such confrontations are either rare or seriously contested.[37] It is hard to see that moral disputes could possibly be as reliable as, or more compelling in this regard than, those in the sciences. But if so, then MacIntyre's strategy must be seen to be transparently ideological. If reason (hence, if virtue) is no more than an artifact of shifting history, then the charge of global moral disorder cannot be more than a prejudice; but if the charge is valid, then history can be no more than the local setting in which contingent options are brought into accord with the essential *telos* of practical life. (The second option is simply that of Aristotle's *Ethics*.) I see no way in which MacIntyre can escape the dilemma.

As I say, the matter can hardly be confined to the fortunes of moral theory. Its classic forms appear, of course, in Thomas Kuhn's *The*

Structure of Scientific Revolutions.[38] Kuhn had hoped to be able to show that rational choices between "rival" scientific paradigms could always be resolved in historically confined terms; all the while the indicated preferences would lead "progressively," by their own internal logic, in the direction of an objective (ahistorical) grasp of the invariant structure of independent reality. In pursuing this prospect, Kuhn sets the same paradox for science that (much later) MacIntyre sets for moral theories (of the Aristotelian stripe). You will not, however, find an explicit admission, in MacIntyre, of that connection; for MacIntyre does not mention Kuhn in his official account. But I can see no difference in their original strategies, unless it lies with the difference between the prospects of science and the prospects of morality. Furthermore, both fail – and for the same reason. For Kuhn never relented enough to replace his adequational account of theoretical reason (fashioned by the positivists and Popper) by an existential (historicized) conception of rational choice, although he finally despaired of ever surmounting the implied relativism. MacIntyre remains more sanguine, but he overtakes relativism by essentialist fiat – which is to say, he fails.

You may glimpse their convergence (and difference) from the following juxtaposed remarks. First, Kuhn:

> Like the choice between competing political institutions, that between competing paradigms proves to be a choice between incompatible modes of community life. . . . When paradigms enter, as they must, into a debate about paradigm choice, their role is necessarily circular. Each group uses its own paradigm to argue in their paradigm's defense. . . . In these matters neither proof nor error is at issue. The transfer of allegiance from paradigm to paradigm is a conversion experience that cannot be forced.[39]

Then, MacIntyre:

> If the only available standards of rationality are those made available by and within traditions, then no issue between contending traditions is rationally decidable. . . . The relativist challenge rests upon a denial that rational debate between and rational choice among rival traditions is possible; the perspectivist challenge puts in question the possibility of making truth-claims from within any one tradition. . . . What I have to do, then, is to provide an account of the rationality presupposed by and implicit in the practice of those enquiry-bearing traditions with whose history I have been concerned which will be adequate to meet the challenges posed by relativism and perspectivism.[40]

Between them, Kuhn and MacIntyre capture the sense in which, in both theoretical and practical matters, truth and objectivity are mortally threatened by the *existential* notion that the rational capacity to judge is itself an artifact of cultural formation. Kuhn is tempted by the (adequational) commitment of the unity of science program. He never quite escapes its charm, but he also admits he cannot reconcile its presumption with the insuperable historicity of inquiry. Kuhn comes down on the side of existential historicity – which was, of course, the apostasy the strategists of analytic philosophies of science perceived. MacIntyre acknowledges the same dilemma in moral and practical matters – but he assures us very plainly that it *is* surmountable, without invoking privilege or essentialism. But that cannot possibly be shown. I see in this the curious convergence, from absolutely opposite poles of philosophical reflection, between the "Aristotelian" MacIntyre and the "Kantian" Rawls.[41] It is the result of the self-imposed (but necessary) *epistemic* weakness of certain forms of constructivism and historicism. Kuhn treats the resolution of incommensurable paradigms as nonrational. MacIntyre treats it as rational. Both are too extreme. Kuhn does not concede enough to the accommodating powers of historical reason, and MacIntyre is too sanguine about overcoming the historicist and relativistic limitations of critical reason. Kuhn worries, therefore, about the realism of science in the face of competing paradigms, and MacIntyre is too confident that there is a uniquely adequate morality that we preserve through all the vicissitudes of history.

I take this to be the touchstone of all English-language philosophy at the close of our century. It poses a dilemma that cannot be resolved in objectivist terms: that's to say, in adequational terms, once the historicist option is embraced. Apel pretends to resolve it, but he does so by an apriorism that simply ignores the possibility of the historicist option. Rawls pretends that the historicity of reason has no inning at all. Kuhn confronts the dilemma but admits its insuperability despite vestigial longings to the contrary. MacIntyre admits the same dilemma but claims, mysteriously, to overtake it:

> The rival claims to truth of contending traditions of enquiry depend for their vindication upon the adequacy and the explanatory power of the histories which the resources of each of those traditions in conflict enable their adherents to write.

The upshot, MacIntyre affirms, is the discovery of "how the justification of first principles is to be carried through": hence that

> *prima facie* at least a case has been made for concluding ... that those who have thought their way through the topics of justice and practical

rationality, from the standpoint constructed by and in the direction pointed out first by Aristotle and then by Aquinas, have every reason at least so far to hold that the rationality of their tradition has been confirmed in its encounters with other traditions.[42]

MacIntyre apparently means that the Aristotelian–Thomist tradition of rationality *is* dialectically superior to all its competitors; *and*, working through incompatible moral claims relativized to different historical conceptions of rationality, we find *objective* or *rational* resolutions of such claims in spite of *not finding* "standards of rationality, adequate for the evaluation of rival answers [to questions of justice and practical rationality], equally available, at least in principle, to all persons, whatever tradition they may happen to find themselves in and whether or not they inhabit any tradition" – relative (it seems) to inter- as well as intra-tradition disputes.[43] In this sense, MacIntyre is committed to historicity and denies a changeless, transhistorical form of rationality. But he nowhere holds the line.

There is some charm in MacIntyre's insistence. But I find no argument in it. To mention a few vexed applications: I cannot see how the Aristotelian–Thomist tradition could possibly presume to settle one way or another (that is, bivalently) the morality of contraception, abortion, suicide, euthanasia, or homosexual relations. I confess I find the idea that there is, or could be, such a general strategy preposterous. What is wanted is not mere coherence but moral coherence – conceptual coherence that is demonstrably moral, normatively binding in the moral way. MacIntyre never arrives at such a verdict.

All of MacIntyre's arguments in favor of his doctrine rest on the validity of a single conception: "the notion of goods internal to a practice"[44] – which (I believe) is utterly unconvincing and questionbegging. The counterargument is straightforward enough. "By a 'practice'," MacIntyre explains,

> I ... mean any coherent and complex form of socially established cooperative human activity through which goods internal to that form of activity are realized in the course of trying to achieve those standards of excellence which are appropriate to, and partially definitive of, that form of activity, with the result that human powers to achieve excellence, and human conceptions of the ends and goods involved are systematically extended.

Now, it is entirely possible that MacIntyre means that the relation between "practice" and "good" is, in internal terms, simply tautological. But if so, his examples belie the idea: architecture, farming, the inquiries of physics, painting and music (all of which he mentions), work "sustaining . . . communities – . . . households, cities, nations – [each] is generally taken to be a practice in the sense in which I have defined it."[45] It would hardly be worth the bother to construe the matter tautologically; I have, in fact, no reason to think MacIntyre sees it that way.

But if so, then it stares you in the face that, generally, and particularly in modern times, although there are goods internal to a practice, practices (in the sense intended) *support plural and "rival" values* (goods or their associated "virtues") equally well: there is usually no uniquely (bivalently) valid way to identify *the* goods internal to and definitive of such practices. There is no way to settle the question by historicist norms – to conform, say, with any of the principles (mentioned above) that MacIntyre would have had to favor if he were to win his argument or to confirm the superiority of the Aristotelian–Thomist tradition. (I have mentioned three principles: those concerning essentialism, bivalence, and reason.)

The strategy is a failure, therefore, unless it is supplemented by a theory of virtues (goods internal to a practice, that may be practised apart from that practice) that may be shown to be independently "objective." But then, MacIntyre would have "overcome" (superseded) the historicized forms of reason he pretends to favor. One sees this if, bearing Kuhn's account in mind, the inquiries of physics were, as MacIntyre suggests, genuine "practices." Kuhn, who discusses the matter (where MacIntyre does not), admits he cannot restore our theory of physics to objectivist presumptions. How, if Kuhn fails, does MacIntyre propose to succeed in moral and practical affairs? There is no answer.

I hesitate to say that MacIntyre's account is as straightforward as I have made it out to be. For instance, when he says:

> Virtues . . . stand in a different relationship to external and to internal goods. The possession of the virtues – and not only of their semblance and simulacra – is necessary to achieve the latter; yet the possession of the virtues may perfectly well hinder us in achieving external goods,[46]

I am not sure I can "save" MacIntyre's account from a Hobson's choice between a questionbegging tautology and an Aristotelian–Thomist essentialism. I can "save" it all right, but I cannot do so without utterly subverting its original claim. MacIntyre comes down, finally, on the side of privilege, on the "adequational" side. I see little difference, strategically (*not* doctrinally, of course), between MacIntyre's (Aristotelian) account and Apel's (Kantian) account. Both fail. If I may count all that has already been said as dialectical evidence collecting on the question, I am bound to say that the radical possibilities of the "existential" strategy (in particular, the historicized, even relativistic, options that are now surfacing) begin to appear more plausible than before, if indeed they can be made out to be coherent. That issue remains to be resolved, but I should like to offer it a better debut.

I have treated Kuhn's and MacIntyre's accounts as matched attempts to come to grips with the possibility that reason (or rationality) in theoretical and practical affairs is a historicized construction that, one way or another, reflects and embodies the cognitive and active powers of this or that enabling culture. Together, they confirm that existential and adequational theories of persons and objectivity cannot be reconciled. MacIntyre pretends to discern a strongly bivalent or essentialist resolution regarding all, or most, important rival moral claims within the dialectical resources of historicized reason; that is, *in spite of his having rejected any invariant, transhistorically accessible, species-specific norms of rationality*. MacIntyre secures his argument by an (unearned) optimism regarding what amounts to a rational consensus on each individual contest between either incompatible or incommensurable alternatives.

It is for this reason that I take the absence of any mention of Kuhn to betray the Kuhnian theme in MacIntyre – joined to a distinctly un-Kuhnian confidence in a single, a putatively superior tradition of rationality. It's true that Kuhn supposed there were a number of criteria-like considerations – theoretical simplicity, fruitfulness, and the like – that bore on rational preferences among rival scientific theories,[47] but Kuhn abandoned, in the same setting, the very idea of a neutral epistemic stance[48] (which, of course, incurred Donald Davidson's extreme but unsecured displeasure).[49]

MacIntyre's resolution of incompatible and incommensurable rival moral claims is disarmingly generous in a way that belies the historicity he espouses:

> The only rational way [he claims] for the adherents of any tradition to approach intellectually, culturally, and linguistically alien rivals is one that allows for the possibility that in one or more areas the other may be rationally superior to it in respect precisely of that in the alien tradition which it cannot yet comprehend.[50]

MacIntyre's intention is to outflank "modernity," which he perceptively characterizes as the "ability to understand everything from human culture and history" within the terms of one's own horizon, culture, or language.[51] The rational resolution of incommensurability, therefore, always rests with the perception that a problem has arisen that one's local tradition cannot resolve within its own terms but may resolve *in the incommensurable terms* offered by some "alien" culture that it cannot yet understand. But, of course, there is no reason to suppose a similar incommensurability (one that does not generate incomprehensibility) never arises within our own sprawling "plural" practices; although if such contests obtain (as plainly they do) then MacIntyre's optimism and adherence to an exclusionary bivalence would be utterly misplaced. For instance, on abortion or suicide, there may be no disjunctive finding possible within a modern tradition, and there may be no formal or dialectical possibility of ensuring same by reference to any historicized forms of reason not already secretly essentialized along Aristotelian–Thomist lines or the like. There is no better prospect there, and all the ones there are are hardly neutral.

You may appreciate the rejoinder if you bear in mind the arbitrariness or vacuity of MacIntyre's account of "goods internal to a practice." For, for MacIntyre, a would-be "practice" is not a genuine practice *if* there are no "goods internal" to it that *define* that practice (normatively) as such. There are then two possibilities: (1) the arbitrary or vacuous sense just mentioned; (2) a sense in which "goods" and "virtues" may be defined in terms of antecedent "practices," but only for reasons that are *independently* compelling, *not* through any supposed conceptual necessity or logical entailment or cognitive privilege or in any way that precludes, by logical fiat, alternative options not compatible with a bivalent logic.[52] It's not clear, also, whether (1) and (2) must, if drawn from actual traditions, accord with Aristotle's notion of the human *telos*. I understand, for instance, that the devastating Japanese attack on Port Arthur in the Russo-Japanese war was made without a formal declaration of war, which the Japanese regarded as honorable and the Russians as a violation of acceptable international conduct. The Japanese apparently regarded their behavior as entirely in accord with the strict code of *bushido*. They might have claimed to have met MacIntyre's notion of there being an internal relationship between virtue and historical practice. But I cannot see how they could be faulted on MacIntyre's grounds or how, in the face of an obvious incompatibility and incommensurability, there could be a neutral resolution "in accord with reason" unless one fell back to essentialist norms of an obviously arbitrary kind. I hasten to add that I cannot see that the Japanese are indisputably vindicated in their own judgment either. The whole idea is too simplistic . . . one might well say absurd.

Certainly, the greatest challenge to MacIntyre's thesis would come from instances in accord with (2) that may not accord with the "Aristotelian–Thomist" tradition.[53] That possibility seems to be characteristic of contemporary societies. MacIntyre discounts it. But he cannot secure his argument without falling back to the dilemma already adduced. He has little else to say. In general, there is no reason *not* to suppose, either with regard to Kuhn or MacIntyre, (1) that the "rational" resolution of a significant "incommensurability" is itself a consensual artifact rather than an objectivist discovery of some sort; (2) that resolutions in accord with (1) are usually plural, divergent, irreconcilable in bivalent terms; (3) that it is unlikely that there is any "tradition" (like the Thomist) that is discernibly superior to all others in resolving the usual puzzle cases and incommensurabilities; and (4) that a bivalent logic will be inadequate for resolving the puzzles that arise, in ways that antecedently eschew essentialism or cognitive privilege.

IV

We have reached a stalemate here. We have found (1) that adequational theories of the self, whether cognitivist or constructivist, are prone to claim privilege (on the competence required for objective judgment and commitment), or that such theories (as in the constructivist option) may have suppressed the evidence of such privilege; (2) that existential theories problematize the supposed competence of practical reason, whether cognitivist or constructivist, but do not by themselves resolve the objectivity question; and (3) that cognitive and rational competence cannot fail to be conceptually inseparable from the standing of our theories of the human subject, whether in morality or science.

My original point, remember, beginning with Rawls, was that twentieth-century moral philosophy characteristically avoids, denies, or otherwise diminishes the existential complexities within which our cognitive and rational competence first functions. The strongest arguments for favoring the existential over the adequational are these: first, that, on the cognitive side, no part of the natural world is sufficiently transparent (if, indeed, norms and values may be objectively discovered there) to ensure a simple realism of such norms and values, or their direct perception or their discernible fixity or reliability; and, second, that, on the side of practical reason, reason is itself an artifact of changing history and enculturation. My catalogue of specimens confirms that leading theorists often eschew explicit privilege and yield in the direction of history; but it also shows that they cling in the last resort to vestiges of invariance and cognitive transparency that illicitly entrench their own moral ideologies. All that is gone now, if the foregoing arguments are admitted.

The question remains: Can we recover moral objectivity under the double condition (1) that privilege is denied; and (2) that practical reason proves to be an artifact of history? At any rate, (1) and (2) are surely the commanding (existential) constraints imposed on relevant speculation – not merely in moral theory but in general epistemology and the philosophy of science as well. I am entirely sanguine about the prospects of moral theory under these new constraints, if for no other reason than that the most recent efforts in the philosophy of science are also noticeably sanguine in proposing plausible theories of objectivity that conform more and more closely with the economies of (1) and (2). I admit all the pertinent differences between science and morality, but I see no *a priori* objection against our claiming an objective morality. I say only that the disputes I have aired surely set the terms of reference under which the philosophical contests of our time may be judged to be responsive to the lessons of historicity. My intuition is this: we may secure a sense of objectivity in the moral domain (as in the scientific) only by way of a diminished *posit* based on a critical assessment of what we may suppose is not altogether preposterous or illicit. (I shall call this, finally, a "second-best" objectivity.)

Contemporary moral philosophies are very strongly drawn to the magisterial doctrines originally offered by Aristotle and Kant. But, although they appear to require one or another of the forms of invariance Aristotle and Kant espouse – the theoretical grasp of the human *telos*, the universalized rules of reason – they are, for the most part, unwilling to claim such invariances directly or initially. They hit upon them, cleverly enough, in open inquiry; they find them dialectically entailed or reasonably idealized from diverging contingencies, or similarly detected. It is nearly impossible to mention a single salient theory that gives up invariance altogether. That is the point of the convergences I find among Rawls and Apel and Habermas and MacIntyre. But that is also what I have – obliquely – now called into mortal doubt. I have uncovered, here, the executive doctrines these theorists espouse, by way of examining the larger strategies they favor. But I have not offered the full resources of the new options I suggest: those that adhere to items (1) and (2) of the last tally. Such an effort calls for a fresh beginning. For the moment, it should be enough to fix our sense of how large a change of vision that would require. (I suggest that it amounts to the abandonment of "First Philosophy.")

Let me mention a theory or two, more for the sake of strategy than of doctrine, in order, in closing this preliminary skirmish, to collect evidence favoring the existential over the adequational and, within the existential, themes robustly in accord with (1) and (2). The specimens I have in mind are hardly successful, I admit. But that is not their most important feature. Rather, one begins to see in them – through their very weakness – the prospect of a radical escape from the iron grip on moral theory that Aristotle and Kant (and their successors) have exercised down to our own day. The novelty I have in mind rests with the enabling complexities and constraints of history. They are absent from Aristotle and Kant; and the figures I've reviewed (chiefly, Rawls and MacIntyre) have, in only tentative – quite inadequate – ways, reached out to history.

Contemporary feminism affords some of the most plausible specimens. Among these, I single out Catherine MacKinnon's manifesto: partly because it is so explicitly existential and opposed to (what I have been calling) the adequationist's stance, partly because it relies on and then criticizes and seeks to enlarge one of the most important sources of existential critique (the Marxist), partly because it grasps in a clear way the link between the presumed "objectivity" of the adequationist and the effective hegemony (in class or gender terms, according to MacKinnon) of such a presumption in politics and law, partly because it applies its best critique of ("male-dominated") liberal hegemonies unperceived in the work of such figures as Rawls and Ronald Dworkin,[54] and partly because it palpably fails to achieve its own objective (a "feminist theory of the state"). For all these reasons, it affords a clear sense of the problematic of shifting from an adequational to an existential point of view.

Here is a sample remark of MacKinnon's, which, read as strategy rather than doctrine, poses the legitimative question all adequationists ignore – from Aristotle and Kant to Rawls and MacIntyre:

> Formally, the state is male in that objectivity is its norm. Objectivity is liberal legalism's conception of itself. It legitimates itself by reflecting its view of society, a society it helps make by so seeing it, and calling that view, and that relation, rationality. Since rationality is measured by point-of-viewlessness, what counts as reason is that which corresponds to the way things are. Practical rationality, in this approach, means that which can be done without changing anything. In this framework, the task of legal interpretation becomes "to perfect the state as mirror of the society." Objectivist epistemology is the law of law. It ensures that the law will most reinforce existing distributions of power when it most closely adheres to its own ideal of fairness. Like the science it emulates, this epistemological stance cannot see the social specificity of reflection as method or its chance to embrace that which it reflects. Such law not only reflects a society in which men rule women; it rules in a male way insofar as "the phallus means everything that sets itself up as a mirror."[55]

The most important feature of these remarks – the book is replete with observations of this sort – lies with the fact that *they challenge the*

supposed objectivity of a particular moral political, or legal tradition or
practice in terms that its own adequational champions cannot admit or
accommodate. They cannot, because to admit MacKinnon's charge is
(1) to construe objectivity and rationality as a problematic construction,
in the existential sense, and (2) to subordinate the epistemic credentials
of the adequationist's claims as legitimatively dependent upon existential
considerations. It is no small part of MacKinnon's acuity that she notes
(in a footnote to the passage just cited) that Rawls's "original position is
a version of [what she calls] the objective standpoint."[56] It shows at a
stroke, therefore, the enormous power of certain versions of what I have
been calling the existential strategy regarding human subjects. In my
own mind, that strategy is most compellingly associated with the work
of figures like Marx and Nietzsche and Michel Foucault. But that is
neither here nor there for my present purpose, since I am featuring the
strategic rather than the doctrinal aspects of MacKinnon's account. I am
happy, however, to acknowledge whatever validity may be accorded
MacKinnon's specific critique of American law.

You will have noticed that, *if* MacKinnon's strategy is honored, then
the appeal to the neutrality or objectivity or universality of "reason" is
instantly rendered doubtful. The point is not whether it can or cannot
be vindicated – ultimately. The point is rather that the challenge cannot
rightly be ignored. What I have demonstrated, in effect, is that the
legitimation of reason (whether theoretical or practical) has not been
squarely met in Rawls and Apel and MacIntyre; and that the challenge
is not due merely to the advocacy of an alternative doctrine but, more
profoundly, to the advocacy of an alternative philosophical strategy.
What MacKinnon helps us to see is how, precisely, questions about
Rawls's "original position" suggest the reasonableness of stalemating his
claims (as well as Apel's and Habermas's and MacIntyre's) *before* he has
satisfied us on the matter of existential sources – in particular, regarding
the extent to which those sources mask certain deeper hegemonies.

I confess I don't find MacKinnon's comparison of the Marxist and
feminist critiques entirely apt; but then, I find the exposé of widespread
institutional "male dominance" unanswerable. It is in this sense that I
feature MacKinnon's remarks – as suggesting the power of an existential
strategy rather than as merely a feminist doctrine. But let me offer a
sample passage from MacKinnon's theory that leads us ineluctably to
generalize about the underlying strategy:

Sexuality [she says] is to feminism what work is to marxism: that which is
most one's own yet most taken away. Marxist theory argues that society
is fundamentally constructed of the relations people form as they do and

make things needed to survive humanly. Work is the social process of shaping and transforming the material and social worlds, creating people as social beings as they create value. . . . Implicit in feminist theory is a parallel argument: the melding, direction, and expression of sexuality organizes society into two sexes: women and men. This division underlies the totality of social relations. . . . As work is to marxism, sexuality to feminism is socially constructed yet constructing, universal as activity yet historically specific, jointly comprised of matter and mind.[57]

Here, MacKinnon instantiates the most radical possibilities of the feminist and existential critiques, combining in one statement a doctrinal and a strategic extreme. For, for one thing, the existential strategy construes cognitive and rational competence as an artifact of the conditions of human life; and, for another, the feminist and Marxist doctrines historicize that existential theme. Once we allow ourselves to be guided, at the level of strategy, by the joint import of these conjectures, we cannot plausibly retreat to any (doctrinally) privileged or (strategically) adequational maneuver.

Moral dispute instructs epistemology and the philosophy of science here. One grasps the lesson easily by turning to another sector of inquiry altogether: by acknowledging, for instance, that, in the work of analytic philosophers like W. V. Quine and Donald Davidson, the entire philosophical game is completely decided by one's *initial* entry (*adequationally*) into the space of debate. I think there can be little doubt that all the dissatisfactions with Rawls's conception of reason, in *A Theory of Justice*, similarly depend on the initial construction of the "original position" and the seemingly invincible use to which it is immediately put. At the risk, therefore, of confusing matters by citing a few remarks from Quine that have nothing really directly to do with moral questions (but that do bear on their fate nevertheless), let me remind you of the opening lines of the second edition of *Pursuit of Truth*. Quine sets his problem very cleverly there – I mean to draw an important parallel to Rawls at least:

> From impacts on our sensory surfaces, [Quine says,] we in our collective and cumulative creativity down the generations have projected our systematic theory of the external world. Our system is proving successful in predicting subsequent sensory input. How have we done it?[58]

The full relevance of these remarks may elude you. What I make of them is this. Quine speaks of our "theory of the external world," which he says is "projected" from "impacts on our sensory surfaces" and which has proved "successful" about further such "sensory input." The language is devilishly clever. Quine manages to frame his puzzle *initially* so that "impacts on our sensory surfaces" are *already* construed as emanating from the "external world" *from which* we (then) "project" *a theory about the external world that includes those same impacts*! Nothing could be prettier. Quine's words form both an "externalist" view (insisting on an independent world the features of which do not depend on our cognitive interventions) and an "adequational" view (presuming that our cognitive competence matches the mentioned features of the world itself). I cannot discuss Quine's epistemology here. I have no intention of doing so. But I must emphasize that Quine *sets* his problem in a most authoritative way by his externalist and adequational stance; and that that stance is put at serious risk only by raising an existential question about Quine's initial entry: Why should we begin as Quine begins? we ask. Quine flatters us by acknowledging "our collective and cumulative creativity" and, at the same time, he insinuates that the problem *he* thereby sets *is* the essential problem for American (indeed, for all of Western) philosophy.

If one had doubts about all this, Quine dispels them systematically. First of all, he distinguishes between "propositional attitudes *de re*," which presuppose a relation of *intention*, between thoughts and things intended, for which I [that is, Quine] conceive of no adequate [scientific] guidelines," and "propositional attitudes *de dicto*," which favor "annexation to scientific language." (This marks, of course, Quine's famous elimination of Brentano's notion of intentionality. But *he himself* has already exploited intentionality in order to dismiss it.) Secondly, he explains, "each perception [referring back to sensory inputs] is a single occurrence in a particular brain and is fully specifiable in neurological terms once the details are known."[59] These cannot be anything but adequational remarks: as such, they render our doubts inoperative. The upshot is that Quine *confines dispute within the space he first defines*. That *is* the adequationist's way – whether Quine's or Rawls's (who is, of course, not a cognitivist in moral matters). The opponent of either will seem to proceed in an arbitrary or unfair or even irrelevant way, in not being willing to begin with the common ground that Quine (or Rawls) lays down. But if you consider that the question is not merely one of hearing Quine out (or Rawls) but of formulating (as both concede) the best account of the rational undertaking each examines (science or morality, respectively), then the existential challenge to the work of each will not seem intemperate or ill-mannered.

Still, I am reluctant to allow the matter to be decided as a question of mere manners. The truth is: Quine's opening remarks *are*, already, a way of entering and shaping the conceptual dispute he offers the profession at large. He never discusses *that* maneuver (existentially)! But it already implicates (in the intentional sense he sets aside) "our collective and cumulative creativity," which he then ingeniously *confines* to what (alone) *may follow from* those putative "impacts on our sensory surfaces" – which (as a consequence) are no longer subject to the same "creativity" but merely ground it. There you have the clue to the counterstrategy I am applying to Rawls. In short, Quine ingeniously conflates the elements he needs from existential and adequational sources. Quine is no apriorist in Kant's sense; nor is he a noetic theorist in Aristotle's. But he *does*, within his naturalistic and pragmatist proclivities, invent imperceptible analogues of both. I am suggesting that Rawls's pared-down apriorism is not noticed within the space of American moral philosophy for much the same reason Quine's holism and behaviorism (by which Quine entrenches his particular epistemology and metaphysics in a seemingly neutral account of logic and language) is similarly not seen to exploit a "transcendental" presumption. There you have the them of late Anglo-American "naturalism," which claims to banish legitimative questions.

I apologize for the detour, but it does confirm the deeper relevance of the existential challenge and, of course, the parallel between the theory of science and moral theory. If we eschew cognitive privilege – with or without history – we cannot allow the initial entry into the space of science or morality *to be taken as given in that sense in which only an adequational account of subjects or cognizinq aqents is admitted.* There's the flaw of analytic moral theory. I cannot see any difference here between analytic moral philosophy and analytic epistemology.[60] (It is the reliable mark of a closet First Philosophy.)

The truth is, Rawls has suppressed the initial question on which the reasonableness of first entering the space of moral debate in the way he does may and must be assessed. Rawls's "externalism" (the counterpart of Quine's) assures us that practical reason may be counted on to be constant and uniformly objective in the "original position" – also, to remain essentially unaffected by the vagaries of history and changing cultures. But the assumption is never tested and objections are never really allowed. (The sheer coherence and plausibility of MacKinnon's existential assumption shows at a stroke why Rawls's liberal conjecture cannot go unchallenged.) There is no discussion of the matter in all of Rawls's work, in spite of the fact that he assures us he's examined the principal alternatives to his own analysis. There is no argument in Rawls to show that the moral, political, or legal order of social life he favors could *not* be anything but an "expression of an underlying natural order." This last phrasing is due to Roberto Unger[61] – directed against all forms of naturalistic liberalism (as much perhaps against Ronald Dworkin as Rawls): that is, directed against the general assumption that human nature, human reason, human interests are essentially fixed by and in a "natural order" rather than being (in some significant degree) the changing artifacts of a changing history.[62]

I must of course resist the temptation to follow these intriguing leads. We are, after all, only at the point of recommending a change of strategy. You must not imagine that very much can be gained by such preliminaries alone. No, the puzzles of moral theory will seem even murkier when one accepts the change. At any rate, it completely baffles our older expectations. The problem is to define anew what may rightly be expected of moral philosophy – in shifting from the adequational to the existential, from the invariant to the historicized, from the privileged to the merely conjectured. You will find all this adumbrated once again in MacKinnon. The word "Toward" in her book's title is the entire sum of what she offers in the way of a positive resolution. She captures the distinction between the adequational and the existential admirably enough:

> A jurisprudence [she says] is a theory of the relation between life and law. In life, "woman" and "man" are widely experienced as features of being, not constructs of perception, cultural interventions, or forced identities. Gender, in other words, is lived as ontology, not as epistemology. Law actively participates in this transformation of perspective into being. . . . What female ontology can confront male epistemology; that is, what female epistemology can confront male ontology? What point of view can question the code of civil society [the liberal vision]? The answer is simple, concrete, specific, and real: women's social inequality with men on the basis of sex, hence the point of view of women's subordination to men. Women are not permitted fully to know what sex equality would look like. . . . Equality will require change, not reflection – a new jurisprudence, a new relation between life and law. Law that does not dominate life is as difficult to envision as a society in which men do not dominate women, and for the same reasons.[63]

But where are her instructions regarding a new use of "ontology" and "epistemology"? There are none. More than that, MacKinnon seems to be saying that there cannot be any way of recovering "objectivity." But where's the argument?

If she had construed the work of justice as a straightforward matter of correcting inequalities, she would have fallen back to the liberal vision. MacKinnon will have none of that. But, if the "corrective" were nothing but the expression of a feminist conviction, then "actional" resources would be nothing but ideology and bare hegemony. What then is the feminist *theory* of the state? You see the dilemma. "Disaffected from objectivity, having been its prey, but excluded from the world through relegation to subjective inwardness," MacKinnon affirms, "women's interest lies in overthrowing *the distinction itself*."[64] Yes, of course, but what then?

I may perhaps add without elaboration that it has been borne in on me that, in the Muslim and African and other countries, the question of the just treatment of women hardly ever takes the extreme disjunctive form it takes in American feminist terms. The plight of women through-out the world is plain enough (sexual slavery, institutionalized rape, physical abuse, forced abortion, the killing of female infants) and may well require a change of moral vision; but such a change need not be polarized (as by MacKinnon) between the "feminist" and the "patriar-chal" although the pattern also clearly gives the advantage to men.

V

There you have a clue to the essential *aporia* of contemporary moral (and epistemological) theory. "Objectivity" is now seen ("existentially") to be an artifact of history and hegemony. But if Kuhn and MacIntyre are right at all in supposing that a "paradigm shift" may yet be vindicated in objective and rational terms, we need to know how the strategy works. For the moment, we have only the barest clue that the prospect is thought not to be incoherent. We cannot count on Kuhn or MacIntyre, for they are not entirely consistent on the matter of an independent or invariant reality; they also do not satisfactorily explain what may be meant by overcoming, by rational and objective means, the conceptual incommensurabilities of opposed traditions or ways of life – regarding either science or morality.

Richard Bernstein, who has pursued the matter in two substantial volumes is right of course to query whether there is "some third way of understanding critique that avoids – passes between – the Scylla of 'groundless critique' [Max Weber] and the Charybdis of rationally grounded critique that 'rests' upon illusory foundations [Apel and Habermas]?"[65] Bernstein is sanguine about such a "third way." But the best he can offer is to recover the pragmatist's notion of "fallibilism," and that is not enough. Bernstein rightly sees that MacIntyre's resolution of the incommensurability problem harbors "an *implicit* cultural imperi-alism," the supposed objective superiority of the "Aristotelian–Thomistic tradition."[66] That is, Bernstein rightly sees that MacIntyre's solution violates the historicism MacIntyre himself espouses. But Bernstein fails to see that fallibilism (in Peirce's original sense) violates the same constraint; and that, if the charge may be set aside (possibly along the lines of a Deweyan reading of Peirce), then we would be back again – but with a vengeance – to MacKinnon's dilemma.

Bernstein sees the whole of late twentieth-century philosophy as focused on finding a third way between "objectivism" and "relativism" – in effect, between a privileged grasp of an independent, ahistorical, changeless reality (adequate for morality as well as science) and the denial of any single, "overarching" conceptual framework that can ensure "objectivity" against the splintering of indefinitely many conceptual schemes radically relativized to whatever perspective we happen to inhabit.[67] Bernstein's project is to secure "objectivity" without falling back to objectivism and without yielding to relativism. In a way, it is the idealized concern of all the theorists I have mentioned. MacIntyre, of course, emerges as the closest, and therefore the most opposed, of all of these, since he is the only one among them (besides Bernstein) who features the incommensurability problem and who claims to have found a (third) way to secure the objectivity of moral judgment – while accepting a robust form of historicism and overcoming the threatening chaos of relativism.

Bernstein's countermove simply does not work. (I pursue it here in spite of the fact that it opens up a vast new set of puzzles – that I cannot do justice to.) I remind you, however, before taking a closer look at this last confrontation, that all the doctrines so far considered should be regarded as so many specimen expressions of the adequational and existential strategies I have been tracking. Rawls and Apel and MacIntyre and Habermas are certainly among the principal moral philosophers of our time. MacKinnon and Unger and Bernstein are probably not. The irony is that the latter have a better grasp of the contest between adequational and existential strategies than the former; but the former are, for doctrinal reasons, more influential than the latter – and deservedly so. There is always a danger of being blinded by the sheer proliferation of arresting details. They do indeed serve to collect a vivid image of our age. But no one doctrine by itself commands our allegiance, and our sense of a reasoned moral philosophy (or epistemology) demands a certain dialectical patience.

In any case, the common ground between Bernstein and MacIntyre is registered by Bernstein in the following terms:

The rational superiority of a tradition can be vindicated without (falsely) presupposing that there are universally neutral, ahistorical standards of rationality. There is no "rationality as such." However it is possible to show that a specific tradition – say the Aristotelian tradition – can be rationally vindicated and shown to be rationally progressive by its own "standards of rationality."[68]

MacIntyre had (wrongly) supposed (Bernstein thinks) that it could be decisively shown that "rival and incommensurable traditions fail, not only according to Aristotelian standards of rationality, but according to their own standards of rationality"; and that, as a result, a particular tradition's (the "Aristotelian–Thomistic" tradition) could be shown to be superior to all others. The trouble is not, Bernstein thinks, that that can never be shown in any particular contest. It is, rather, that the verdict is always openended and no tradition can claim the prize for all future contingencies – or (in MacIntyre's vocabulary) for all future "epistemological crises."[69]

Bernstein is right, of course, but he also misses the point. For, first of all, if "there is no 'rationality as such'," then any would-be "standards of rationality" cannot rightly be fixed once and for all, are always merely abstracted from a tradition's ongoing practice, punctuated, arrested for an interval, idealized, made plausible as a summary of a tendency never actually operative or binding as such. Secondly (and even more compellingly), although it is true that our "standards of rationality" belong to different living traditions, *there are* no determinate particular traditions to which they belong!

The incommensurability problem requires that we formulate determinately many individuated *doctrines* that may be pitted against one another. "*Tradition*" is a dummy term, a holding-place for some holistically intended space of societal life within which reflexively constructed rules, principles, "standards of rationality," norms, criteria, and the like are thought to capture, heuristically and perspicuously (in the interval in which they are advanced), the orderly practice of this society or that. *That* is why MacIntyre cannot gain his point: the "Aristotelian–Thomistic" *doctrine* is either a series of Zenonian points thought to approximate to a living *tradition*, or it is a separate doctrine justified by some privileged grasp of independent reality; the first reading renders the claim quite pointless, the second renders it inconsistent with MacIntyre's own larger commitment to history. But Bernstein can fare no better.

If I may say so, the insight is the same that is shared, quite powerfully, by Wittgenstein and Gadamer. For, for Gadamer, we belong to a tradition, but there is no tradition to which we belong; and, for Wittgenstein, in sharing a form of life, we act according to rules, but there are, normally, no rules according to which we act.[70] This collects my reading of the notorious paragraphs 201–202 of the *Investigations*: it signifies both that a (living) practice *is* openended, may be extended in ways that cannot be antecedently confined by determinate rules; but that, at any point in that practice, apt practitioners are normally able to formulate a retrospective rule that effectively fits their living practice.[71]

Gadamer makes a similar point in speaking of one's tradition, except that, unlike Wittgenstein, he treats tradition as historicized and he treats selves as social constructions of some sort. In any case, Gadamer (whom Bernstein professes to admire in the relevant regard) explicitly holds – it is surely one of the central doctrines of his hermeneutics – that:

> The historical movement of human life [within a tradition] consists in the fact that it is never utterly bound to any one standpoint, and hence can never have a truly closed horizon. The horizon is, rather, something into which we move and that moves with us. Horizons change for a person who is moving. Thus the horizon of the past, out of which all human life lives and which exists in the form of tradition, is always in motion. It is not historical consciousness that first sets the surrounding horizon in motion. But in it this motion becomes aware of itself.[72]

Now, what I wish to emphasize – in favoring the existential over the adequational and, in particular, in historicizing the existential – is that neither Bernstein nor MacIntyre can convincingly solve the incommensurability problem, either in the punctuated or episodic sense or in the inclusive sense that ranges over all future "crises." It cannot achieve the first, because it cannot demonstrate that there is *ever* an exclusively apt or "correct" resolution if there is an acceptable resolution; and it cannot achieve the second, because it is *never* possible to generalize over all future moral or epistemological "crises." The denial of the first requires a privileged view of bivalence;[73] the denial of the second requires a privileged view of the invariance of human reason (which Bernstein and, more equivocally, MacIntyre reflect). But that brings us back to what was unsatisfactory in Rawls and Apel (the secret reliance on invariant first principles).

I close this discussion by reminding you of Peirce's conception of fallibilism and by indicating why Bernstein cannot avail himself of that conception *in countering MacIntyre's claim*. The matter is a subtle one but of the greatest strategic importance. In fact, it marks in a particularly instructive way the fatal lacuna in nearly all current attempts to bypass historicity in reclaiming objectivity (Rawls, Apel) or to reconcile historicity with the recovery of objectivity (MacIntyre, Habermas). I am convinced that something like Peirce's optimistic doctrine – fallibilism – lies behind nearly every form of progressivism featured in our time, whether in science or morality: for instance, in Popper, in Kuhn, in Lakatos, in science; and in Dewey, in Habermas, in Putnam, in Bernstein, in moral and political matters.[74]

Bernstein espouses fallibilism – as providing the required third way. He attributes the doctrine to "Peirce and the pragmatists," but that is because he holds that "fallibilism is characteristic of the experimental habit of mind [and] that philosophy itself is intrinsically fallibilistic. [That is, p]hilosophy is interpretive, tentative, always subject to correction."[75] Now, *this is* Dewey's formula, but it is definitely not Peirce's. The first is insufficient or epistemically vacuous, the second is adequate to the task, but incompatible with historicism and the denial of invariance and privilege. The distinction is crucial: in effect, Dewey is an evolutionist (a Darwinian more than a Hegelian) who consistently repudiates all essentialisms, all modal necessities and invariances; but Peirce is a Kantian (or a Hegelianized Kantian) who believes that indefinitely extended human inquiry (Peirce's approximation to the Hegelian process of history by way of evolution) yields, in the limit ("the long run") the invariances of reason regarding knowledge and practice that Kant originally thought he could discern transcendentally. In a word, to espouse fallibilism in the Peircean sense would be to commit Bernstein to the "objectivism" he (rightly) opposes in MacIntyre (and should oppose in Rawls and Apel); and to espouse fallibilism in Dewey's sense would commit Bernstein's "third way" to being no more than an expression of "philosophical hope" – an optimism or ideology without any validating grounds at all – characteristic (in diverse ways) of Habermas's "American" confidence, of Hilary Putnam's and Bernstein's own confidence, and even (in a dampened form) of Richard Rorty's moral and political optimism.[76]

It would serve no purpose to pursue Peirce's notion in depth here. The relevant points of importance are: (1) that fallibilism in the original Peircean sense *is* objectivist and progressivist; (2) that Dewey's is neither, but in being neither, is committed to progressivism in a completely blind and arbitrary way or one that has no principled relevance at all for determining objective truth (unless sheer optimism is a "principle"); *and* (3) that there cannot possibly be a plausible reason for invoking fallibilism – as in the manner of Bernstein, Putnam, or Habermas – with respect to either science or morality, once objectivism and relativism are disavowed. The lacuna that Bernstein has effectively discerned cannot possibly be filled by fallibilistic options; either such options would be fallbacks to the very objectivism being opposed, or they would be irrelevant because inherently inadequate.

You may grasp all this at a stroke if you bear in mind that Peirce expressly held (as early as 1897 – a view from which he never strayed) that "fallibilism cannot be appreciated in anything like its true significancy until evolution has been considered."[77] But, of course, evolution, in Peirce's hands, is a very complex doctrine – one that, in particular, requires a distinction between *mind* and *consciousness*, since that (alone) enables Peirce to admit the operation of "mind" or "habit" or the habituation that we call a "law of nature" or "Thirdness" in the real world *independent* of our subjective or psychological states. But that is simply a retreat (even if at the limit of inquiry) to objectivism. Dewey does not commit himself (quite rightly, I should say) to such an Emersonian-like notion in his mature work. But then, in *not* adopting it, Dewey effectively denies the very ground on which Bernstein and other (liberal) progressivists ultimately depend. They don't see the untenability of their position, however.[78] Its exposé follows at once from what Peirce calls his "conditional idealism" – that is, his pragmatism, in which he characterizes fallibilism thus: "I hold that truth's independence of individual opinions is due (so far as there is any 'truth') to its being the predestined result to which sufficient inquiry *would* ultimately lead."[79] Peirce says very plainly that "there is a definite opinion to which the mind of man is, on the whole, and in the long run tending. . . . Everything, therefore, which will be thought to exist in the final opinion is real, and nothing else."[80] But it would be a great mistake to suppose – in the liberal or inductivist sense – that mere (Deweyan) "self-correction" separated from Peirce's ontological optimism regarding the evolution of "objective" mind could possibly justify the appeal to fallibilism as a principled "third way" in Bernstein's sense. (Certainly, the relationship between fallibilism and constructivism needs still to be worked out.)

I have taken the trouble to spell out this weakness of liberal pragmatism because it is so much in vogue and because it is so easily taken to be a promising alternative to all the failed options I have been canvassing. Or, more likely, it is the principle that those failed options implicitly accept. For instance, I should say that it (or something very much like it) lies behind the work of Rawls, Habermas, Putnam, MacIntyre, and Bernstein. The short way to defeat it is to recognize tht it is merely a version of a privileged adequational strategy that masquerades as existential and free of privilege. Apart from all that, it confirms what I have been at pains to emphasize, namely, that questions of moral and epistemological theory are ultimately inseparable and altogether uncompelling if they are not rightly grounded existentially.

2

Moral Philosophy in Four Tiers

I

The theorists I have featured – John Rawls, Karl-Otto Apel, Jürgen Habermas, Alasdair MacIntyre – are what I call "second-tier" moral philosophers. The term is not familiar, but it is not intended to be derogatory. I mean by it to draw attention to the obvious fact that all four theorists (as well as many others) are chiefly occupied with (1) formulating a determinate vision of the objective standing of certain traditional moral norms by which human life is thought to be rightly guided or governed, and (2) formulating something of the rationale by which such visions can be and are legitimated. The term is purely classificatory. What is important about second-tier thinkers is their being convinced that the genuine validity of what they offer under the terms of (1) can be reliably confirmed in accord with (2). There's hardly anything in the way of legitimatize doubt about them: they form a backdrop, therefore, for a deeper probe.

I shall say that candidate views in accord with (1) are first-order (moral claims or judgments or convictions), and that candidate views in accord with (2) are second-order (rationales). Again, the distinction is purely classificatory. I suggest we construe it in as relaxed a way as possible. Candidates for (1) may include prima facie moral beliefs apparently or actually operative in this society or that, regardless of whether they *are* objectively valid or can be shown to be. If we apply this small rule in the relaxed way I recommend, what we should collect as its specimens may be called *moral ideologies* – meaning by that nothing more than doctrines confidently affirmed in the spirit of (1)–(2)

but not yet actually confirmed and possibly not even capable of being confirmed. Second-tier thinkers are, I say, straightout morel ideologues. "Third-tier" thinkers fasten primarily on the actual validity of second-order rationales for ensuring the objective standing of moral ideologies.

There's an equivocation in this adjustment: one might suppose, for instance, that the doctrines Rawls and MacIntyre espouse are false or illegitimate, without hurrying to conclude that all second-tier views need be such; or, one might suppose it impossible, in principle, to demonstrate that any candidates within the range of (1) could ever be confirmed in accord with (2). Speaking with care, then: theorists who favor the second reading may be called *moral skeptics*.

Third-tier moral philosophers are those – I shall say – who (1) believe that second-tier theory is inherently problematic, who are (a) outright moral skeptics, or (b) not convinced by the legitimative work of particular (or the usual) second-tier thinkers, or (c) still sanguine about some further untried ways of legitimating the objective standing of moral norms and values. Speaking carefully again: *moral realists* are those contemporary theorists among the company of (c) who specifically believe they can meet the charges brought by the adherents of (a) and (b) against the usual realism of norms and values and can do so on cognitivist grounds. "Moral realist" is an attribution of art, now in general use, signifying the important difference between *realists* of the second-tier sort (MacIntyre, for instance, but hardly Rawls) and those occupied with the questions raised by (a)–(c). Among the leading third-tier theorists one cannot fail to include such figures as David Wiggins, John Mackie, Sabina Lovibond, John McDowell, Thomas Nagel, Peter Railton, and Mark Platts.[1] These are theorists of vastly different dialectical skills and very different points of view. Most (excepting Mackie) form a family of sorts, if not an actual school ("moral realism"). Late analytic moral philosophy is largely occupied with the prospects of moral realism, or perhaps it is already at the cusp of searching beyond such prospects. It is an essential part of the argument I am offering that second-tier theories cannot possibly succeed and that third-tier theories are therefore committed to a hopeless rearguard action. But the force of saying so depends on coming to see that the preponderant part of contemporary moral philosophy is occupied with the dialectical connections between second- and third-tier thinking. You will not fail (I assure you) to find my third-tier specimens disappointing; you may, therefore, judge my classificatory scheme to be a little forced. I concede the point: I am hoping that the labor of assessing the work of my third-tier specimens will make you impatient for the eventual corrective.

It is perhaps an accident of history that late analytic moral philosophy that is sanguine about moral objectivity is also sanguine about moral realism. It would not be unfair to read both Apel and Habermas and the communitarian thinkers they have influenced (primarily in Germany) as, to some extent, third-tier constructivists of the Kantian sort (moral constructivists), who count thereby as the counterpart champions of objectivity to the (third-tier) moral realists. But, generally, it remains true that English-language theorists who link moral objectivity with constructivism – by way of the competence of practical reason (Rawls, preeminently) – are second-tier thinkers more than third-tier thinkers; and even Apel and Habermas nowhere seriously attempt to demonstrate (though they do affirm) that their "pragmatic" strategies succeed (in effect) in third-tier terms. Their way of proceeding seems more one of making a liberal or Kantian ideology more plausible, as arising in accord with the consensual processes of mutual respect rather than of being merely affirmed once and for all by the pronouncements of transcendental reason. But, in saying this much, we may already anticipate that third-tier thinking is likely to fail.

I think it must fail, largely because it sets out its own projects primarily in accord with the terms of reference of second-tier thinking, which, as we have seen (in chapter 1), is fatally flawed. (In fact, MacIntyre may be read as a third-tier critic of a second-tier MacIntyre.) By and large, third-tier thinking is a stopgap phase of Western moral philosophy: it confirms, by straining the limits of legitimation, that the resources of second-tier thinking (and extensions of same) are played out; it blinds us thereby to strategies of an entirely different sort ("fourth-tier" thinking) that might otherwise be able to reclaim a measure of moral objectivity – of a sort that would be noticeably diminished (in scope and pretension) from the work of second- and third-tier thinking, or would be both more frankly ideological in inspiration and philosophically more accommodating (with regard to opposed ideologies) than the usual theories have proved to be.

Third-tier thinking – chiefly, moral realism – is, therefore, a transition of sorts. I should say that its trajectory is most interesting if read as spanning the conceptions of John Mackie and Thomas Nagel at its most conservative and least inventive and the conceptions of David Wiggins and Sabina Lovibond at its most imaginative. It forms an interlude that (in my opinion) fails as thoroughly as any second-tier thinking fails. But it betrays certain strategic possibilities that render quite unnecessary all of its best efforts. That is not likely to be believed, but that is what I wish to set out. Its theories are disappointing in what they accomplish in a positive way; but it is hardly disappointing to discover that what makes them disappointing is what they have missed "on the way" and what, tantalizingly, was always within the grasp of their best practitioners.

Here, I shall go no further than include an analysis of David Wiggins's argument, which permits us to arrive at a certain convenient closure. My own view is that Lovibond's contribution is the most promising of the lot, because it begins, intuitively, to incorporate the *lebensformlich* themes of Wittgenstein and the *sittlich* themes of Hegel within the terms of analytic philosophy – which is instructively opposed to such accommodations. It fails as well as the more conventional specimens. But, in failing (it dawns on us), it points the way to a conceptual constraint *without which there is no prospect of ever capturing a plausible form of moral objectivity*. Here, I divide the labor: I leave Lovibond for a better inning and I close the discussion with Wiggins. The result is something short of making a new beginning. (I warn you again that you may experience a certain impatience in the labor. I share that impatience. But there is a need to show in a detailed way the futility of the principal strategies of our time.)

I am concerned, then, to map the largest possibilities: to suggest (but hardly more) that the failing of third-tier thinking is the pivot for an entirely new direction; to emphasize a possibility that is nowhere perceived in second- and third-tier thinking, namely, that analytic philosophy (reading moral philosophy as an exemplar) can ensure its own rigor only if it is suitably entrenched in the *Lebensform* or *Sitten* of historical societies. I shall not argue the case in this chapter, I mean to bring us to the edge of the new terrain. Even that bland adjustment, however, marks (for me) the difference between inevitable failure and the possibility of success in philosophical work of every kind. I hold all that in abeyance here, and focus rather on the local infelicities of certain leading third-tier thinkers.

By and large, contemporary moral philosophy is centered on the play between second- and third-tier thinkers, where – significantly – third-tier moral realists aspire to be more effective second-tier realists. Even the moral skeptic supposes that if moral philosophy were objective, it would be objective in the way second-tier thinkers favor. Since second-tier thinkers are ideologues, there is a fair suspicion that third-tier thinkers who are not skeptics – which, by the way, makes room for "Kantians" as well as "Aristotelians" (and moral realists and the self-appointed progeny of even lesser masters) – are also ideologues. In any case, the primary focus of current philosophical debate about moral matters shuttles between second- and third-tier theory. I regard that fact as a sign of impending failure.

If you have penciled in my distinction between second- and third-tier thinking, you have implicitly before you my entire catalogue. For what I call fourth-tier thinking is nothing but that line of speculation that (1) is convinced of the futility of second- and third-tier contests and (2) is open to new lines of theorizing about objectivity and legitimation committed to such themes as (a) the historicity of thinking, (b) the rejection of any principled disjunction between theoretical and practical reason, (c) the treatment of rationality and objectivity as social constructions or artifacts of societal life, (d) the repudiation of any and all forms of cognitive privilege or claims to have discerned some neutral or universal or necessary or objectively independent norms, and (e) a tolerance for applying to matters of moral judgment and commitment logics that are not exclusively bivalent. I endorse fourth-tier thinking – but not yet. A preliminary labor is still needed to show that third-tier thinking is genuinely hopeless. The need for fourth-tier strategies springs from that perception. The point to ponder is the self-impoverishing tendencies of second- and third-tier thinking that has largely denied to itself the resources of all those strategies that bear on the topics I've just collected as (a)–(e). In general, I associate the latter with the work of "continental" philosophy – with figures usually dismissed out of hand by the analytic tradition. By surveying third-tier thinking, one begins to see how those ignored resources are drawn to our attention, dialectically, by the palpable deadend to which such thinking leads.

"First-tier" thinking is more labile. Nothing strenuous hangs on the distinction. You must bear in mind that my specimens of second-tier thinking – Rawls and company – are pared-down descendents (in our own time) of "Kantian" and "Aristotelian" strategies-and-doctrines. If you allow that Rawls and Habermas are "Kantians" and that MacIntyre and Martha Nussbaum are "Aristotelians" (you may well not wish to do so), then, by first-tier thinking, I mean (loosely) any specimen views of a provenance earlier than that of contemporary theories, that mediate as relatively compelling versions (chiefly) of the "Kantian" or "Aristotelian" sort, that have an important formative influence on second-tier thinkers – or else, Kant and Aristotle themselves. For example, Thomas Aquinas is, in my scheme, a first-tier Aristotelian – certainly with respect to MacIntyre; and Charles Sanders Peirce might (somewhat more adventurously) be read as a first-tier Kantian with respect to Karl-Otto Apel or Hilary Putnam or Richard Bernstein.

Under these conditions, Kant and Aristotle are the principal first-tier paradigms. I mean two things by that: one, that the strength and weakness of most second- and third-tier theories cannot be disconnected from the strength and weakness of the original exemplars – and must be studied in their company; and, second, that, particularly with regard to

English-language moral philosophy, it is very likely that every other lesser first-tier figure – Hobbes, say, with respect to David Gauthier, Hume with respect to Annette Baier, Bentham and Mill with respect to J. J. C. Smart, and so on – are not likely to be able to claim to have escaped the general limitations of the principal forms of second- and third-tier disputes. I count all that a promissory note I need not redeem here. (I trust the inherent weakness of moral intuitionism and moral empiricism are reasonably clear, for instance.)

If you have all this before you, I can direct your attention at once to the central contest of third-tier thinking, in particular to the fortunes of moral realism. Consider only this: "Objectivity," Thomas Nagel affirms, "is the central problem of ethics. Not just in theory, but in life."[2] For his part, John Mackie confronts our age no less directly, declaring in the very first sentence of his *Ethics*: "There are no objective values."[3] I have no doubt Nagel construes his own work as meeting Mackie's challenge. The arguments of both, however, are distinctly flawed – flawed in such a way that a close study of what they offer contributes to the gradual dismissal of the entire third-tier undertaking. (It's for that reason that my catalogue is little more than a convenience.) But the argument is lacking. Its burden, as you may guess and as I shall argue, is that the very idea of moral objectivity is flawed: that we should dismiss the converging vision of objectivity in all first-, second-, and third-tier thinking but that, in doing that, we may yet recover a sense of objectivity (a "second-best" objectivity) that belongs to fourth-tier thinking and that has been all but ignored in the philosophical tradition. So the labor has a positive outlook.

II

I offer three third-tier specimens: John Mackie and Thomas Nagel, because they invoke something like Kant's condition of legitimation (universalized reason, categorical obligation) and because they draw from that utterly opposed verdicts about objectivity; David Wiggins, because he favors a more cognitively oriented (eccentric) strategy armed with a clear awareness of the impossibility of recovering any naturalism of the eudaimonistic sort; all three together because their patent failure is due to certain shared considerations, certain exaggerated expectations about what is legitimatively possible or necessary, and the absence of any mention of resources (*fourth-tier* resources) that might have brought legitimation within actual reach.

They play a riskier game than second-tier thinkers, but they also offer little in the way of substantive moralities. Their speculations confirm, I believe, that any seriously sustained effort to recover a Kantian or Aristotelian (or lesser) legitimative strategy is ultimately misguided: in particular, that moral philosophy has been led up the garden path by first- and second-tier maneuvers; that the absurdities of third-tier strategies are patent symptoms of a profound – insuperable – mistake that nonetheless is easily avoided by a mere change of basic strategy; and that there remains before us a perfectly straightforward (neglected) line of reasoning by which to recover what may still be termed an objective form of moral legitimation.

In a word, what I claim is that *everything* third-tier thinkers judge to be problematic (and then cleverly pretend to redeem) *can* be recovered at a stroke by a simple adjustment of our philosophical vision along the lines already tallied as items (a)–(e) but not otherwise. That leaves the legitimative question still unanswered but recovers the moral world well enough to put the question in a new light. I say again, therefore, that to thread our way through the best third-tier work is to come upon the fourth-tier prospect in a natural way. I am aware, of course, that to characterize the work of still-active, even leading theorists in this diminished way will hardly endear my prose to many. It will have to make its own way.

There's the challenge. Now the argument.

Mackie's claim has drawn the greatest fire:

> The claim that values are not objective, are not part of the fabric of the world is meant [Mackie says] to include not only moral goodness, which might be most naturally equated with moral value, but also other things that could be more loosely called moral values or disvalues – rightness and wrongness, duty, obligation, an action's being rotten and contemptible, and so on. It also includes non-moral values, notably aesthetic ones, beauty and various kinds of artistic merit.[4]

It's much too easy to misunderstand Mackie. He does *not* mean to deny that people in general (even the "moral skeptic" – Mackie himself) regularly make judgments of the sorts mentioned, or do so in an orderly way. *No*: making moral judgments one way or another, affirming or denying that there are moral values, counts as "first order moral views, positive or negative; the person who adopts either of them is taking a certain practical, normative stand."[5] Doing that *is* part of "the fabric of the world." Mackie insists on it. He opposes only "a second order view, a view about the status of moral values, about where and how they fit into the world." "First-order" and "second-order" views apparently address entirely separate and independent matters. But that is hard to maintain. "Moral skepticism" (on Mackie's reading) views his original charge as a "second-order" claim: "The kinds of behavior to which moral values and disvalues are ascribed are indeed part of the furniture of the world, and so are the natural descriptive differences between them; but not, perhaps, their difference in value."[6]

Mackie is so familiar by this time that it may seem unnecessary to remind you of what he actually says. I should like you to concede that Mackie is right on *both* "first-" and "second-order" grounds; but that admitting *that* does *not* confirm that, in the "second-order" sense, "values are *not* objective "*not* part of the fabric of the world"! On the contrary, the "first-order" admission (Mackie's) confirms – *when rightly understood* – *that* there *is* a "second-order" sense in which values *are* part of the fabric of the world; that Mackie's reading of what a "second-order" view requires is entirely arbitrary, incompletely worked out, unnecessarily severe (on internal grounds), much too Kantian in any case (given his own outlook), and easily replaced by an alternative "*second-order*" reading that, trivially, defeats the moral skeptic out of his own mouth. You may not believe all that, but that is what I claim.

Moreover, related arguments can be convincingly mounted against Nagel and Wiggins as well, although they are plainly persuaded that they can recover an objective morality on their own grounds. Their particular errors, therefore, take an entirely different turn. Nagel is too confident that a legitimative maneuver of a Kantian-like sort can be satisfactorily recovered. (I say it cannot be.) Wiggins relies too heavily on dredging up a supposedly necessary connection between "the meaning of life" and a pared-down form of legitimation along cognitivist lines; but either there is no such connection or whatever there is presupposes a deeper analysis than Wiggins ever considers – which defeats the very point of Wiggins's gymnastics. In any case, my third-tier specimens are paradigms of the entire tribe: their failure is the tribe's failure.

Mackie's mistake lies in not recognizing that what *he* admits (in the "first-order" sense) is already too strong to disallow *every* "second-order" claim about the objective standing of moral norms and values; hence, that the reason his argument seems compelling lies entirely with the too-easy acceptance of a *first-tier* sense of *what* legitimation should require (without his actually adopting a first-tier vision himself). Deny the credentials of the Kantian legitimative line and Mackie seems quite arbitrary. Oddly, Nagel shares the same Kantian impulse that Mackie favors: the difference is that Nagel is a self-styled realist and Mackie, a skeptic. Nagel's realism cannot, however, be sustained and Mackie's skepticism is too extreme: both defeat themselves by their own words.

Wiggins is more careful and more adventurous; he also rejects (convincingly, I should say) both the Aristotelian and the Kantian options. But he has no real clue about alternative legitimative strategies. He has no other options. So he makes too much of the supposedly necessary connection between moral truth and "the meaning of life." A double disaster follows: first, because none of the tortured strategies my specimen theorists offer is genuinely tenable or really necessary in itself; second, because there are (in the philosophical wings) more promising ways to gain what *is* minimally needed for morality's objective standing; and, third, because, what is available in the way of replacement strategies utterly obviates the skeptical *and* realist (or objectivist) legitimative detours. The argument, therefore, suggests a rationale for fourth-tier strategies. Together, my specimens exhaust the resources of the most salient third-tier thinking. (As I say, I am holding back on Lovibond.)

But what we shall find, meanderingly, is that Mackie (by his skepticism) and Wiggins (by his insistence on the problem of the "meaning of life") touch on the essential clue regarding the recovery of moral objectivity – but veer off in ways that are merely "loyal" to the defective strategies of analytic philosophy; and that Nagel (by his eclectic caution and good sense) is immobilized in his own effort to recover objectivity and legitimative grounds – so that he and the others incontrovertibly betray the self-defeating strictures of third-tier analytic philosophy. We are the beneficiaries, in the sense that we find ourselves forced thereby to consider whether there are any (and what may be the) more promising ways of boarding the question.

III

The argument against Mackie is the easiest to mount. Remember: Mackie holds that "moral skepticism [is] the denial of objective moral values," where that doctrine is not to be "confused with any one of several first order normative views, or with any linguistic or conceptual analysis." It is (said to be) "an ontological thesis."[7] By itself, the claim fails to offset the fact that *if* "first-order" moral behavior *is* part of the fabric of the world (as Mackie concedes), then *that* too is "an ontological thesis"; and then, there cannot be a knockdown argument to the effect that moral values cannot be "objective" in the required sense, or that a diminished strategy for legitimative norms could never succeed. (I mean, by "diminished," a reasoned alternative to specifically Kantian-like legitimative demands but not necessarily a reliance on Kantian doctrines.) On the one hand, Mackie goes too far in requiring a Kantian-like legitimation of morality if any legitimation is to be had: he is too much of a skeptic to justify recommending any such extreme. On the other hand, he does not go far enough in searching out the resources of legitimation if (as he concedes) the "fabric of the world" includes our "first-order normative views" and their conceptual analysis: he is already too generous "ontologically" (his own term) to be the extreme skeptic he professes to be. Analytic moral philosophers hardly notice the extent of Mackie's paradoxical pronouncement because they, too, tend to be unfamiliar with the implications of admitting the world of human life and human culture to full realist standing. I find the same defect, for instance, in Nagel and Wiggins.

At this point Mackie distinguishes between "descriptivism" and "objectivism":

> Descriptivism [he says] is ... a doctrine about the meanings of ethical terms and statements, namely that their meanings are purely descriptive rather than even partly prescriptive or emotive or evaluative, or that it is not an essential feature of the conventional meaning of moral statements that they have some special illocutionary force, say of commending rather than asserting. It contrasts with the view that commendation is in principle distinguishable from description ... and that moral statements have it as at least part of their meaning that they are commendatory and hence in some uses intrinsically action-guiding. But descriptive meaning neither entails nor is entailed by objectivity.[8]

This is not a particularly felicitous view, though its improvement would still leave Mackie's skeptical intent intact. For, surely, *if* "first-order moral views" *do* involve "taking a certain practical, normative stand," then either first-order views are *not* merely "descriptive" or else (contrary to what Mackie says) descriptivism at the "first-order level" *is* sufficiently robust, ontologically, sufficiently "objective," *to support prescriptive, commendatory, action-guiding direction.* I cannot see how tht can be denied: merely admit a rational link betwen belief and action, and *some* prescriptive consequence will "follow." I take Mackie to have subverted his own position; but I do not mean by that that his intended claim against the (full Kantian-like) legitimation of objective values fails for that reason alone. It does, however, set the stage.

Still, Mackie's formulation is an inadvertence of sorts – more telling than he realizes. His intention is clear enough, as one sees from the following:

> The subjectivist [that is, the skeptic] about values ... is not denying that there can be objective evaluations relative to standards, and these are as

possible in the aesthetic and moral fields as in [any field that calls for expertise and invokes standards]. But the statement that a certain decision is thus just or unjust will not be objectively prescriptive: insofar as it can be simply true it leaves open the question whether there is any objective requirements to do what is just and to refrain from what is unjust, and equally leaves open the practical decision to act in other ways.[9]

Notice that judgments of what is just or unjust *might* well occur *in* first-order discourse; hence, they may be prescriptive *in a first-order sense. without reference to second-order considerations.* There *is* an "objective requirement" there but *not* the one *that is categorical in Kant's sense.* Mackie says as much: "we may make [the] issue clearer by referring to Kant's distinction between hypothetical and categorical imperatives." You may object that Mackie is no Kantian. You would be right; but Mackie does say that "the objective values which I am denying would be action-directing absolutely, not contingently . . . upon the agent's desires and inclinations": "A categorical imperative [he adds] would express a reason for acting which was unconditional in the sense of not being contingent upon any present desire of the agent to whose satisfaction the recommended action would contribute as a means."[10] So the distinction between the "descriptive" and the "prescriptive" is misleading. *If* the linkage between the descriptive and the action-guiding depended primarily on constraints of rationality, then it would be preposterous to deny that "first-order" evaluations had action-guiding import; and if prescriptive ("second-order") action-guiding import depended primarily on the objective standing of categorical norms, then the failure of an objective morality would have little to do with the logical connection between the descriptive and the action-guiding.

Although Mackie is not a Kantian, he believes that genuinely *objective* moral values *would be* such only if they *could* support a Kantian-like categorical obligation. When, therefore, he says there are no "objective values," he means that there are none that support a Kantian-like legitimation. But the argument is a *non sequitur*. From the fact that Mackie argues that, if moral values were "objective" in the second-order sense, something like the Categorical Imperative would obtain, it hardly follows that if *we* reject Mackie's premiss, we must also reject the possibility of legitimating moral values as objective or as having some prescriptive force. Mackie has stacked the cards in a most unlikely way. But that captures perfectly what he means by "the [notorious] argument from queerness":

If there were objective values, then they would be entities or qualities or relations of a very strange sort, utterly different from anything else in the universe. Correspondingly, if we were aware of them, it would have to be by some special faculty of moral perception or intuition, utterly different from our ordinary ways of knowing everything else.[11]

About this remark, it may be said: first, that it is hardly a serious argument; second, that Kant's argument is (as it happens) fatally flawed in terms of its own presumption;[12] third, that Mackie nowhere shows that any and every attempt to recover "objective values" must adhere to the Kantian-like condition – that nothing conceptually or "ontologically" slimmer could possibly do the requisite work; and, fourth, that there are in fact strategies for securing "objective" legitimation *if only we abandoned Kantian obiectivism (and Aristotelian essentialism) as ideal models, and looked to the full import of Mackie's concessions.* The irony is that Mackie's boldness is undercut by his own appeal to a first-tier vision that he himself opposes. Also, of course, there is no need to insist that the real world already *includes* first-order moral behavior. Mackie himself never denies the fact.[13]

Consider only this. The question of moral objectivity arises in a serious way only if the human world is real, as real as physical nature. What the concession of such a realism entails is obviously problematic. Mackie nowhere examines the matter in depth. He intuitively concedes enough about it, however, to admit, in first-order terms, moral and normative behavior in general and our reasoning about such behavior. So he admits that we think and act in terms of would-be moral norms and that we take ourselves to be rightly guided and obliged by the relevant reflections. He demurs only at the point of a certain strenuous *second-order* worry: namely, whether any of these first-order episodes can possibly yield grounds secure enough to confirm anything like a Kantian sense of categorical obligation. Very few commentators seem to be aware of how much Mackie has conceded.

He says that an affirmative answer would entail "queer" entities. But how does he know that, if he has already conceded an "ontology" of the human world robust enough in realist terms to include our first-order moral habits? He nowhere explains his judgment, and the matter has been largely ignored. It would hardly have the force it has if we (or Mackie) relented on the *need* for a Kantian-like legitimation in the first place. For, if we could find a middle ground between mere "hypothetical" and (Kantian) "categorical" obligation – remember: Mackie himself invokes the distinction – then we might well ensure a ground for legitimation that would no longer implicate "queer" entities. I don't deny that Kantianism requires "queer" entities, but Kant might already have conceded that much. The question remains: on what grounds does

Mackie claim (1) that legitimation must be Kantian if it is anything at all; or (2) that if we allowed a "diminished" form of legitimation, it too would entail "queer" entities? Mackie has no answer.

I conclude that Mackie's argument is a failure. He nowhere shows the propriety of invoking the Kantian (or, indeed, any counterpart Aristotelian or lesser) legitimative test. The truth is, he has no inventions of his own to offer: he simply falls back to the most conventional forms of legitimation.

IV

Turn back to Nagel.

There is an odd quality in Nagel's running remarks: on the one hand, Nagel seems to believe that there is no method in place for securing the objectivity of morality and practical life; on the other hand, be believes he has found an effective way to recover objectivity.[14] Consider this:

> In theoretical reasoning objectivity is advanced when we form a new conception of reality that includes ourselves as components. This includes an alteration or at least an extension of our beliefs. In the sphere of values or practical reasoning, the problem is different. As in the theoretical case, we must take up a new comprehensive viewpoint after stepping back and including our former perspective in what is to be understood. But there the new viewpoint will be not a new set of beliefs, but a new or extended set of values. We try to arrive at normative judgments with motivational content, from an impersonal standpoint. We cannot use a nonnormative criterion of objectivity, for if values are objective, they must be so on their own right and not through reducibility to some other kind of objective fact. They have to be objective *values*, not objective anything else.... Normative realism is the view that propositions about what gives us reasons for action can be true or false independently of how things appear to us, and that we can hope to discover the truth by transcending the appearances and subjecting them to critical assessment. What we aim to discover by this method is not a new aspect of the external world, called value, but rather just the truth about what we and others should do and want.[15]

I risk citing the passage in full because it might otherwise seem that Nagel has simply recast Kant's central notion (in the *Foundations*) by an economy that sets aside Kant's own doubtful metaphysics. Nagel is obviously not a Kantian here, and he is obviously countering Mackie's claim. We are left, however, with a dualism just as severe as Kant's:

theoretical reason aspires to a truth about the world that is said to rest on experience but is not confined to experience, a truth that embodies the epistemic neutrality of "the view from nowhere"; practical reason, building on that, is said (it seems, at least at first) to *add* to it – to reconcile it with – a "motivational" vision, "a view from nowhere" as well, that catches up "what we and others should do and want." One might go the extra mile and suggest that either Nagel has in mind Rawls's model of a "naturalized" Kantian-like proposal,[16] or else he means to offer a proposal (of that kind) of his own. ("Normative realism" is not easily characterised.)

That is not my concern. To pursue it would be to construe Nagel as a second-tier thinker. I am more interested in him as a third-tier thinker; but you can already see how natural it is to suppose that second- and third-tier questions go hand in hand. (By parity of reasoning, it would not be difficult to suppose that Rawls and Habermas and MacIntyre and Nussbaum also suppose they *have* addressed the third-tier issue. But they invariably withdraw from the riskier, more frontal *second-order* questions now before us. That's just what I mean by "*second-tier*" thinking.) *At* the third tier – the more courageous front – Nagel admits that if "a richer metaphysics of morals" were wanted (than what he offers), *he* cannot guess what it would be or would be like. He summarizes matters in a pared-down Kantian-like way: regarding science, he says, we must ask, "What can we see that the world contains, considered from [the, or an] impersonal standpoint?"; and, regarding morality, we ask, "What is there reason to do or want considered from this [same] impersonal standpoint?"[17] This now begins to clarify the sense in which (as I originally remarked) Nagel thinks "the standpoint of morality" *combines and reconciles* "the subjective and objective standpoints." But Mackie's fine challenge (to Nagel and to us) was to oblige us to explain precisely how moral values *could* be objective in a second-order sense.

Nagel hardly meets the question. He sees his project as one of resisting skepticism, solipsism, "Humean subjectivism,"[18] reduction to "materialistic psychology,"[19] and (of course) Mackie's specific thesis. Fine. But what is the grand strategy he intends? "The first type of [counter]argument," he says, "depends on the unwarranted assumption that if values are real, they must be real objects of some ... kind [other than what is found in the first-order world of science, they must be 'queer', as Mackie says]."[20] What Nagel means is: (1) that values are not "real occult entities or properties" *in* the "first-order" world of science; (2) that the answer to questions of moral or practical values are validated by offering justificatory reasons; (3) that "reasons play no role in causal explanations" (in first-order science); (4) that the worlds of theory and practice are disjoint in this respect though conceptually reconcilable; and (5) that "normative realism" is focused on supplying valid reasons – "claims about values and about what people have reason to do [that are] true or false independently of our beliefs and inclinations."[21] Science concerns truth and fact; morality, what it is rationally right to do, what is "motivationally" right. Nagel is responding to Mackie's challenge, but what he says is not entirely responsive. What I mean is, he offsets Mackie's worry by denying that values are "queer" *entities*; he construes values "motivationally." But he does not seriously address the question of whether a motivational account *can* accommodate, objectively, anything like the "categorical" sense of obligation. He offsets Mackie's "ontology" but not the need for pertinent realist resources, and he does not secure the latter. Strange victory.

Nothing could be more Kantian than Nagel's sense of the question, except that his (third-tier) answer is (finally) not Kantian at all. It does not fail for *that* reason, but it fails nonetheless. Nagel's failure, joined to Mackie's (which, you remember, invoked the Kantian test as well), goes a long way to closing down a large legitimative industry that, rightly pursued, would reach to Rawls and Habermas – and beyond, by analogy, to the Aristotelian wing of the reigning philosophical conglomerate. It is an industry that is completely played out. But the *question* is not played out.

It's at the second step of his argument that Nagel's ingenuity shows itself:

> If we push the claims of objective detachment to their logical conclusion, and survey the world from a standpoint completely detached from all interests, we discover [he says] that there is nothing – no values left of any kind: things can be said to matter at all only to individuals within the world. The result is objective nihilism.[22]

This is also Kantian – and distinctly promising. I shall come to it in a moment. But notice that what Nagel offers signifies that (1) it *is* possible to form a science "detached from all interests" (which *I* personally deny, but won't pursue here) and which – that is, the denial of which – entails the denial of any principled disjunction between theoretical and practical reason; and (2) normative "objectivity" requires some deep conceptual analogy between the possible disinterestedness of "motivation" and the detachment "from all interests" said to hold in perceptual and theorizing inquiries of the sort science favors.

Since Nagel is *not* a full-fledged Kantian – he does not argue that we *must* begin from a *concept* of practical reason capable of confirming a certain "universality" and "necessity" – he is bound to supply a heterodox rationale. (Otherwise, he would simply have had to fall back to a first-tier Kantian thesis, which would have been uninteresting.) The fact is he never shows *that there is* "a view from nowhere" – *in* science or in morality! (He offers an adjustment here.) I say there is no such view; that no such view is needed; that no such view can be demonstrated; that no such view is entailed or presupposed by either science or morality; and that no one has ever supplied a convincing criterion for recognizing any such view. Objectivity or neutrality, on any compelling theory, is an artifact of our conjectures. Is that self-contradictory?

It is hard to *appear* to do full justice to Nagel's third – the decisive – step (which I have yet to supply). Quite frankly, the third step is a disaster; but I need you to confirm that conclusion independently, drawing on what Nagel actually says. The point of pursuing these details would be lost if we permitted ourselves to tire too quickly. We need to see how third-tier thinking exhausts itself.

Nagel is canny about the difficulty of the task. For instance, he says: "No completely general argument about reasons can show that we must move from the admission that pleasure and pain have relative value to the conclusion that they have neutral value as well."[23] That is: although it is true that "we have reason to seek/avoid sensations we immediately and strongly like/dislike," we cannot be sure that this is a sufficient ground for claiming "neutral value" – the "agent-neutral" perspective.[24] He's right, of course. Nevertheless, he also insists – after making this concession – that (3) "it is conceivable, but false, that pleasure and pain provide only agent-relative reasons for action."[25] (So he falls back to a thin essentialism, after all, by way of Locke and motivational options.) There's no advantage in starting a quarrel here. The question remains whether all that is needed for full moral objectivity *can* be reasonably drawn from a Kantian-like beginning or from such a beginning *plus* such a thin essentialism. The matter is inherently doubtful; on Nagel's argument, it is impossible.

Here is the clue. In the introductory chapter of *The View from Nowhere*, after having introduced the two standpoints, Nagel observes (I cite the entire remark):

> The distinction between more subjective and more objective views is really a matter of degree, and it covers a wide spectrum. A view or form of thought is more objective than another if it relies less on the specifics of the individual's makeup and position in the world, or on the character of the particular type of creature he is. The wider the range of subjective types to which a form of understanding is accessible – the less it depends

on specific subjective capacities – the more objective it is. A standpoint
that is objective by comparison with the personal view of one individual
may be subjective by comparison with a theoretical standpoint still farther
out. . . . An objective standpoint is created by leaving a more subjective,
individual, or even just human perspective behind; but there are things
about the world and life and ourselves that cannot be adequately understood from a maximally objective standpoint.[26]

It takes a moment to grasp the peculiarity of what is being said. First of
all, it departs from Kant's view, in the *Foundations of the Metaphysics
of Morals*, by making the distinction between the subjective and the
objective "a matter of degree." That's not fatal in itself, though it is
plainly incompatible with Kant's thesis; for Kant's notion is a purely
formal one. Secondly, Kant does not pretend to determine moral or
practical objectivity on the basis of any true substantive view of actual
human interests; Kant's claim invokes only a universalized formal
constraint (imposed) on *whatever*, contingently, answers to actual
human interests. Nagel relies on some inchoate (motivational) reading
of normative human nature. Thirdly, there can be no approximation to
the universality Kant requires; any generality that fails to take a
universalized form would be instantly inadmissible. Nagel endorses
approximations. Fourthly, Nagel pretends that, in the sciences, there *is*
"a maximally objective standpoint" (one that might even "leave behind"
the "human perspective") that needs to be contrasted with the "motivational" (the interested) stance of the moral agent; but, surely the point
of the contrast is put in jeopardy if, as seems reasonable, the supposed
neutrality of the "objective standpoint" is itself an artifact, under
reflexive conditions, of our own "interested" perceptions of the world.
The entire scheme collapses.

   For Nagel, "objectivity" is continuous with "subjectivity," a matter
that presupposes some initial sorting of the substantive interests and
purported human needs relative to which *increased generality is then
judged to be equivalent to increased objectivity*. Suppose, for instance,
one had to decide whether the Marxist notion of the dictatorship of the
proletariat was objectively more valid (morally) than global capitalism,
or whether a conversion to Catholicism was more valid than a respect
for private religious conscience, or whether a benignly intended public
instruction along the lines explored by the Marquis de Sade was more
liberating than the unmonitored hit-and-miss discoveries of naive children. *How* should we apply Nagel's doctrine? In what way should
pleasure and pain be relevant? I see no prospect of ever distinguishing,
on Nagel's grounds, between increased generality with respect to doubt-

ful interests and lesser generality with respect to interests inherently less "agent-relative" than others. Surely, any ramified provision along competing lines could not fail to reflect (and confuse) "abstract" but partisan interests (the generalizing of interests *of* a partisan nature) and putatively neutral concerns "abstracted" *from* all partisan interests. You see, of course, the sense in which the continuum of the subjective and the objective is needed (by Nagel) to ensure the objective moral standing of pleasure and pain; and you may also see here a somewhat tortured analogue of Mill's worries about Bentham's calculus.

The trouble is due to a confusion. Nagel rightly grasps that if he is to offset Mackie's worry, he must replace a reading of moral values and norms as objective "entities" with something like a "subjective" motivational account. Fine. But, as a realist, he must also recover the *objective* standing of values, so conceived, robustly enough to legitimate something like the Kantian notion of categorical obligation. Apparently, he thinks this can be done by yielding in some essentialist direction – minimally perhaps, along empiricist lines: hence the appeal to pleasure and pain. But he has not laid a proper foundation. In fact, Mackie could easily complain that the "motivational" account is little more than a masquerade for a normative reading of human nature along essentialist lines: in which case, Nagel would not have escaped the charge of "queerness."

I see no reason to think that Mackie would not be right. Nagel's maneuver is, after all, little more than a failed analogue of Mill's *aporia* (in *Utilitarianism*) about deducing the "desirable" from actual episodes of "desire". I concede that the use of a "motivational" account explains reasonably well how normative judgments may be "action-guiding" without implicating "queer" entities; but I cannot see how Nagel could ever have supposed he had recovered moral objectivity in a suitably strong second-order sense. The disjunction between the "factual" and the "action-guiding" (Mackie's move – also, Wiggins's, as we shall see) is really the result of a conventional disjunction between theoretical and practical reason. Grant that the human agent in science and morality is (1) one and the same, and (2) rational (in the way of smoothly reconciling beliefs, desire or interest, and action – which is what Nagel has in mind), and it becomes implausible to suppose that mere factual judgments are in principle precluded from being action-guiding at all. I cannot see how anyone can deny this who reflects on the significance of what is common (in the use of the copula "ought") in saying to a morning angler, "The sun ought to rise before six this morning," and saying to a penitent gambler, "You ought to pay back the money you've taken, even though you've lost it."

The failure of Nagel's formula affects Aristotelian-like objectivity as much as Kantian-like objectivity, and consequentialism as much as intentionalism. The weakness disqualifies a line (or two) of possible arguments for third-tier theorists: namely, a tolerance for approximative tactics of a Kantian-like sort said to be concerned with what is rational (as in Habermas); or a progressive mixing of "essentialist" and "Kantian" measures such that acknowledging what is "neutral" or "liberal" in regard to human nature counts as ensuring the universality and objectivity of practical reason's deliberations (as in Rawls).

At the very least, Nagel has not succeeded in meeting Mackie's challenge – which he initially accepts – either in the first-tier Kantian way or in the diminished and eclectic way he favors. He fails, but in failing he reinforces our sense of the excessive demands of first- and second-tier presumptions. We begin to see that third-tier thinking is not likely to fare better.

I have no wish to exaggerate the importance of Nagel's and Mackie's arguments. They seem to be remarkably ineffectual. But that, in a way, is my point. It's not merely that they fail – in failing to mount as strong an argument as they might have. It's rather that their failure is symptomatic of the best that third-tier thinking can produce. My claim, you remember, is that third-tier thinking is pretty well the work of a scruple that views moral philosophy as more or less confined to the options of the classic first-tier sort or of the second-tier sort that dominates contemporary canonical speculation. That was the original reason I sought out the views of Rawls, Apel and Habermas, and MacIntyre at least. Second-tier thinking rightly activates third-tier scruples, but third-tier scruples are pretty well addressed to saving second-tier objectives. All that can now be seen to fail – *utterly*. To say so may not be of much importance *sub specie aeternitatis*, but the fact remains that Western moral philosophy is largely occupied with the projects of second- and third-tier thinkers, and their strategies are hopelessly impoverished. I trust you will find my report of the scope of current moral theory more of a shock than the mere failure of any particular specimen theory. The first is a symptom of philosophical and moral bankruptcy; the second, no more than a sign of a contingent frailty.

V

Turn, finally, to Wiggins, the subtlest of my three third-tier theorists. Before we do that, however, let me review what has been accomplished.

My argument against Mackie rests with the fact that Mackie believes that *if* moral objectivity may be saved it must be saved by meeting some strong first-tier condition (like Kant's) that ensures "categorical" or "absolute" or "unconditional" obligation. There is no such argument, Mackie claims. Quite right. Nothing, however, follows from that that bears on the final prospects of moral objectivity! Why should Mackie have fallen back to a Kantian requirement if *he* has already rejected the bare relevance of the Kantian thesis? As he says, it is downright "queer."

My argument against Nagel rests with the fact that, taking up Mackie's challenge, Nagel believes he *can* supply an answer (that straddles second- and third-tier considerations) that abstracts moral objectivity from obviously partisan or subjective interests (by a policy of measuring increasing generality). But he cannot show that any merely formal generality abstracted from admittedly partisan or egoistic interests, or any seemingly altruistic or natural interests, can rightly count as progressively "objective" in any pertinent sense at all. Such a strategy would have no way of distinguishing mere ideology from a pretended objectivity. A conformist society would be likely to rate best on such a scale; and any independent adjustment might well fall back to a form of essentialism, which Nagel means to avoid.

Wiggins begins at a much greater remove, but he eventually brings his answer back to the question of objectivity. His argument is remarkably original – even eccentric; yet in the final analysis it leads us back to quite conventional options. The significance of that rests with the dawning sense of the self-imposed limitations of nearly all analytic strategies of the third-tier sort. *They literally have no prospects* – for whatever is *now* promising goes contrary to the analytic canon. (This must still be shown.) By his failed inventiveness, Wiggins (inadvertently) makes us aware of bolder possibilities that lie at land that cannot be pursued without calling into doubt the entire philosophical commitment of third-tier strategies.

I confess I am hard on Wiggins. I suppose the reason lies with Wiggins's strong perception of the failed resources of conventional moral theory and with his retreat, in spite of that, to positions that are nearly impossible (or impossible) to defend except front one or another epistemic vantage of the sorts he appears to repudiate. Thus, he is a kind of cognitivist though he opposes standard forms of cognitivism. He is even a kind of intuitionist (or "commonsense" intuitionist), though he cannot possibly subscribe to strict intuitionism. He finds "non-natural" moral properties in the world, though he never explains their objective standing. He favors some decisive "mentalistic" contribution of the moral "consciousness" of individual persons, but he nowhere explains its "metaphysics" (a term he himself admits springs to mind). He has a *lebensformlich* bent, but he does not explicitly avoid a kind of methodological solipsism.

He resists characterizing himself as a "moral realist" but that is chiefly to accommodate the "mentalism" mentioned which also makes room for a measure of subjective "relativity' and the unlikelihood of universal agreement along those lines.

Certainly, Wiggins is not a moral realist in that familiar sense in which an adherence (in moral matters Wiggins's adherence) to "mentalism," "undetermination" by whatever we may concede are the features of the independent world, a "relativity" of pertinent "subjective" convictions that "converge" (in their own terms) forcefully enough to count as "really" true do not yet reach to the sense of "plain truth" the exemplary moral realist is likely to espouse. The qualifications I've piled on are all drawn from Wiggins's own texts. But their virtue lies more in marking Wiggins's demurrers against the positions he means to avoid than in formulating some well-defined alternative that he actually means to defend. It is entirely fair to say, therefore, that, in his own terms, he is a diminished, if heterodox, moral realist or a theorist much closer to moral realism than to any noncognitivism. I say he is a moral realist persuaded that the usual moral realists have gone too far – that the epistemic resources and convictions he and they share are insufficient to secure *their* strongest claims and that his own are not yet secured. I agree with Wiggins, therefore, but he still falls back to the idiom and persuasion of moral realism. In any case, I ask you to construe my reading of Wiggins in the light of these qualifications; otherwise, what I say may not seem temperate enough. The following passage may help to fix the general sense of Wiggins's orientation:

> What cognitivism does is only to add one new twist. It takes seriously both the possibility that mentalistic explanations will never be supplanted, and the possibility that mentalistic explanations themselves for some actions and thoughts will never be able to dispense with the moral properties that consciousness finds for itself in the world. But for such properties as these to be indispensable and irreducible, and for *vindication* to be one indispensable element in the explanation of thinking and acting, this is surely what it is for consciousness not merely to arrive in the natural world, but for it to make itself at home there. For by critically determining the presence there of valuational properties, we colonize that world; and, by treating the vindication of thought as both indispensable to understanding what happens in the world and irreducible to any other ideas that pull their weight in the description of that world, we demonstrate practically the irreducibility of that consciousness.[27]

Wiggins anticipates the unlikelihood of ever recovering objectivity by way of any of the usual first- or second- or even third-tier strategies.

Hence the inventive extravagance of first invoking the question of the "meaning of life" and then presuming to demonstrate how *that* is linked to resolving the standard question of objective moral truths. I cannot hide the fact that I find the argument entirely uncompelling – even ultimately vacuous. I offer it as a specimen, because it demonstrates the self-limiting liberties third-tier thinkers are prepared to take in order to recover objectivity without falling back to the resources of first- and second-tier strategies and without departing from the canonical policies of analytic philosophy.

Wiggins is the best of the third-tier thinkers. He is not the most promising. (I save that epithet for Lovibond.) He is the best, because he avoids the pitfalls of Mackie's and Nagel's strategies. He is not the most promising because, doing that, it turns out that he has, literally, *no legitimative options that he can turn to*. His skill keeps him from repeating the old Aristotelian and Kantian and empiricist and utilitarian mistakes. But he is unwilling, or unable, to strike out in a fresh way that is not already defined by a thinker like G. E. Moore reflecting on all the failures just collected. He cannot, it seems, reach out to fourth-tier strategies. I take that to be a benefit (didactically), though not a virtue (philosophically). As a result – or so it seems – he invents a final, rather desperate maneuver for reclaiming objectivity. It is partly a form of intuitionism, or "non-naturalism," and partly a blending of that with legitimate speculations tied to resolving the question of "the meaning of life." If I understand his argument correctly, the appeal to certain moral intuitions is vindicated in the conceptual "space" recovered by answering the question of the meaning of life: doing that enables Wiggins to avoid the usual traps of first- and second-tier thinking.

The trouble is, the legitimative strategy fails in the most elementary way: either the question of the "meaning of life" can be answered arbitrarily (in which case, it has no particular philosophical importance) or it can be answered trivially (in which case, though it is important, it cannot serve to answer whatever is left of Mackie's question), or its "proper" answer already prepares the ground for a suitable exercise of intuitionism (in which case, the independence and priority of the matter of "meaning" over moral "truth" cannot but be a charade).

Here, I merely anticipate the argument: by the first horn of this trilemma, Wiggins cannot answer (as he claims to do) Richard Taylor's (empiricist) defense of a meaningful life (for Sisyphus, with respect to Camus's version of the story); by the second, he cannot legitimate intuitionism (or any similar substantive doctrine); by the third, he cannot but beg the question. Still, Wiggins has a very clear sense of the limited effectiveness of such third-tier thinkers as Mackie and Nagel; and he leads us to a point at which the excessive demands of "Kantian" requirements as well as the paradoxicality of "Aristotelian" conditions are effectively exposed. The fact is, he brings us to the doorstep of fourth-tier strategies by his own deadend.

Wiggins encourages in his better readers an appetite for radicalizing legitimative strategies, without *his* being able or willing to satisfy such tastes. That is the clinical import of his perseveration on the "meaning of life," all the while he neglects the historicized and collectively encultured sense in which (paradigmatically) *life proves "meaningful" at all.* In this sense, Wiggins demonstrates the exhaustion of third-tier thinking.

In the first section of his important paper "Truth, Invention, and the Meaning of Life," Wiggins says very plainly:

> In what follows, I try to explore the possibility that the question of truth and the question of life's meaning are among the most fundamental questions of moral philosophy. . . . My finding will be that the question of life's meaning does, as the untheoretical suppose, lead into the question of truth – and conversely. Towards the end I shall also claim to uncover the possibility that philosophy has put happiness in the place that should have been occupied in moral philosophy by meaning.[28]

This is an extremely condensed announcement. It offers something of an analogy regarding the difference between Freud's and Jung's psychoanalytic conceptions: the one, emphasizing libidinal gratification; the other, a meaningful life. It explains Wiggins's astute criticism of Aristotle and Spinoza's reversal of Aristotle's formula, and the point of his own replacement of "happiness" by "meaning." Wiggins cites Aristotle's remark (*Metaphysics* 1072a29), which is a variant of the question posed in Plato's *Euthyphro* bearing on the objectivity issue: "We desire the object because it seems good to us, rather than the object's seeming good to us because we desire it." Wiggins counts this an "error." It is not, he thinks, as serious an error as the one he draws from Bentham's *An Introduction to the Principles of Morals and Legislation* (which, in turn, reminds us of Nagel):

> Strictly speaking, nothing [says Bentham] can be said to be good or bad, but either in itself, which is the case only with pain or pleasure, or on account of its effects, which is the case only with things that are the causes or preventives of pain and pleasure.

Wiggins's subtle objection (if I understand it rightly) is this: (1) Bentham's formula is false to the facts, since "many . . . conscious states" have intentional objects, are states of striving for "objects" that are not themselves conscious states, and include states that assign "a non-instrumental value" to their intentional objects;[29] and (2), even more significantly – now, against Bentham, Aristotle, and Spinoza together – any version of the strategy that disjoins or merely conjoins conscious states and their "valued" objects will fail to account for "the meaning of life."[30]

It's at this point that Wiggins provisionally concludes:

> But maybe it is the beginning of real wisdom to see that we may have to side against both Aristotle and Spinoza [*Ethics*, part III, proposition 9, note] here and ask: "Why should the *because* [of Aristotle's remark, as cited] not hold both ways round?" Surely an adequate account of these matters will have to treat psychological states and their objects as equal and reciprocal partners, and is likely to need to see the identification of the states and of the properties under which the states subsume their objects as interdependent.[31]

Remember: we are reviewing Wiggins as a third-tier thinker. I am prepared to concede that Wiggins's objection to Bentham and the others is reasonable and shows a reasonable way of linking the question of moral values and the meaning of life. But I don't believe the link Wiggins provides has any (or much) strategic importance for objective moral legitimation. There's the fatal weakness.

Nearly half the essay pursues a pointed attack on a clever discussion by Richard Taylor of Camus's Sisyphus myth, in which Taylor tries to explain how Sisyphus's meaningless life *might* be converted into a meaningful life.[32] Taylor actually *does* show that Sisyphus might, for reasons *we* should probably think monstrous or preposterous, come to believe his life to be meaningful; Wiggins *fails* to show that that is unlikely or false or impossible. But Taylor's argument is entirely beside the point, as far as genuine legitimation is concerned, and Wiggins's "correction" is equally pointless because it pursues an irrelevancy. Neither Taylor nor Wiggins explains the connection between the meaning of life and the objectivity of moral values. The connection is *there*, but they miss it. (Taylor offers no more than a first-order answer. Wiggins permits himself to be drawn into a complete blind alley.) My own interest is not to demolish Wiggins's argument here (though it invites the strongest objections). I wish to show rather that Wiggins has missed the important lesson of his own argument; that it explains as well the pointlessness of both Mackie's and Nagel's (third-tier) strategies; that it helps us to form an impression of the "second-order" excesses of an entire tribe of thinkers (the "moral realists")[33] who have sought to apply the benefit of Wiggins's ingenious argument (or others like it, as in Sabina Lovibond and John McDowell); and, most important, that it leads us beyond its own resources.

VI

Wiggins's attack on Taylor is an attack on "noncognitivist" views of morality and meaning (both of meaning *in* life and of the meaning *of* life). But in defending a form of "moral cognitivism," Wiggins explicitly distances himself from both Kant and Aristotle: hence, from (all the usual) first- and second-tier strategies. (That is generally the intent of the moral realists.) In this sense, Wiggins combats Mackie (on the one hand) and (on the other) finds Nagel too obscure or too concessive in slipping back to Kant or Aristotle or both. But the truth is, it is unlikely – granting the failure of second-tier thinking, and with due attention to its bearing on both Aristotelian and Kantian strategies – that the recovery of legitimative objectivity can have very much to do with a strong disjunction between cognitivist and noncognitivist (or constructivist) options. Wiggins seems to have been distracted by his preference for Moorian intuitions over empiricist convictions. But that is really too slight a matter for the larger issues at stake.

Let me, therefore, cite (without prejudice) Wiggins's explicit rejection of the Kantian and Aristotelian options. (I find his objections forceful and compelling; but he invariably deflects the argument from its principal target.) Against the Kantian, Wiggins affirms:

> there is no such thing as a pure *a priori* theory of rationality conceived in isolation from what it is for us as we are to have a reason; and that even if there were such a thing, it would always have been irrelevant to finding a meaning in life, or seeing anything as worth while.[34]

The local reason for pressing the charge is to disallow the noncognitivist (Taylor) any plausible grounds for recovering "the meaning of life." But Wiggins's elaborate argument is no more than a corrective for a puzzle of his own devising; it is otherwise completely irrelevant to the meaning issue. Similarly, reviewing the well-known line in Aristotle's *Nicomachean Ethics* (1094a23): "Will not knowledge of the good have a great influence on life? Shall we not, like archers who have a mark to aim at, be more likely to hit upon that right thing?," Wiggins adds:

But in reality there is no such thing as *The Good*, no such thing as knowledge of it, and nothing fixed independently of ourselves to aim at. Or that is what is implied by the thesis of cognitive underdetermination.[35]

Here, too, Wiggins has a local reason for mentioning his stand against Aristotle: he supports a strong disjunction between *matters of fact* and *matters of practice* (practical or action-guiding matters) – which presumably bears on moral objectivity.

Wiggins presses his objections against Kant and Aristotle largely in the service of defeating Taylor, but the issue of linking meaning and value is (I fear) lost in the bargain. Furthermore, although the disjunction between fact and practice seems reasonable on its face, Wiggins wishes to contrast the point of *that* disjunction with the point of a favorable continuum linking *matters of fact* and *evaluative matters*. As I have already suggested (reviewing Mackie), the continuum between the *factual* and the *evaluative* ineluctably supplies a ground for admitting a continuum between the *factual*, the *evaluative*, and the *action-guiding*. Once you grasp that, there is no longer any point to intruding the question of the "meaning of life," as if the answer to *that* would justify bridging the divide between the factual and the evaluative and also justify ensuring the disjunction between that continuum and the practical or action-guiding. But it won't work (as we have already seen, reviewing Mackie). It is no more than a distraction.

The first continuum, Wiggins thinks, subverts Taylor's strategy for recovering meaningful life (for Sisyphus). In veering off in this way, Wiggins simply misses the clear link between the meaning of life and moral objectivity – which, I suggest, would support a fourth-tier strategy. I take this to be symptomatic of analytic third-tier thinking – especially moral realism. In any case, *if* Sisyphus finds his own meaningless life suddenly made meaningful – by a crazy self-delusion that would never help *us* – what's to prevent its being admitted to be effective *for Sisyphus*? And if *we* require more, how will Wiggins procure what would "rightly" serve us?

We are near the nerve of Wiggins's theory. Have patience. Wiggins is a moral cognitivist, of course: he means us to understand that value judgments address the real world, take truth-values, enter into explanatory discourse, and are no different in these respects from scientific statements.[36] He is (also) specifically committed to treating moral values as "non-natural" (in G. E. Moore's sense) but *not* in any sense in which they might be said to be "supervenient" upon "natural" properties (as in the way of the dubious theory advanced along different lines by Donald Davidson and Jaegwon Kim).[37]

When, however, Wiggins explains the sense in which *he* takes values to have a realist import, he retreats (if that is the right term) to the model of a very strong objectivism regarding "facts." Apparently he believes that if he weakened his objectivism in either science or morality (say, in the direction of relativism), he would not be able to defend moral realism at all and perhaps would not even be able to distinguish his own cognitivism from something close to Taylor's noncognitivism. He seems to think (wrongly, I believe) that if he yielded in the noncognitivist direction (in at least the constructivist sense, say), he would effectively be unable to answer the question of "the meaning of life" and, as a consequence, he would be unable to answer the question of how to legitimate objective moral truths or how to ensure their prescriptive function. I'm afraid there's a serious blunder there. (These topics are not sufficiently pursued by Wiggins or the moral realists, although they obviously belong to the context of Mackie's third-tier question.)

Let me suggest, for the time being, that *if* one concedes the realist standing of the human world – what I call *cultural realism*, a realism regarding what Wittgenstein means by the human *Lebensform* or what Hegel means by *Sitten, then it no longer matters* – as far as moral objectivity is concerned – whether one is a cognitivist or a constructivist. I don't deny that there are important differences between "Aristotelian"-like and "Kantian"-like moral strategies (or between those and intuition-ist, empiricist, liberal, libertarian, communitarian, and similar strategies); but, in that regard, those differences have little to do with gaining or losing a proper ground for moral objectivity. That is what Wiggins fails to see. It explains at a stroke the extravagance of his entire treatment of the "meaning of life" question. (There would be no point to insisting on the lesson, were it not for the fact that it is the nerve of some of the best "moral realist" thinking and that its collapse confirms the failure of the entire tribe.)

There's a lacuna in Wiggins's argument. Worse still, Wiggins cannot defend his own account except by retreating to some first- or second-tier doctrine (possibly neither Kantian nor Aristotelian: probably Moorian) that actually forces the third-tier question on us. The irony is that it is the very plausibility of his attack on Aristotle and Kant that drives him to a kind of intuitionism and (joined to that) a sense of the exaggerated importance of defeating empiricism. The result is: within the impover-ished resources of analytic moral philosophy, Wiggins sees no way of recovering legitimation except by an eccentric reading of the "meaning of life" issue. But he is no better off in this than Taylor, whom he excoriates for his would-be recovery of Sisyphus's life. Wiggins brings his entire strategy before us in the following:

The cognitivist will see nothing in modern evolutionary theory, or in any other branch of modern science, that forbids us to allow to thoughts themselves and the standards to which these thoughts are answerable the explanatory role that he himself attributes to them when he endorses as explanatory such claims as: "Everyone thinks that $7 + 5 = 12$, because, in the end, there is nothing else to think" or "We converge in the belief that the slaughter of the innocent is wrong because, in the end, there is nothing else to think on this question." If the cognitivist sticks his neck out anywhere, it is here. What he refuses to allow is that non-natural properties are explanatorily inert.[38]

We must consider how cannily crafted and lean these remarks are. The operative phrase is "there is nothing else to think." In the same vein, Wiggins speaks of "the passion to get the answer to this or that moral or political question *right*," or to press moral explanation to the point at which it fastens finally on "the only opinion that would survive reflection."[39] I cannot see how such a confidence can ever be counted on in the sciences. It is surely a kind of intuitionism *manqué*. Why should we suppose it would be more reliable in moral matters? The least sense of the diversity of history should make this clear. It makes a blackmail argument of every resistance to our own convictions. (Strawson had warned us of this long ago.)

The irony is that Wiggins holds the decisive clue in his hand but cannot fathom it. The clue is this: the "meaning-of-life" issue is trivially resolved – *everywhere*! *There's no need to pursue it: it solves itself*! It brings us back (in an ampler space) to the finding I mentioned but did not pursue against Mackie: namely, that Mackie's admission of "first-order" morality *already* sets the stage for the objectivity of "second-order" morality, *if* only we abandon the untenable reliance on first- and second-tier forms of legitimation. (There's the nerve of my fourth-tier proposal.)

All right. Wiggins combines two notions: first, that the continuum between meaning and truth ensures a *cognitivist* solution to the question of the "meaning of life"; second, that, once granted, "evaluative" claims match the objectivity accorded "factual" claims – so that the moral cognitivist may "reach the state of mind where one thinks that *p* because there is nothing else to think but that *p*."[40] The trouble with this picture is this: first, it does not bear at all on the meaning of life; and, second, it is supremely unhelpful in just the way intuitionism generally is. Wiggins never probes beyond these slim objections.

He defends a very strong disjunction between "pure valuations" and "pure directives": he insists that "the fact–value distinction and the is–ought or is–must distinction" are not the same; that evaluative discourse is continuous with factual discourse (in the way of taking truth-values) but that directive discourse is not similarly continuous.[41] (That is an unnecessary – even pointless – extravagence; for, as I have already remarked, once you admit a rational link between belief and action, you obviate the need for a disjunction between the "factual" and the "directive.") By these strenuous devices Wiggins defeats the noncognitivist; for, on Wiggins's reading, "life is *objectively* meaningless" *for* the noncognitivist, and meaning is supposed to be infused (for Sisyphus) only by a "subjective" *addition* of values (to what is objectively meaningless).[42]

That won't do at all, I'm afraid. For, *if* obligation belongs to the "evaluative" side of discourse as much as to the "directive" side, then copulas like "ought" and "must" must belong to the evaluative side as much as to the directive; and *then*, the "practical" force of directive discourse cannot fail to be "logically" or "pragmatically" or "rationally" entailed (in standard cases) by the evaluative force of what is being *factually* affirmed.[43] For, even non-evaluative factual truths can have "directive" force for rational agents; and if that is so, then (1) we hardly require an answer to the "meaning of life" question in order to ensure such a linkage; and (2) we hardly require an intuitionist or cognitivist (Moorian-like) resolution of the "meaning of life" question in order to ensure an "internal" connection between evaluative and motivational concerns. There is literally no philosophical work that Wiggins's maneuver performs.

Wiggins opposes all such arguments but he fails to say why. He needs the disjunction in order to make the case against the noncognitivist. *He does not need it anywhere else.* But it siphons off all his philosophical energies. He loses the point of his own argument thereby; in any case the issue about "meaning" is conceptually trivial. *If* the empiricist (speaking for Sisyphus) holds life to be "objectively" meaningless, then he has no option but to impose meaning ("subjectively") on a meaningless life; in that case, Sisyphus succeeds, but only locally. *If* life must be meaningful (if it is meaningful) on the "inside" because it is in the same conceptual "space" that we decide the question of meaning *and* the question of objective moral truth, then nothing *need* follow from Wiggins's argument except that we are as arbitrary as Sisyphus (about meaning) and as arbitrary (about objective values) as the moral ideologue. I cannot see how Wiggins escapes his own trap. I cannot see that he answers Mackie successfully.

VII

I must bring this tedious argument to a close; but you may already see that its being closed is nothing but a new beginning. I must take advantage of Wiggins once again to bind up loose ends. I draw attention, therefore, to what may be Wiggins's essential mistake as well as the *ur*-clue to the need for fourth-tier strategies. Here is what Wiggins says, speaking against the Aristotelian thesis, that is, speaking against the thesis that "Happiness = the End" (meaning by that to link moral truth and the meaning of life):

> Inasmuch as invention [Mackie's term] and discovery [the term Wiggins shares with Nagel] are distinguishable, and insofar as either of these ideas properly belongs here, life's having a point may depend as much upon something *contributed* by the person whose life it is as it depends upon something discovered. Or it may depend upon what the owner of the life brings to the world in order to see the world in such a way as to discover meaning. This cannot happen unless world and person are to some great extent reciprocally suited. And unluckily, all claims of human adaptability notwithstanding, those things are often not well suited to one another.[44]

Further on, he explains why Aristotle's view that "*eudaimonia* [is] not exactly happiness but a certain kind of success – [is] absurd":

> This is not to deny that Aristotle's doctrine can be restored to plausibility if we allow the meaning of the particular life that accommodates the activity [in question, the activity (say) of ditch-digging to help a neighbor] to *confer* intrinsic worth upon the activity. But this is to reverse Aristotle's procedure (which is the only procedure available to a pure cognitivist). And I doubt we have to choose. At its modest and most plausible best the doctrine of cognitive underdetermination can say that we need to be able to think in both directions, down from point to the human activities that answer to it, and up from activities whose intrinsic worth can be demonstrated by Aristotle's consensual method to forms of life in which we are capable by nature of finding point.[45]

This is the heart of Wiggins's entire effort: first, to redeem Aristotle against himself; second, to read Aristotle along somewhat Wittgensteinian lines; third, to recover the very point of Nagel's later (and lamer) union of the "objective" and the "subjective"; fourth, to satisfy Mackie's challenge; fifth, to launch thereby an entirely new form of objectivism (moral realism).

Wiggins's effort fails, I say, but, *in failing* provides the clue to a full recovery. (That is very nearly the sole point of this interminable aside.)

What Wiggins misses stares him in the face. *If* the defeat of Aristotle's doctrine is reasonable because *we* are able to find meaning in certain "forms of life," then Wiggins should have realized that the meaning of life is already inherent *in* those "forms of life" (the *Lebensformen*) he himself marginally invokes (from Wittgenstein) – *by which we first emerge* as the competent selves we are. Grant that much, and you must admit that resolving the question of the meaning of life *is already decided in the lebensformlich way – holistically*. It makes no sense to suppose that life *becomes* meaningful only when each of us *in addition* confers a personal meaning on our lives, *if in being formed* as creatures capable of doing that we have already internalized the very "meaning" *of* our form of life! (To insist that that is not enough is to invite Sisyphus to improvise as he does!) The error is the mate of that famous error that appears in social contract theories (from Hobbes to Rousseau) in which we first agree to function in a certain politically rational way as a result of a contract to which we could not be party if we were not already so disposed and apt.

Life *is* "meaningful": not because each of us, individually, first finds or makes life meaningful, and *then* engages in certain social activities in order to promote the point of such meaning, but rather because the "meaning of life" *is no more than* the collective form of life we share and spontaneously promote *in* our individual lives. Analytic philosophy is largely "solipsistic" in methodological terms: there, the social, the societal, the cultural, the linguistic, the institutional, the traditional is ultimately explained in terms of *relations between* putatively autonomous, well-formed individuals.

How did they ever become well-formed? you ask. There you have the clue to the impoverished conceptual resources with which Wiggins is prepared to conjure. Yet he himself has hit on the essential postulate that moral speculation presupposes and depends on, *that it cannot secure by any of the miserly resources of the analytic tradition*. It's no surprise that English-language philosophy has, in incorporating Wittgenstein, resisted the collectivist import of Wittgenstein's own notion of the *Lebensform*; and it's no surprise that Russell and Moore intuitively conspired to drive out Hegelian thinking from the university world. The result, I claim, is the utter collapse of third-tier thinking. The important lesson is that that failure is at the point of its most inflexible inspiration just where we need to remind ourselves of the mortal contest between the fundamental philosophical options we must consider. At the very least, moral realism must be seen to be completely bankrupted, though it is also near to victory.

The extraordinary thing is that Wiggins *has* indeed isolated the essential issue – but only by a lucky hit. He misses the elementary point that life *is* "meaningful" in the sense that human life is already culturally formed, collective, historically local; he misses it in the sense that each of us, *in* being formed as individual persons, selves, "subjects," linguistically competent agents, are already constituted as beings *who find life meaningful in that way*. Whatever other idiosyncrasies we bring to that question cannot but be secondary: it takes on primary importance only in pathological cases – in Sisyphus, for example. And there, marginally, anything goes!

The importance of this is immense. It marks the difference between third- and fourth-tier thinking. It marks a fundamental shift in philosophical orientation. It turns us away from "adequational" questions to "existential" ones. Wiggins's distinction lies in his searching for a new source of moral objectivity that eschews all those first- and second-tier strategies that are linked to Aristotle and Kant (or lesser paradigms). Some of the more perfunctory third-tier thinkers – Mark Platts, for instance – simply announce (against Mackie) the equality of moral and scientific realism: they offer no grounds at all for what they claim.[46] Others – John McDowell, for instance – appeal to strategies that clearly fail to grasp the profundity of Mackie's challenge (which Mackie also failed to grasp): they speak, for instance, of treating moral values in the way of Lockeian secondary qualities.[47] Others, Railton for instance, fall back to supervenience in order to secure a form of moral naturalism.[48] Wiggins senses the need for a new departure. He has it in his ken, but he cannot seize it. He fastens on the *need* for an internal relation between evaluative (factual) and motivational (directive) considerations. Finding that relation absent in the empiricist and noncognitivist conjectures he examines, he invests in a Moorian sort of intuitionism *in which* an internal connection and a moral objectivism are explicitly preserved. But it is a completely superfluous effort, because the "meaning of life" question is (as I say) always trivially resolved (in *lebensformlich* terms); it is also an entirely uncompelling answer, because, without the link to the "meaning" question, Wiggins cannot distinguish his own position from that of the ordinary intuitionist.

My sense is that Wiggins cannot see the whole matter because third-tier thinking is committed by long philosophical habit to a certain analytic model: individualistic, objectivistic, opposed to the social construction of the human self, indifferent to historicity, committed to a strong disjunction between realist and idealist sources, puzzled by the conceptual (rational) link between the factual and the directive in human thinking.

Wiggins is the best of the English-language third-tier practitioners. Hence, *his* failing is the best key to the failing of the tribe. (Otherwise, the close reading I've favored would have no dialectical benefit beyond the worst academic niggling.) I am trying to isolate a clue that lies before our eyes that the entire community of analytic moral philosophers has utterly ignored. I am trying to isolate it by means that cannot be faulted by reference to the best virtues of analytic practice itself. I might have hurried on to the same discovery by other means. But the intended gain requires the acknowledgment of the best of the moral realists. (I mean to enlist their support.)

Wiggins prepares the ground, then, for the eclipse of third-tier thinking. One sees it in his having linked Aristotle and Wittgenstein. Wittgenstein, of course, captures the collective and consensual character of societal life – -in which alone all our cognitive and active commitments have meaning and effect – which, remarkably, analytic philosophy "reduces" in assimilating Wittgenstein. (Wittgenstein himself has no interest in the historical formation of our *Lebensformen*. Remember that.) The closest the moral realists come to fourth-tier thinking appears – under Wiggins's strong influence – in Lovibond. For it is only in Lovibond that Wittgenstein begins to be Hegelianized.[49] The *passage* of pertinent transformations is clear: Aristotle's consensus of civilized reason is made *lebensformlich*, and the *lebensformlich* is made *sittlich*.[50] By that maneuver both the realism of moral values and the answer to the question of the meaning of life are assured – but not yet the answer to Mackie's question! Lovibond herself falls back to third-tier analogues of Wiggins's failing. So we are brought to the edge of a great advance, but we cannot yet cross over. My own sense is that the entire moral realist vein is played out, entirely exhausted and unpromising; but the confirmation that it could not fail to be played out was worth the labor. Except for a pocket of fresh metal here and there, it's time to close the site.

3

Reasonableness and Moral Optimism

Moral theory is difficult. We cannot escape the nagging thought that we promote our own utopian dreams or distopian fears or cater to our own deep appetites all the while we tell ourselves we are being "neutral," "fair," "objective," "disinterested," "morally responsible." I cannot see how objectivity in moral questions can be freed from whatever profound convictions we find ourselves harboring about the meaning of life and how it should be lived; and, about such convictions, I cannot see that there is any simple right or wrong to proclaim.

The history of moral philosophy is largely the history of ingenious minds that have not worried too strenuously about such questions. They see complexity everywhere all right; but, by and large, they get on with the business of working out what they suppose is the best rule of reason. If, for instance, it were true that, as the animals we are, humans regularly manifested nearly intractable cannibal proclivities (or, more realistically, cruel and potentially oppressive dispositions or various forms of sexual deviance), some philosophers might announce (perhaps on Aristotelian grounds) that it was reasonable to accord them a well-defined place in a responsible eudaimonism; others (possibly on Kantian grounds) might regard the repudiation of such proclivities as prima facie evidence of the appeal to pure practical reason. If cannibal appetite were a fact of life, then, I suggest, we might never be altogether sure that there was *any* reasonable moral instruction that would favor either policy exclusively – or any other, for that matter – except the entirely vacuous instruction that we should, somewhere, somehow, come to terms with our natural dispositions. Possibly, each response might be incorporated into a "reasonable" account of an exemplary life. I should be prepared to honor each *prima facie* – without yielding to either finally – and I should not be troubled by the certainty that, at the very least, they would be incompatible with one other.

In a bookish way, I have always been impressed with Sophocles's immense humanity (and conceptual aplomb) in composing the *Antigone*, and even more with Aeschylus's sense, in the *Oresteia*, of the historical contingencies under which one great vision of justice supplants another without quite eliminating the first. I see no reason to think my little parable could possibly put to rest such grander conflicts of irreconcilable judgment. (The resolution of the *Oresteia*, I remind you, was the work of a very human *deus ex machina*.) The assurance that such conflicts can be resolved I regard as hopelessly utopian. The conviction that moral theory is for that reason pointless I regard as extravagantly distopian. And the blithe pursuit of one or another theorizing response, to the exclusion of others incompatible with its own presumption, I regard as a kind of cannibal appetite on the theorizing side.

Most of the finest work in moral philosophy is written in that trancelike state in which fixed principles, indubitable intuitions, endlessly adequate reason, the inherent wisdom of human nature, the universal brotherhood of creaturely understanding, sheer humanity and fair play, moral neutrality, the telic confidence of all our blind approximations of same hang on our conceptual trees for easy picking. All of it is bombast – thrilling enough even on repeated readings, infectious, conspiratorial, but still pure bunkum. And yet, valid and reasonable and objective and humane moral visions *are* possible. They are possible, but they are our own construction; and we, as a consequence, are also our own construction, the openended, ongoing, reconstructed ensemble of ourselves.

I

I have in this spirit noted with particular interest John Rawls's citation, in his recent book *Political Liberalism*,[1] a delicious remark of Bossuet's: "I have the right to persecute you [Bossuet declares] because I am right and you are wrong."[2] Of course! The trouble is, contemporary moral philosophy is – at least secretly – unsure of any such grounds. It is right to be unsure. I take moral philosophy to be scrupulous in its heart but not, reliably, in its printed word or public pronouncement. In any case, to worry the point is to call into profound doubt any presumption that one could ever simply recognize the exclusively reasonable treatment of the supposed *fait* of our cannibalistic nature. Could it be that the presumption that we do know what such a treatment would require is already hostage to opposed philosophical scruples? I think so. More to the point, Rawls, who holds very definite views about what a *reasonable* moral and political vision involves, is entirely captured by Bossuet's pronouncement despite his fine effort to escape it.

Rawls is worth quoting on the matter:

> Since many doctrines are seen to be reasonable, those who insist, when fundamental political questions are at stake, on what they take as true but others do not, seem to others simply to insist on their own beliefs when they have the political power to do so. Of course, those who do insist on their beliefs also insist that their beliefs alone are true: they impose their beliefs because, they say, their beliefs are true and not because they are their beliefs. But this is a claim that all equally could make; it is also a claim that cannot be made good by anyone to citizens generally . . . . reasonable persons see that the burdens of judgment set limits on what can be reasonably justified to others, so they endorse some form of liberty of conscience and freedom of thought. It is unreasonable for us to use political power, should we possess it, or share it with others, *to repress comprehensive views that are not unreasonable.*[3]

"Views that are not unreasonable"! Splendidly civilized phrasing. But what does it mean?

Rawls has put his finger on the decisive question. I don't mean the question of moral liberalism extended to political behavior. There is that, of course; and, in that regard, *Political Liberalism* is the clear sequel to *A Theory of Justice*,[4] which it (that is, the new book) builds upon (and corrects).[5] I mean that Rawls implies a principled distinction between the presumed *truth* (Bossuet's) of one or another variously opposed substantive doctrines and their being, jointly, morally and politically *reasonable* even if opposed (or, of it being "liberally" reasonable to make room for their political play *as* no more than "reasonable" doctrines).

Frankly, I cannot see how, *if* there is no assured ground on which to vote in Bossuet's favor, it is possible to vote (*still* in Bossuet's favor or against it) by sorting out what is "reasonable" and what "unreasonable" in the way of moral or morally informed political doctrine. There's the problem: how can the morally or politically "reasonable" possibly be separated from what is normatively *true* or normatively *right*? (Morality and politics are inseparable, of course, whether one thinks with Rawls or Nietzsche or with Aristotle or Kant.)

I cannot see how to show that a sincere moral agent – convinced that Bossuet has gone too far (as a realist of some sort about moral or political values) but convinced as well that *he* (the agent) *can* still

distinguish between those doctrines that are merely politically "reasonable" and those that are not – *would not then be able to do* Bossuet's
dirty work for him with an entirely clean conscience, arguing all the
while that he (the agent) never supposed he had Bossuet's truth tucked
up in his back pocket. I don't see the principled difference between the
supposed *objective truth* of Bossuet's claims and the *objective reasonableness* of Rawls's claims, except that the latter may be expected to be
more generous than the former and except that the explanation of the
entailed policy might involve setting aside a bivalent logic (although it
never risks that much in Rawls's hands). Furthermore, on Rawls's
argument, the force of political dispute – as distinct from moral dispute
– can never be more compelling than the other, since it presupposes the
prior fair resolution of the problem (or at least an awareness of the
problem) of defining moral justice.

The matter is enormously complicated, as you see: I can afford only a
few remarks in summarizing Rawls's very large thesis. The point is this:
in *Political Liberalism*, the (liberal) moral theory of "justice as fairness"
functions only as a "module" influencing no more than the "basic
structure" of a political constitution. Rawls means that "the political
conception of justice . . . is, of course, a moral conception," but it applies
only to a particular constitutional structure (Rawls prefers "a modern
constitutional democracy") – that is, it applies in the main only procedurally. The "political conception of justice" that results is "a free-
standing view"; that is, "it offers no specific metaphysical or
epistemological doctrine beyond what is implied by the political conception itself."[7] Hence, it is *not* a form of moral or political knowledge or
correctness (as it would be for Bossuet). The individual persons who
participate politically certainly possess their own "metaphysical or
epistemological doctrine[s]" that color *their* political roles. But the *liberal*
judgment of what is "reasonable," or "unreasonable," to allow *as*
politically fair interventions is *not* informed (as it would be for Bossuet)
by any metaphysical or epistemological privilege. That is the claim all
right. But how in the world can it be made valid – objectively?

My charge is that, as a matter of principle, Rawls (as a stand-in for all
of us) cannot draw a demarcation line between questions of reasonableness that are merely procedural and questions of reasonableness that
accord with whatever is substantive in "the political conception itself";
and that, as a consequence, he *cannot* draw a principled demarcation
between Bossuet's claim and his own. (None of us can.) To fail in that is
to confirm the futility of treating "justice as fairness" – restricted to the
politically normative space for which it was originally intended – as the
objective, neutral, consensually universal practical policy it is said to be.

But *that* hardly confirms the futility of moral and political theory! You may see in this puzzle (about what is "reasonable") the full range of the reflection in which a second-tier Rawls risks a third-tier worry about his own commitment. The entire project of liberalism (and its competitors) hangs in the balance.

II

Imagine, to come to cases, that I believe abortion to be wrong. More than that, although I recognize that there are many in my society who believe abortion to be morally acceptable and, believing that, scrupulously work at formulating a moral doctrine to back the claim and locate it in a suitable "metaphysical and epistemological" space. *I* believe, from the vantage of my own "comprehensive" view, that *their view is both morally and politically unreasonable*. How so? you ask. Well, I say, the matter of taking "an innocent life" is too deeply entrenched in my vision to permit me to concede that *any* doctrine that opposed it, while not demonstrably false or wrong, was at least morally or politically unreasonable. How could you *show* that *I* was *wrong*, or politically (even "liberally") *unreasonable*? Barring cognitive or rational privilege, there cannot be a principled ground for such a claim. For *if we can't know what is morally true or right, then we can't know what is morally reasonable either*. And if that is so, then moral and political liberalism collapses of its own weight. Even that most decent of moral theories (liberalism) must then be deluding itself beyond the scruple of the original caveat with which I began. And if that doctrine fails, what could possibly succeed? Either the notion of what is "reasonable, procedurally" *is* ontologically or epistemologically freighted (as it is for Kant and Apel) or there is no reliable, known basis on which the validity of procedural and substantive norms can be disjoined. (It is a dogma of liberalism that they can be disjoined.) There is no way to disjoin (and defend) what is morally or politically reasonable (in the way of practical reason) from what is morally or politically true (in the way of theoretical reason).

Don't misunderstand me. I am not saying that, if we give up Bossuet's sense of the confident discovery of what's "objectively" right and wrong, we must give up the serious debate about what is "reasonable" to allow to compete in the moral or political marketplace. I am not recommending moral skepticism or nihilism. I say only that we cannot *know* or rightly *judge* what is morally reasonable and unreasonable if we cannot *know* or *judge* what is true or right in moral matters. To shift from the true to the reasonable is not to replace a (normative) substantive policy by a (normative) procedural one but to replace one epistemic and ontic policy by another. The collapse of liberalism may be no more than a by-product, but it is the salient "by-product" Americans live by. (There are counterpart doctrines embattled in other parts of the world.) East of Eden, we construct our moral theories as the creatures we know ourselves to be: creatures who cannot claim to have any *reliable inkling* of what is "naturally," "rationally," "reasonably," "universally," "necessarily," "certainly," "objectively," "independently," "neutrally" true or right in the way of moral norms and values. (That is still the inescapable lesson of Mackie's failed critique.)

Remember: Rawls makes a brief reference to the abortion issue. He speaks in terms of respecting "three important political values: the due respect for human life, the ordered reproduction of political society over time . . . , and finally the equality of women as equal citizens. . . . Now I believe [he says] *any* reasonable balance of these three values will give a woman a duly qualified right to decide whether or not to end her pregnancy during the first trimester."[8] I don't find the argument any-where in Rawls. (In fact, I don't find the argument anywhere. *Why* the restriction to the first trimester, for instance?)

I happen to share Rawls's "prejudice" about what is "reasonable" here; but, at this point in the argument, that's all it is – an attractive prejudice. I cannot see how it can be suitably universalized for those who oppose it; and I cannot see why, in its universalized form, it cannot be reasonably affirmed against its opponents. *And* I cannot see how the argument would work in terms of Rawls's original notion of justice and rights or in terms of political liberalism (or in terms of any alternative policy of comparable strength). Rawls, of course, is no more than a ideologue here. We need to be honest scoundrels if we must be philosophers. The entire legitimative game is a sham *if* it is played according to the rules of *real or rational moral values invariantly or objectively discerned or judged to be rightly or truly such*. No such assurances can ever be given. Once we give up Bossuet, it's sand all the way down! There is then no principled difference between what is right or true and what is reasonably judged to be such.

In support of this objection, I offer three intuitions with which nearly all of the best-known moral and political theories are in conflict: first, conjectures in the empirical sciences noticeably converge over time, without yet necessarily arriving at any universally or apodictically affirmed judgment or explanatory theory, whereas the reverse obtains in moral and political matters; second, not only is there no general agreement about norms and values, there is no general agreement about how to decide whether there is agreement or not about the validity of moral and political judgments; and, third, there is no principled distinction between what it means to say that anyone knows, or reasonably believes, this or that general moral and political truth and how to show that anyone actually does know, or reasonably believe, this or that in particular cases.

Let me make this clearer. If I say abortion is wrong, you may suppose that I mean that, if it is wrong, then (1) it is wrong for all in *similar* circumstances, and (2) it is wrong for *all* in these and those particular circumstances. Reasoning along line (1) simply ensures consistency of usage and is not morally or politically serious in the abstract, although inconsistency certainly can have moral repercussions. Reasoning along line (2) captures what is sometimes called *moral* universality, which says that whatever is right or wrong for each *is* right or wrong only if it is right or wrong for all (relevantly). (Richard Hare confused the two notions in his early discussions of universalizability.)[9] I say only that line (1) is morally trivial and line (2), morally and politically doubtful.

There is no way to decide – empirically or rationally or reasonably or objectively or disinterestedly, if such differences are supposed to make a difference – whether arguments in accord with (2) *ever* obtain: there is no way to tell, for instance, whether *everyone* – or everyone acting "rationally" or "reasonably" – would agree (or would be found to agree or could be counted on agreeing) with *any* would-be moral or political pronouncement. One cannot but "idealize" here. The trouble is, *every* such idealization presumes to discern what is true or right or reasonable *in the moral or political way. But that* returns us to the difficulty we found in Rawls's reading of Bossuet. It is an insuperable limitation but not a fatal one. It *is* fatal for theorists like Rawls and Habermas and MacIntyre. It is not fatal for Kant and Aristotle, or for Apel or, for that matter, for that part of MacIntyre that subverts the historicizing voice that would temper his own Thomism. Above all, it is not fatal for the future of moral philosophy (of the fourth-tier sort).

III

The conundrum that lies at the base of Rawls's theory is the essential conundrum of the entire tradition of Western moral (and political) philosophy. I am not suggesting that all moral and political theorists are committed to liberalism. Of course not.

The fact is, Rawls has attempted to attenuate the conundrum in an extraordinary way: to treat it as a sort of smoothed-down moral membrane through which we pass with the least conceptual exertion from the factual to the normative, to go from standard reminders of psychological commonplaces to the most minimal admission of normative practice. (That is the moral naturalist's "best" maneuver.) It may help if I caricature Rawls's trick as an analogue of Descartes's attenuation of the physical in the vicinity of the pineal gland so that mind/body interaction begins to seem no longer impossible. The "reasonable" is a bit like what might appear to pass through a moral pineal gland linking ideology and true morality! It's for this reason that I single out Rawls.

Rawls may not have defined the only conceptual strategy for resolving the fact/value conundrum, but he shows us a way to *naturalize* the difference, to make it appear that, in admitting the "reasonable," we have only redescribed the would-be powers of practical reason (adjusted from Kant's unacceptably transcendental characterization) so that its description is hardly more than the description of natural psychological tendencies that manage (nevertheless) to ensure a sense of what is *normatively universal* in ordinary psychological behavior. I see in this an exemplary attempt on Rawls's part to "naturalize" moral and political concerns – in the sense of "naturalize" that Quine offers in his immensely influential paper, "Epistemology Naturalized."[10] In Quine's hands (and among those who have followed Quine), the naturalizing strategy is usually construed in a cognitivist way. What Rawls has managed to do is provide a constructivist alternative specifically fashioned for moral and practical judgment and commitment. It would not be unfair to say that Rawls thereby joins the vestigial universality of some would-be transcendental subject's moral judgments with the contingent convictions of mere human subjects. Rawls constructs an adequational account of liberalism and presents it as an existential finding.

It is at this point that one begins to see the remarkable convergence – despite appearances – between Rawls's project and that of Jürgen Habermas; for what Habermas is intuitively after, particularly in his important paper "Discourse Ethics,"[11] is (once again) a constructivist (or Kantian) naturalizing of practical reason, except that this time (in Habermas) the process is described in terms of so-called "dialogic" habits of mind. The details do not concern us for the time being. The important thing to grasp is the enormous skill with which Rawls manages to recover a sense of moral objectivity – in a way that is (1) naturalized and (2) putatively universal.

I am, of course, in the middle of dismantling that strategy. The point is that what is at stake is not merely the assessment of a single theory, however important, but the assessment of one of the most skillfully formed paradigms of moral philosophy that we can imagine, that shows us how to reclaim the Kantian model within the severe constraints of late twentieth-century analytic options. Otherwise, my having singled Rawls out in the way I have may strike you as no more than an odd detour. It is meant to be no such thing: it is the reclamation and critique of certain third-tier themes applied within the terms of certain of the principal second-tier theories.

Consider Rawls's picture of a liberal political society that (as Rawls sees matters) precludes anything like Bossuet's pronouncement:

> In a reasonable society, most simply illustrated in a society of equals in basic matters, all have their own rational ends they hope to advance, and all stand ready to propose fair terms that others may reasonably be expected to accept, so that all may benefit and improve on what every one can do on their own.[12]

If one knew the answer to what was morally true and false about the "ends" of human life, there would be no need for political liberalism: it would be superfluous. Not knowing that, we fall back (Rawls believes) to "fair terms" that tolerate the idiosyncrasy of the "ends" of others *within our political order.* "Political liberalism," he says, "takes for granted not simply pluralism but the fact of reasonable pluralism." Rawls asks us to consider the question: "How is it possible that deeply opposed though reasonable comprehensive doctrines may live together and all affirm the political conception of a constitutional regime?"[13]

To the counterquestion: "What is the 'reasonable'?" Rawls answers:

> The first basic aspect of the reasonable ... is the willingness to propose fair terms of cooperation and to abide by them provided others do. The second basic aspect ... is the willingness to recognize the burdens of judgment and to accept their consequences for the use of public reason in directing the legitimate exercise of political power in a constitutional regime.[14]

Rawls means that (1) the liberal is justified in using force, politically, to disallow *unreasonable* "comprehensive doctrines" (or judgments or commitments that they subtend), but (2) the liberal is not justified in doing so with regard to *reasonable* "comprehensive doctrines." Now, however diminished, isn't that simply Bossuet's outlook in a gentler guise and in terms that replace a cognitivist approach by a constructivist alternative?

I must put one final clue in place before pronouncing sentence. It is a finding that the collapse of Rawls's strategy cannot dislodge. It's this: *thinking has (or is) inherently a history*; what is *rational* or *reasonable* is an artifact of human history; *there is no reason common to the human species that is timelessly such*, completely ahistorical in structure – whether in logic or science or morality. Rawls is wrong to think that *if* Bossuet cannot legitimate *his* claim, *we* may still legitimate what is morally "reasonable"; and Mackie is wrong to think that if realism in moral matters fails, we are driven to skepticism.[15] There's the grand mistake (I find) in nearly the whole of moral philosophy. It's the perseveration of thinkers like Rawls that makes Mackie's complaint seem plausible and that drives postmodernists like Richard Rorty to their very sly complaisance.[16] We need to pin Rawls down all right; but the clue I glimpse beyond the failure of his "pineal" resolution is this: *liberal political justice, like the "reasonable," which it is supposed to embody and which in turn is supposed to embody a minimal morality is inherently historicized.*

Here is the last bit of evidence:

> Let's say that reasonable disagreement is disagreement between reasonable persons: that is, between persons who have realized their . . . moral powers to a degree sufficient to be free and equal citizens in a constitutional regime, and who have an enduring desire to honor fair terms of coopera-tion and to be fully cooperating members of society. *Given their moral powers. they share a common human reason*, similar powers of thought and judgment: they can draw inferences, weigh evidence, and balance compelling considerations.[17]

You see the slippage (I've italicized the evidence.) Rawls begins with the supposed *uniformities of ideal reason*. To these he adds our skills in resolving what he calls "the burdens of judgment." Most of these have to do with such self-marginalizing matters as "hard cases." But not all the "burdens" are like that. Rawls eventually comes to the essential, the most difficult "burden," the one that subverts his entire strategy, the one that disallows a distinction between objective morality and moral ideology, the one Isaiah Berlin correctly marks in the following way: "Some among the Great Goods cannot live together. That is a conceptual truth. We are doomed to choose, and every choice may entail an irreparable loss."[18] Rawls accepts Berlin's instruction without qualifica-tion: "any system of institution," he says, "has, as it were, a limited social space."[19] Remember that.

The point is: *if* Rawls is right, then; (1) liberalism cannot claim to be *reasonable* in the universalizing sense – *ever*; (2) if (1) is true, then no moral or political philosophy that is not already committed to something like Bossuet's strong thesis (or Aristotle's or Kant's, of course) can be *reasonable* in the universalizing sense – *ever*; and (3) if (2) is true, then no moral or political philosophy can – *ever* – be legitimated, *if* legitimation must accord with the universalizing constraint. In the analytic tradition, the upshot of admitting (1) – (3) is simply moral skepticism.[20] I claim, however, that we can avoid that conclusion – which analytic moral philosophy cannot – if we but historicize reason: *a fortiori*, if we historicize justice and whatever other normative notions we invoke. (To historicize reason, I should add, is to accommodate relativism[21] and to regard strict universality, whether in science or morality, as an idealization from one contingent perspective or another.) But if we see matters thus, we cannot be liberals in Rawls's sense; and if we cannot, then we cannot legitimate any moral vision by reference to the (universal) resources of the "reasonable" or the "rational."

The nerve of the argument is this. Either we claim (1) to know what is morally right and wrong (Bossuet, metonymically); or, failing that or not invoking such a claim in the political context, we fall back (2) to what is morally rational (the "original position"), or we fall back (3) to what it is reasonable to allow in a certain constitutional space (liberal democracy, say). We pretend to recover "objectivity" in accord with one or another of these three strategies. In the first, we fall back to metaphysical and epistemological realism; in the second, we fall back to an attenuated constructivist alternative (as when we fall back to "justice as fairness" under "the veil of ignorance"). It seems that we do not do the same (in the third strategy) under the "modular" terms of political dispute: there, we appeal "only" to what is universalizable among "reasonable" agents who know they have systematically different and opposed interests but who share, "modularly," the same principles of justice that define *their* political space! (If *that* is Rawls's position, then there is really no great difference between Rawls and Rorty: the question of objective norms cannot then arise.) On the argument, however (Rawls's argument), neither the second nor the third maneuver can be distinguished in practice or in principle from a temperate version of Bossuet's assurance. There's the final *reductio*.

There are at least two serious difficulties with Rawls's notion of the "reasonable": for one, he supposes he can disjoin the question of normative political procedures from that of substantive moral or practical norms – but he cannot (the argument from Bossuet); for another, he supposes the question of normative (liberal) political procedures is entirely a matter of accommodating some form of pluralism – but it is not (the argument from Berlin). Rawls believes he has escaped the Bossuettian difficulty, but he fails to answer the charge that he pretends to *know* which norms (governing what is moral and what is politically congruent with what is morally normative) would be so judged by ("pure") practical reason. He does not believe he can escape Berlin's difficulty, but he does believe it can be attenuated in a "reasonable" way because the idea of what is (liberally) "reasonable" has to do *only* with accommodating plural values. But – in this – he has failed to answer the charge (1) that Berlin's "burden-of-judgment" cases *cannot be reconciled* with any merely generous (or procedural) pluralism and (2) that, more generally, *there cannot be any pluralistic resolution at all if there is no "reasonable" finding about substantive goods, compatible with a bivalent model of judgment on which "all" can agree.* So Berlin's worry falls within Bossuet's range – which is precisely what I had anticipated.

The problem may be pressed a little further. *Pluralism*, in practical matters, is a policy of tolerance within an appointed range of options. It cannot be supposed to tolerate just *any* would-be option at all. Hence, pluralism always risks a conflict at the limit of "reasonable" options – at which it ceases to function. Pluralism cannot be merely procedural, therefore. In this sense, Rawls contradicts himself when he denies that a "liberal" or pluralist or "procedural" rule of (political) fairness advocates "no specific metaphysical or epistemological doctrine" beyond the requirements of the procedural matter itself. Furthermore, pluralism is also an analogue, in regard to practical tolerance, of the theoretical admissibility (for instance) of all the "objective" alternative "appearances" of some particular thing under variable perceptual conditions. That is, pluralism, like the admissibility of different appearances, *precludes*, in principle – within the terms of its proper tolerance – *any logical or criterial conflict at the level of appearances* (or their practical counterparts). If conflict of Berlin's sort arises, then only three lines of resolution are possible: (a) we can fall back to a Bossuettian judgment (privilege); (b) we can deny that there is an objective solution possible (skepticism); or (c) we can replace a bivalent rationale with a relativistic rationale. My own recommendation is (c); but the point is simply that Rawls wishes not to invoke (a); to oppose (b); to admit that pluralism cannot accommodate Berlin's difficulty; but to be unwilling to admit (c).

We begin to see, therefore, the fundamental difference between pluralism and relativism *and* just how moral relativism gains in plausibility wherever *we are not prepared to disallow normative judgments that on a bivalent logic (but not now) would produce contradictory or incompatible findings.* (I call such judgments – now, valid relativistically – "incongruent.")[22] In any case, neither a liberal morality nor a liberal politics can survive the import of Berlin's challenge. Put another way, there is no satisfactory liberal "procedure" by which a conflict along the lines Berlin introduces can be read always and everywhere as a mere contingency compatible with a pluralistic policy. For pluralism requires that there be *some* generic (objective) Good that may be validly instantiated (along bivalent lines) in different forms (that may occasionally come into practical conflict). Berlin's thesis concerns, rather, the principled incompatibility among all the "Great Goods" themselves. My claim is that you cannot admit Berlin's "Great Goods" doctrine without invoking relativism (if you deny cognitive privilege or the privilege of practical reason), and you cannot square the resultant conflicts with a bivalent logic or with moral or practical liberalism. QED.

"Reasonableness" in the moral or political sense, therefore, fails as a separate policy. Pluralism cannot but be a doctrine of tolerance within the terms of *some* substantive Good, whether determined in accord with theoretical or practical reason. Relativism, on the other hand, is the option of all those who deny privilege (but not conviction or belief) in theoretical and practical affairs alike, who construe universality as an artifact of idealizing from one contingent perspective or another, and who are prepared to replace bivalence with a many-valued logic in virtue of which "incongruent" judgments may, in context, be deemed pertinently valid. I have already touched on the analogy between Quine's treatment of the "indeterminacy of translation" and Rawls's liberalism. But it may help to add that both are pluralists, not relativists, and that Quine's pluralism would make no sense unless one conceded that (Quine's) "holophrastic sentences" must be capable of being shown to be true on objective grounds that are *not* themselves pluralistic but vindicate our subsequent plural "parsings." Quine nowhere attempts to justify this first principle. It cannot be done without falling back to some form of cognitive privilege. That explains (by way of analogy) why Rawls cannot fail to be a Bossuettian.

IV

We have turned a corner. Most contemporary moral philosophy is of the "second-tier" sort. Even "third-tier" philosophy – Wiggins's, Lovibond's, Nagel's, McDowell's – aspires to restore second-tier assurances. I have argued that all these ventures fail. I have tried to show that Rawls's argument is, clinically, the most decisive second-tier specimen (much as Wiggins's is the decisive third-tier specimen), because it attempts (by naturalizing tactics) to provide the slimmest possible grounds for legitimating (1) objective rationality or reasonableness regarding practical norms and (2) a certain normative universality as a consequence of (1). All that would be rendered untenable at a stroke if, as I suggest, we simply began with the postulate that human reason is historicized, grounded in the contingencies of human *praxis*, open to a valid choice of norms and values that cannot, in the aggregate, be reconciled with a bivalent logic. That, of course, is what I offer as the key to my "fourth-tier" strategies. I am trying to show how our interest in such strategies grows out of the utter failure of the usual first-, second-, and third-tier literature.

But second-tier philosophies divide in a further respect: some, I shall say, are *assured*; and some, merely *optimistic*. Rawls and Habermas are "moral optimists"; Apel is definitely "assured," although he coopts the optimist's ground. MacIntyre argues as an optimist as far as he can, but he always falls back to assured terrain. Bernstein is an optimist (regarding both science and morality) but without ever advancing any grounds apart from a vacant appeal to "fallibilism" in the Deweyan sense. Optimists, I should say, subscribe to the sheer hope that the play of moral dispute will, in the limit, yield a kind of neutrality and universality that all rational persons can support; those who are assured claim a principle on which such a hope may be reliably grounded in an epistemic way. Obviously, there are ready parallels in the philosophy of science. Kuhn, for instance, is an optimist, as are also Lakatos and Popper. Salmon requires assurance, precisely because Reichenbach, his mentor, was an optimist in a way Salmon thought insufficient to secure the laws of nature.[23] Peirce is the supreme optimist in the philosophy of science, and, for that very reason, reclaims assurance at the end of "the long run."[24] You may perhaps begin to see the point of the contrast. Fourth-tier theories will be neither assured nor optimistic.

I should also mention that neither Nietzsche nor Foucault are second-tier philosophers: neither is "assured" and neither is "optimistic." But then, neither is prepared to offer a reasoned defense of an "objective" morality – and that is what we (usually say we) need. So neither is a fourth-tier thinker. Each avoids being systematic in a way that would approach the work of first- and second-tier theorists; but then, neither is a skeptic or a postmodernist. They are, I should say, "poststructuralists," meaning by that that, although they oppose every pretense of assurance and optimism, they also have no interest in anything like fourth-tier thinking. Foucault and Derrida are quintessentially poststructuralists (certainly not postmodernists) whereas Nietzsche is a poststructuralist only by courtesy – *avant la lettre*. In the philosophy of science, Ian Hacking and Arthur Fine are, perhaps, the closest to being poststructuralists as any figures one might imagine.[25] What is common to fourth-tier thinking and what I am calling poststructuralism is simply the repudiation of all forms of privilege assigned to theoretical or practical reason –

metonymically, whether of the noetic (Aristotelian) or transcendental (Kantian) sort. In a word, fourth-tier strategies admit only human subjects, the culturally formed creatures that we are, shorn of any pretense of sharing a further godly power apt for discerning or judging neutrally and universally what is binding on the normative direction of human life. No one can demonstrate that we possess such a resource. Accordingly, moral philosophy, like the philosophy of science, cannot exceed that limitation.

The distinction between the "assured" and the "optimistic" is obviously problematic. But it is considerably more important than the fate of liberalism. What I mean is, the entire tradition of Western moral philosophy has risked itself on more and more attenuated maneuvers meant to bridge the convictions of second-tier thinking and the legitimative uncertainties of third-tier thinking. Rawls, of course, has thrown in with the liberals. But the fact is he has done so as an "optimist."

We have now recovered the insoluble dilemma that confronts Rawls's strategy: on the one hand, Rawls risks everything on the optimism of the "reasonable"; on the other, he falls back to the assurance of the "rational." To hold to the first is to convert any would-be objective morality and politics (liberalism) into plain ideology; to fall back to the second is to subordinate any constructivist morality to the privilege of an ulterior cognitivist model. If you follow the argument out, this means that, of the two great paradigms of moral theory, the Kantian cannot succeed if it insists (as it does) on a constructivism based on discerning (1) the universal or invariant norms of human reason, that (2) are demonstrably necessary or converge toward some ideal necessity in terms of actual practical or pragmatic concerns. It also means that the other paradigm, the Aristotelian, cannot succeed if it insists (as it does) on a cognitivism based on discerning (1) the normative essence of human nature, that (2) is demonstrably invariant or necessary or converges telically toward some ideal invariance in the practices and institutions of social life. On my reading, Karl-Otto Apel and Jürgen Habermas span the "assured" and "optimistic" limits of the Kantian strategy, just as Alasdair MacIntyre and Martha Nussbaum span the same limits of the Aristotelian.

Of course, it is entirely possible that constructivism and cognitivism take other forms: for instance, Marxist, Nietzschean, hermeneutic, Foucauldian in the one; Hobbesian, Humean, utilitarian, intuitionistic in the other. But nothing much hangs on such preferences, *if*, as I argue, Rawls's strategy exposes the essential nerve of the whole of Western moral theory. I insist, therefore, that the "reasonable" will be seen to be illicit wherever it specifies a normative invariance of its own when separated from the foundational pronouncements of (pure!) practical reason (as in Rawls's "original position") or when separated from the privileged discovery of man's telic nature (as in MacIntyre's account of the virtues or even, more curiously, in Rawls's account of invariant human "rights" that a legitimated justice would have to serve).

The trick is that Rawls cannot make the "reasonable" powerful enough in a criterial sense, unless he falls back to the assurance of invariant rationality or invariant human nature (which is what he actually does). In that single move, therefore, Rawls betrays the exhaustion of all second- and third-tier theory. (That is what I meant by mocking his treatment of Bossuet.) Thus Rawls remarks: "Reasonable disagreement is disagreement among reasonable persons." That now means that the criteria of reasonableness must be in place *before* ("reasonable") disagreement sets in. Reasonable disagreement ("within ideal theory") presupposes the notion of justice developed in *A Theory of Justice* (or something close to it). Rawls says as much: "the guidelines and procedures of public reason are seen as selected in the original position and belong to the political conception of justice."[26] Furthermore, the "reasonable" is *substantively* obliged to compromise with whatever is essential to its application in the universalizing sense. That was the "burden" of Berlin's "conceptual truth." Hence, working within the "Kantian" tradition, Rawls conflates (as does MacIntyre, working within the "Aristotelian") the distinction between the assured and the optimistic. Optimism is illicit when separated from assurance; but, in the presence of assurance, it makes no independent contribution at all. It marks no more than the pluralist's dependent contribution.

V

I say Rawls is wrong in this; most of moral philosophy – most of philosophy, in fact – is similarly wrong. Here I draw your attention to the fact that Rawls has an opposite number in current European philosophy: namely, Jürgen Habermas (and, less neatly, Karl-Otto Apel). Habermas actually perceives that Rawls is a natural ally – and a natural opponent. Habermas (mistakenly) believes that the difference between them is merely that Rawls's argument is "monological" whereas his own is "dialogical" (that is, inherently social in its reclamation of what is morally reasonable: "rational," as Habermas prefers to say).[27] Habermas means by this that the mark of what is morally reasonable (not *a priori* in Apel's sense – or in Kant's, for that matter) cannot be worked out "objectively" in the monologic way. (*That*, he thinks, is the fatal weakness of Rawls's "original position," which, it is true, is methodologically solipsistic.)

Habermas insists, however, that what is morally reasonable (or "rational") *can* be discerned, empirically, in the conditions of social communication – in its universalized form. He worries a bit, in passing, about the (same) difficulty Rawls fails to master in embracing Berlin's conceptual truth.[28] Like Rawls and, equally, in the liberal spirit, Habermas fails to come to terms with the implications of idealizing the "reasonable." (In fact, it is not at all certain that Habermas is *not* a solipsist masquerading as a dialogist.) But if that were all there were to say, both Rawls and Habermas might suppose that a little tinkering might restore the doctrine to philosophical health. Here I invoke an argument by analogy.

One says casually enough: it is against reason to offer, as a compelling argument, an argument known to violate the principle of noncontradiction. It is not "rational" to argue by way of violating the principle; and it is "unreasonable" to advance such an argument where a valid argument is required. Both Rawls and Habermas support the claim. I do not need to oppose it. It is completely vacuous in the form given. I go further: I say that, for any *interpreted* use of the principle of noncontradiction, it is always possible to relieve the charge by reinterpreting the terms of the argument. That is: even if the principle of noncontradiction is said to be a necessary truth, it remains true that no *sentence* interpreted as a contradiction is *necessarily* so interpreted. Thus, if you say, with Aristotle,[29] that noncontradiction *is* a necessary truth, then it suddenly becomes important to insist as well on the further truth – which Aristotle would deny – that there is no strictly necessary way to interpret the world or our thinking about the world validly. Aristotle holds *that* to be a false doctrine (arguing against Protagoras), because he believes that there *are* necessities *de re* that have universal scope. (Quine rejects such claims, of course.)[30]

The point of arguing in this way is quite straightforward. There *is* no way of formulating any *prior* rule of reason (like noncontradiction) in purely formal uninterpreted terms that *then convey to* certain interpreted sentences and arguments the modal necessity of the abstract formula. The formal rules of reason are no more than abstracted (perhaps idealized) *from* natural-language usage – from at least the exemplars of such usage. A geometric argument interpreted as contradictory for Euclidean space might not be contradictory if interpreted for some non-Euclidean space. The paradoxes (the contradictions) generated by Bell's theorems for classical mechanics are not paradoxes (or contradictions) if we give up classical mechanics for quantum physics. It is a mistake, some have persuasively argued, to suppose that formal logic and mathematics are merely *applied* to the actual world, after having (somehow) first secured their necessary truths in their own abstract world. No, the argument goes, those "formal" disciplines are really part (even if they are a peculiar part) of the empirical sciences themselves.[31] If so, then there cannot be an ordered hierarchy of what is relevantly "reasonable" or "rational" that proceeds *from* uninterpreted sentential formulas and argument forms *to* interpreted sentences and interpreted arguments. The syntax and semantics of a language are inseparable.

The bearing of this seeming aside is this: just as there is no prior rule of reason that actual discourse must conform to in order to be reasonable or rational, so there is no *prior* sense of "reasonable person" in terms of which Rawls could relevantly claim that "reasonable disagreement is disagreement among reasonable persons." *That's all*! The argument fails – massively – and for a reason analogous to the one that affects Aristotle's argument.

In fact, there are two distinct lines of argument that Rawls pursues that parallel in an uncanny way those that Aristotle favors. One holds that there *are* prior rules of reason that cannot be violated, on pain of violating reason. The other holds that the rules of reason, though entirely formal, somehow *entail* – when applied in an interpreted domain – interpreted (necessary) truths apt for that domain. In Rawls's hands, this now means that the "lexicographical" account of justice offered in *A Theory of Justice* is already the work of "reasonable persons" in the "original position," behind "the veil of ignorance":[32] hence, that, within the further space of a "constitutional regime," the acceptance of the principles of justice lead to the adoption of political liberalism – and *hence* to a "reasonable" policy on substantive matters like abortion. Nothing could be prettier. The only trouble is, it won't do! Where's the argument? Liberals are said to be able to recognize a "reasonable" disagreement because they are already "reasonable persons," having committed themselves to the substantive principles of justice mentioned. In *Political Liberalism*, Rawls "corrects" the failure to distinguish, in *A Theory of Justice*, between questions of "moral philosophy" and questions of "political philosophy."[33] He does not, however, give up or alter in essentials the theory of justice of the earlier book. He (now) admits that the questions a "reasonable person" might raise in the two contexts are not entirely the same. In fact, it may happen that, *in* the political world, one may have cause to wonder whether the putatively "reasonable" theory of justice of Rawls's own (or another's) moral philosophy is actually viable in, or reconcilable with, the realities of political life. It was in this spirit that I drew attention to the implications of Berlin's dictum.

Furthermore, Rawls's philosophical strategy – "reflective equilibrium" – by which he claims to arrive at the doctrine of "justice as fairness" is itself a most curious notion. It apparently proceeds by dialectically reviewing, first, "the conceptions of justice known to us through the tradition of moral philosophy and any further ones that occur to us," which are themselves fitted to our considered judgments on moral matters; what we there discern is then reflectively matched with what, independently and in the widest sense, "would be [the principle of justice] chosen in the original position in preference to other traditional conceptions of justice"; finally, "to be acceptable," "a political conception of justice" [that is, a constitution structured for producing justice] "must accord" with the outcome of the exercise of "reflective equilibrium." By this process, Rawls maintains, "justice as fairness moves us closer to the philosophical ideal; it does not of course achieve it."[34] What could Rawls possibly mean if he does not intend a diminished Kantian or a diminished moral realism? In fact, what he offers is the supposed fruit of canvassing all the actual *human* options that history affords – judged, now, in accord with the powers of practical reason that are not themselves constrained by human history. You would not be wrong to see in this a distant analogue of Aristotle's collecting the constitutions of the Greek (and neighboring non-Greek) states which are to be submitted to noetic certainties regarding the human essence.

VI

What this shows very plainly is that Rawls must have ruled out at the very start the possibility that justice is a historically changing idealization of the actual evolving possibilities of human practice viewed against the accumulating tradition of moral and political philosophy. Certainly, Marx's best vision of an evolving moral and political ideal pursues the latter possibility.[35] An extremely important (but neglected) aspect of admitting anything like Marx's conception of *praxis* is this: at one stroke, Rawls's confidence in being able to *discern*, by way of an unproblematic exercise of "reason," that the relevant moral and political distinctions are suitably the same or different in one or another social space – predicatively – is suddenly called into profound doubt. If we admit that theoretical and practical reason are embedded in a changing *praxis*, then normative assurances about the requisite similarities cannot fail to be inherently partisan or doubtful. For instance, *what, morally, is similar or different* in abortions linked to incest or rape and abortions linked to severely defective embryos? And *how* do we know? (As we shall see, the worry applies with equal force to Habermas and Apel.)

Closer to Rawls's own sense of how to proceed (but opposed to his model), we may take note of the radically historicized conception developed at considerable length by Roberto Mangabeira Unger, which counters both the supposed historical "necessitarianism" of Marx and the static moral and political visions of liberals and libertarians.[36] I am not recommending either Marx's or Unger's thesis. But *both* adopt what may be called "constructivist" conceptions of moral and political justice – of a sort Rawls nowhere considers in sketching the "original position." Unlike Rawls, who also claims to be a "constructivist," both Marx and Unger hold – to my mind, convincingly – that (1) *no* reflection at any single moment of time, or in any series of discrete moments, could possibly capture what is "rational" or "reasonable" in the way of conceiving justice; (2) our moral and political beliefs and ideals are formed by the institutional circumstances of our actual and contingent social life; (3) we are nevertheless thereby empowered to transform the "artifact" that is our society (the one in which we were formed) in ways that could not have been historically imagined before; and (4) the imaginative prospects of justice depend on a critical review of, and projection from, continually radicalizing the evolving possibilities of *actual* social life – against the ahistorical disposition that favors institutional inflexibilities and the thinking that goes with that disposition.

When Rawls introduces his own "constructivism," he contrasts it with "moral realism" (hence the pertinence of my returning to Bossuet). He lays out very cleanly the difference between his own view of "political constructivism" and the vision of "rational intuitionism" viewed as an exemplar of moral realism (or, better, a realism regarding moral matters). The key distinctions (for my present purpose) are these: on the one hand, moral intuitionism holds that "moral first principles and judgments, when correct, are true statements about an independent order of moral values ... that are known by theoretical reason"; on the other, "political constructivism" holds that "the principles of political justice may be presented as the outcome of a procedure of construction ... based essentially on practical reason and not on theoretical reason." There are other considerations but these are the decisive ones. The realist adheres to the standard conception of truth; the constructivist applies no more than "an idea of the reasonable" to those matters that arise in the political sphere;[37] and both admit the principled disjunction of theoretical and practical reason. (The admission of historicism upsets all that.)

The entire issue depends, therefore, on whether the manifestations of reason – the "rational" and/or the "reasonable" *are* or *are not* artifacts of our historical life. For if they are, then the method of "reflective equilibrium" and the presumption of "political constructivism" simply misperceive the enabling condition under which the theory of justice *can* be made out to be "reasonable" at all. On the argument, the concept of justice is not even morally or politically relevant except in historicized terms. I claim that the evidence that shows that Rawls fails to make his case for the invariance of the "reasonable" is actually exposed by his obvious inability to keep himself from falling back to some attenuated form of (moral) realism (Bossuet's challenge), by his inability to accommodate Berlin's dictum (which is not a matter that can be settled by separating the "reasonable" from the "unreasonable"), and by his unsupported assumption that there is a principled (or universal) distinction that holds between the reasonable and the unreasonable (which returns us to the problem of predicative genrality and the uninterpreted principle of noncontradiction).

I draw two conclusions from the foregoing: first, that, if we give up the presumption that there is an independently real moral order which we can discern, then the "objectivity" of the moral and political world can only be consensual, that is, a function of the convictions of those who reflexively judge their own judgments and behavior and actual prospects; second, that if we adopt the consensual view, then, further on the same argument, universalizability cannot serve in any criterial way. Now, I say, Rawls is unwilling to subscribe to the first, and the second goes contrary to his own conviction. That means not only that liberalism fails, but all views fail that make universal consensus decisive without presuming (somewhere) cognitive resources in the "realist" sense (Kant, for instance, Habermas, Apel, Hare, Gewirth, Gauthier at least). *Reasonableness and rationality exhibit no determinate universal form in an interpreted and historical world.* Reasonableness is a "construction," as is moral and political justice – and for the same reason. It cannot function criterially except as a historically provisional posit of consensual practice that is expressly not universalized or known to be legitimated *qua* universalized. There is only one option by which to save the "consensual objectivity" of moral and political judgment – that is, *if* we are not to yield to the opportunistic or the merely arbitrary: *we must historicize justice and reasonableness.* But if we do that we will be relativists and we will have outflanked both the Aristotelian and the Kantian paradigms.

My sense is that that *is* what Rawls trades on but never quite admits. The liberal tradition *can* be recovered – in some way not altogether opposed to Rawls's own vision – by giving up the fiction of the "original position," which already presumes a universally valid strategy, and by giving up the fiction of universal consent, which is both profoundly inaccessible and incapable, as we have seen, of excluding the realist's presumption or of meeting Berlin's dictum or of distinguishing between "reasonable" and "unreasonable" options.

What is distinctive about these findings may not strike you at once. Of course, I give up the presumption of the moral realist; but Rawls is willing to do so as well. I give up the criterial function of universality, which Rawls pretends to be able to invoke, at least by way of approximation. I also historicize reason and the norms of justice. On both of these counts, Rawls is unclear; for, although he regards justice as a construction, he also holds it to be an approximation to the "philosophical ideal" of justice. Apparently, that ideal is not discernibly skewed by any changing history. History, it seems, assists us in approximating to the ideal! But there is no sense in Rawls that the ideal might be itself no more than a moving historical projection judged in accord with what is deemed possible here and now. If the *constructive* role *of history* were conceded, then of course the admission of the "original position" and of reasoning 'under the veil of ignorance" would be worse than useless.

What is telling in all this is that Rawls betrays the insoluble *aporia* of every constructivism that makes justice an artifact of a rational or reasonable process but does not consider *whether reason (a fortiori, the "reasonable")* is itself an artifact of history as well. It is open to us, of course, to fall back to the realist's view, but there is no satisfactory defense of moral realism.[38]

What we see is that there is not likely to be a plausible defense of the moral constructivist's view, *if it fails to explain why reason should not be treated as an artifact of social history*. That single adjustment appears to offer the only way to avoid the *aporiai* of Rawls's position (which, of course, are not merely local to Rawls) or the triumph of the moral skeptic: first, because universality cannot be criterial; second, because a bivalent logic cannot be shown to be adequate to the puzzles of objective justice; and, third, because what are judged reasonable and unreasonable are *faute-de-mieux* claims relativized to what are institutionally thus entrenched. Moral theory proceeds dialectically: *if* these or those doctrines are admitted to be "reasonable," then what you and I *now* offer may be shown (by current lights) to be *not less reasonable* than they.

I offer one final consideration against Rawls's thesis. Grant that, at some time t, a consensus is reached on a hotly contested political issue; grant further that *that* consensus begins to exert a definite causal effect on the ongoing life of the society in which it holds. If so, then what is judged a "reasonable" consensus at time t_k (later than t) will be a function of the causal history of the decision at *t* and will be likely to conform thereafter to a (causally) altered conception of the "reasonable." This shows that it is unreasonable to regard "reasonableness" as ahistorical or ideal or relatively invariant; that what is "reasonable" at any time t_k is bound to depart from any would-be ideal, and is bound to vary from one society to another, from one subsociety to another, from one stage of any person's judgment to another; and that canny politicians, realizing this, are likely to plan gradual policy changes, so that a congruent consensus may actually be built up causally by changing the tolerance of important sectors of a given society bit by bit. I don't say such policies can always be relied on, but they certainly are rational policies on grounds Rawls cannot allow and cannot discount. Principles of reasonableness are inseparable from the actual historical practice and experience of a viable society. That alone exposes the utter indefensibility of Rawls's doctrine.

Needless to say, conflicting values are not a sign of failure either at the level of moral judgment or at the level of moral theory. Once we give up realism, there is no way to avoid admitting, as morally and politically "reasonable," judgments that cannot be confined within a bivalent logic; there is also no way to avoid admitting that reason itself is a historical construction. Rawlsian liberals cannot admit either concession but they cannot offset them either. Hence, liberalism fails. But such a failure is hardly a local affair. Nearly all contemporary (Anglo-American and German) moral philosophies resist these concessions even where they eschew moral realism (for instance, Habermas's and Apel's philosophies). That's why I say, either Rawls's theory leads to moral skepticism or it leads to the two concessions just mentioned. *Tertium non datur.*

The point is important: make no mistake about it. Because, *if* reason is an artifact of history, then moral theory cannot count on universality or idealized consensus or being brought to any principled resolution on the strength of a higher principle. And if that is granted, then liberalism cannot but be an instrumental policy serving some ulterior norm if it is not itself a mere ideology. And if that is so, then there is no basis for insisting, where moral objectivity is at stake, that reasonable arguments must be confined (or are best confined) to a bivalent rather than a relativistic logic. Think, for instance, of what would be required to condemn or validate suicide or euthanasia or abortion *tout court*. (Think of the suffering of untreatable Ebola victims.)

VII

The single most salient, most vulnerable theme of contemporary Western moral philosophy is, I suggest, *moral optimism*. The reason is due, of course, to the pressure of third-tier doubts imposed on second-tier claims – notably, Mackie's skepticism or any challenge that might strengthen its hand. "Moral optimism" is a term of art. I do not mean by it the real thing – genuine optimism about the prospects of achieving the good life in our time. On the contrary, it has an ironic sense: it signifies a kind of philosophical whistling in the wind, the testimony that, although we no longer know how to legitimate first- or second-tier doctrines *in the "assured" way*, we are entitled to carry on – "optimistically" – as if we could. Optimism, then, is the illicit presumption of assurance, or the substitution of some conceptual *bricolage* in its absence. At the risk of appearing frivolous, I remind you that George Bush was heard to say at the end of the Gulf War that the Americans – therefore, the world – had finally banished from the West's political space every would-be moral ideology that threatened the preeminence of liberal capitalism. I view Bush as an intuitive enthusiast of the second-tier optimisms I associate with Rawls and Habermas and MacIntyre. Alternatively, they are the ideologists of a certain privileged part of Western moral and political doctrine tendered on supposedly assured or optimistic legitimative grounds: Rawls, the principal advocate of American liberalism; Habermas, the younger German witness concerned to oppose the resurgence of Nazi energies in the context of blending German and American liberalism; Putnam, the latecomer in search of the biblical sources of liberalism; Cornel West, the black conscience reminding us of the exclusion of minorities; MacIntyre, the sterner voice of the Anglo-Catholic tradition insisting on the excesses of liberal confidence.

Mind you: Aristotle and Kant and Hegel, who, in various ways, are the tutors of all our second- and third-tier theorists, are *not* "optimists" at all. *Optimism*, as I understand the notion, is a legitimative orientation signifying (1) the displacement of invariant *reason* or *nature* by the contingent and variable forms of *reasonableness*, by way of (2) displacing the reliably objective competence of the first in favor of punctuated guesses or a contingently formed consensus in accord with the second. The process of serious inquiry – in any sector of interest: science as well as morality – is "optimistic," *if* whatever might otherwise be supposed to be an "assured" competence apt for discerning the necessary or universal or objective invariances of nature or reason are now thought to be adequately approximated (empirically, phenomenally, reflexively, pragmatically, dialogically) by one form or another of a consensus that no longer requires the epistemic assurance of the first or its criterial use.

In this sense, Bernard Williams is no moral optimist, because he is not prepared to invest in measuring anything like universal reasonableness or any approximation of the cognitive projects invented in the name of moral reason.[39] Karl-Otto Apel is similarly not an optimist, because *he* is an out-and-out Kantian, a complete apriorist about moral matters (albeit a curious Peircean who claims that the *a priori* necessities of the moral world can be drawn out of the ubiquitous conditions of linguistic communication).[40] On the other hand, at least in matters of scientific method, Karl Popper and T. S. Kuhn (somewhat ambiguously, possibly inconsistently) and Imre Lakatos *are* optimists, whereas Paul Feyerabend and Arthur Fine are clearly not.[41] I am persuaded that "philosophical optimism" – whether of the moral or scientific or epistemic sort – now dominates Western thought (partly as the beneficiary of Peircean pragmatism); that it cannot succeed; and that it is particularly transparent in its moral guise. My sense is that it is the vestigial form that belief about the world and thought and conduct takes when we are no longer able to confirm the pertinent invariances of this particular sector of inquiry or that – the laws of nature, the rules of reason, the norms of the moral life – and when we are unwilling to abandon the hope that there remains a reliable regulative principle, a *Grenzbegriff*, even after the (constitutive) grounds for so believing have simply collapsed. The obvious example of such perseveration may be found in Hilary Putnam's recent writings,[42] but it is also a remarkably widespread conviction. It is, I should say, the presumption that there "must be" a valid First Philosophy.[43]

Optimism takes two characteristic forms across the philosophical board: (1) that of claiming a naturalized but reliable progress in accord with the *telos* of reasonable inquiry, and (2) that of a decisive invariance somehow embedded in the flux of nature or reason. The moral theories offered by MacIntyre, Rawls, Putnam, and Habermas founder along these lines. But, more than that, an army of contemporary theorists of all sorts may be shown to be similarly affected. I have already drawn attention in this regard to Gadamer's insistence on the invariance of the "classical." (I am not, however, claiming that Gadamer is a pragmatist!) Analogously, Donald Davidson's advocacy of supervenience (with regard to the mind/body problem) and Alvin Goldman's advocacy of reliabilism (with regard to the problem of knowledge) are, demonstrably, "optimistic" theories.[44]

I cannot pursue these parallels here. I ask you only to bear in mind that optimisms in accord with (1) yield various forms of *liberalism* or *progressivism* (which, in the inductivist and falsificationist options, apply rather neatly to scientific matters); and that optimisms in accord with (2) yield various forms of (what I call) *traditionalism*.[45] MacIntyre, Gadamer, and Rawls, are, primarily, traditionalists; Habermas, Putnam, and Popper are progressivists. (The distinction fits "continental" and "analytic" philosophies with equal aptness.)

VIII

Consider Hilary Putnam's theory. It is the least developed of all those mentioned; perhaps, for that reason, it is also the most transparent. Putnam is explicit about his general agreement with Habermas and Apel. He is a self-styled pragmatist who holds that the rationale for truth in both moral and scientific matters rests with the life of an inquiring community and that objectivity in accord with either may be ensured without retreating to any cognitive privilege. He does not explain how. On my reading, Putnam is an "optimist" who has by now completely undermined his own ("optimistic") view of truth and knowledge – certainly with regard to science, less legibly with regard to morality. He believes that something like the Kantian and Peircean goal can be rescued by replacing *a priori* reason by a consensual *praxis*-centered reasonableness. He retreats from a universalised ethic, but he also confirms the remarkable convergence between pragmatisms developed on either side of the Atlantic (in particular, that between himself and Habermas):

> Habermas and Apel claim – and I agree [he says] – that the notion of a warranted or justified statement [of, say, a moral or scientific sort] involves an implicit reference to a community. . . . It must, in short, be a community which respects the principles of intellectual freedom and equality.[46]

The idea is Peircean – fallibilistic. Putnam is perhaps right to construe Kant as having implicitly defeated Aquinas (*a fortiori*, Aristotle and MacIntyre), since:

> according to the medievals, as Alasdair MacIntyre has reminded us, we possess a capacity to know the human "function" or the human "essence"; whereas (*pace* . . . MacIntyre) Kant understands that this will no longer wash. In the *Grundlegung* he [Kant] says explicitly [says Putnam] that one cannot build an ethic upon this notion of Happiness, because too many different things can be made out to be the content of that notion . . . . The situation is dark because reason does not give us such a thing as an inclusive human end which we should all seek (unless it is morality itself, and this is not an end that can determine the content of morality).[47]

Clearly, Putnam opposes the usual essentialist and cognitivist options. (One remembers Wiggins.)

The important lesson of Putnam's pragmatism, however – drawn from his epistemology and theory of science but presumably applicable to his developing account of morality – is simply that he himself admits its utter failure. (I concede that it is not always clear that he would be willing to admit that failure.) And yet, its failing is due to his adhering to a kind of Kantianism (that combines both apriorist and Peircean elements) which he wrongly believes can ensure the objectivity of science. It is definitely *not* due to the supposed need to return to the foundational "assurances" of analytic naturalism, which, in rather different ways, both Donald Davidson and Richard Rorty champion against Putnam himself.[48]

Nevertheless, Putnam disappoints us on the decisive issue. He holds, correctly, that Kant is mistaken in supposing that "moral philosophy is impossible without transcendental guarantees that can be given only if we posit a noumenal realm."[49] But he never questions the validity of that conceptual power by which what *is* universally binding (what corresponds to Kant's "pure practical reason" – what is *not* mere consensual agreement) can actually be specified.[50] He treats objective science and morality in the same way. So he insists: "what the relativist fails to see [the relativist is irrelevant and inconsistent, on Putnam's view] is that it is a presupposition of thought itself that some kind of objective 'rightness' exists."[51] It is hard to read this as anything but transcendentally intended, although it is obviously not meant to be privileged or *a priori*. It runs parallel to the views of Rawls and Habermas: it replaces a Kantian assurance with a Peircean optimism, but it never offers a supporting rationale. I cannot find its defense anywhere in Putnam, although the conviction (and the hope) that it can always be recovered is certainly constant in Putnam's work.[52]

Putnam closes *Reason, Truth and History*, in which the charge against the relativist appears, with the following final sentence: "The very fact that we speak of our different conceptions as different conceptions of *rationality* posits a *Grenzbegriff*, a limit-concept of the ideal truth."[53] Why that is so is never explained. But *The Many Faces of Realism* now reads like a confession to the effect (also unexplained) that that confidence can no longer be defended; the text is not sufficiently explicit, although *Realism with a Human Face* confirms that Putnam never intended to abandon the idea of "truth as idealized rational acceptability"[54] – which brings him very close to Habermas.[55] There you have the thinnest form of First Philosophy!

There cannot, however, be a *Grenzbegriff* of Putnam's sort (or Habermas's, for that matter) *if* a "Kantian-like" constructivism cannot fall back to apriorist assurances. For, on the argument, any would-be regulative function of truth or reason would then be no more than a contingent artifact of a contingently "constructed" world. There can be no invariant (or epistemically ideal) regulative *Grenzbegriff* (truth) if there is not in place already, among our cognitive powers (our "under-standing"), an actual, invariant, constitutive structure apt for grasping the objective features of the world. Anything less would not be suitably "Kantian," whether or not one gives up Kant's particular version of apriorism. In a way, the issue is shared by Kant and Hegel and Husserl and Peirce and Putnam as well as the analytic naturalists. Once again, pluralism – and progressivism, which is merely a form of pluralism deployed historically – presupposes *some* substantive truth that *can* function regulatively. Quine invokes such a truth illicitly; Rawls presup-poses what he denies; Putman subverts his commitment to such a truth but fails to see that he does.

Putnam criticizes Kant's insistence on a uniquely correct or true account in morality as well as in science. "What we require in moral philosophy," he says, "is, first and foremost, a moral image of the world, or rather – since, here again, I am more of a pluralist than Kant – a number of complementary moral images of the world."[56] By the expression "here again," Putnam means to remind us that, more or less along W. V. Quine's lines – in the matter of the "indeterminacy of translation" and the (rather doubtful) import of the Löwenheim–Skolem theorem – realism must be reconciled with the finding (ineluctable, on Putnam's view of his own "internal realism") that we cannot expect to vindicate a uniquely correct account of the way the world is: "realism is *not* incompatible with conceptual relativity" (he says).[57] The trouble is, the pluralizing function of the Löwenheim–Skolem theorem *cannot* be relevantly called into play *until some suitably strategic scientific truth is first confirmed*. That is the linchpin Putnam never secures. It threatens both the "Kantian" and "Aristotelian" strategies.

That is the point of Putnam's pluralism. Like Rawls, Putnam cannot concede – in the moral sphere as in the scientific – that the conflict between the alternative visions of what is right or true may require (or at least invite as a coherent option) a conceptual tolerance more radical than the one the pluralist supports. I don't say pluralism is incoherent; it is certainly not. But, on an argument already offered, pluralism makes no sense unless *there is* an objectively valid (probably holist) truth that may be interpreted along diverse lines, without the prospect of providing any rule for uniquely deciding the correct "appearance" of the world. The master strategy that Putnam borrows here, on the side of science, I find in Quine's notion of "holophrastic sentences."[58]

But, in any case, (a) pluralism makes no sense unless there *is* a suitable general truth that may be construed or interpreted (or "appears" to us) in plural ways; (b) the Löwenheim–Skolem theorem can be called into play (in a realist sense) only if (a) obtains; (c) Putnam's rejection of the "subjective"/"objective" distinction (in principled terms) precludes the options offered at (a) and (b); hence, (d) truth (and rationality) cannot function as a *Grenzbegriff*. QED. I conclude, therefore, that (a) Putnam's admission of the untenability of the "subjective"/"objective" distinction, (b) his adoption of a pluralistic constructivism, and (c) his insistence on the constant regulative function of truth or reason, form an inconsistent triad – whether applied to science or morality.

Putnam never goes far enough. Truth, he claims, has a regulative function, that of "*idealized* justification [of truth-claims], as opposed to justification-on-present-evidence." In this, he merely opposes Michael Dummett's "anti-realist" thesis, since, for Dummett (it seems), "one can *specify* in an effective way [*now*] what the justification conditions for all the sentences of a natural language are."[59] (Dummett has the seeming advantage of a naive realism. That is, his "anti-realism has no particular epistemic force": it contributes no more than a procedural caution. In fact, Dummett's anti-realism is ultimately meant to buttress a conventional realism.)

For his part, Putnam holds that justification but not truth is a matter of degree and may be lost; justification is idealized but its idealization cannot be stated once and for all; and the conditions for truth itself cannot be given in terms of any theory of meaning. Here is Putnam's most careful reading:

> truth is independent of justification here and now, but not independent of *all* possibility of justification ... truth is expected to be stable, or "convergent" .... In my view, [he says,] as in Quine's, ... justification conditions for sentences change as our total body of knowledge changes, and cannot be taken as fixed once and for all.[60]

Putnam construes this along the lines of the Löwenheim–Skolem theorem – that "*the same objects* [in the actual world] can be what logicians call a 'model' for incompatible theories [indefinitely many interpretations of *those* objects, compatibly with 'internal realism']"[61] But the careful reader will remember that, thus construed, *truth* and realism are "expected to be stable, or convergent"; that the argument is meant to hold in moral matters as in science; *and* that, according to his latest adjustment, this is no longer a reliable supposition in the way it was once supposed to be.[62] Putnam yields on privilege, but tries to recover the benefits of privilege "by other [by pragmatist] means." That is what I understand an "optimist" to be committed to – an untenable or indemonstrable position. I find variant forms of the same weakness in Rawls, Apel, Habermas, and Putnam, except that Habermas and Putnam are explicitly opposed to any form of apriorism. I think this explains Putnam's otherwise curious insistence (perseveration, almost) that relativism cannot but be incoherent. The other side of the same coin is that he has no other argument to offer, except that the denial of a *Grenzbegriff* (in science and morality) would instantly render all pertinent inquiries as incoherent as relativism. But he never makes the case. In short, as I have already remarked, the rejection of a principled distinction between the subjective and the objective, the advocacy of a (realist) constructivism, and the insistence on truth (or reason) as a *Grenzbegriff* form an inconsistent triad. The force of this paradox is hardly confined to Putnam.

I have been pressing Putnam because his account of the "idealized" (regulative) function of truth – in both science and morality – undermines the pretense that the processes of *reasonable* consensus (under the conditions of actual social life) *could* ever be counted on to yield an approximative recovery of the (strictly nonconsensual) universality of (anything like) Kant's supposition regarding "pure practical" *reason*. Putnam abandons altogether the "'Objectivist' picture of the world" (in Husserl's sense of "objectivist") and holds instead that "The deep systemic root of the [philosophical] disease [he means to root out] is in the notion of an 'intrinsic' property, a property something has 'in itself', apart from any contribution made by language or the mind."[63] He concedes that "Internal realism is ... just the insistence that realism is *not* incompatible with conceptual relativity"; but, against the "relativist," he still insists that realism continues to oppose (opposing Richard Rorty in particular – and Donald Davidson more obliquely) the thesis that "there is no truth to be found ... 'true' is just a name for what a bunch of people can agree on'."[64] But I find no argument in Putnam to explain how this may be determinately shown or what "regulative" function truth plays.

Still, Putnam no longer speaks robustly of what is "stable" or uniquely "convergent" in the way of truth (or justification); he even draws a parallel between science and ethics in exposing the "mistake of supposing that 'Which are the real objects' [in the world] is a question that makes sense *independently of our choice of concepts*."[65] He now says flat out:

> the enterprise [of distinguishing disjunctively between appearance and reality, between "what is 'simply true' and what has only 'assertibility

conditions'; or the cut between what is already true or false and what is an 'extension of previous use' (albeit one that we all make in the same way), or between what is a 'projection' and what is an independent and unitary property of things in themselves"] isn't worth the candle. The game is played out. We can make a rough sort of rank ordering (although even here there are disagreements), but the idea of a "point at which" subjectivity ceases and Objectivity-with-a-capital-O begins has proved chimerical.[66]

I take this to signify the collapse of Putnam's (the "optimist's") thesis with respect to *both* morality and science, but I am quite certain that that is not the intended purpose of the remark. So that when Putnam announces that "the value of Equality is, perhaps, a unique contribution of the Jewish religion to the culture of the West" – for instance, most notably, in the "principle":

> There is something about human beings, some aspect which is of incomparable moral significance, with respect to which all human beings are equal, or whose contribution to society is the least, are deserving of respect

– he *can claim no possible legitimative basis for his dictum*, except his unexplained adherence to a certain liberal or humane conviction (which, ironically, pretty well commits him to something hardly more compelling than Rorty's candid ethnocentrism).[67] Putnam is either unwilling or unable to acknowledge that the defeat of (postmodernist) ethnocentrism is not tantamount to ensuring a ("Kantian-like") *Grenzbegriff*. Clearly, Putnam means to preserve the regulative function of truth under his own form of (pluralized) constructivism. But when he abandons apriorism (may I now say: Peirce's as well as Kant's), he abandons that very possibility. There is no option open to him except something like Quine's "holophrastic sentences." But they, of course, both privilege truth in an unexplained way and provide the theoretical foundation on which pluralism (in science or morality) can claim a *Grenzbegriff*. But there is no rationale for Quine's assumption. It is incompatible with other of Quine's doctrines (for instance, his treatment of the analytic/synthetic dogma); and, in any case, Putnam makes no explicit use of it.

IX

I move on, therefore, to Apel, who is more Kantian than Putnam. I shall not explore Apel's apriorism in any depth. I note that Apel's characterization of the *a priori* (not his strategy for recovering it) is thoroughly Kantian. Apel expressly rejects the "scientistic notion of normatively neutral or value-free 'objectivity'" and (like Peirce) affirms that "logic – and, *at the same time*, all the sciences and technologies – presupposes an ethic as the precondition for its possibility." "The logical validity of arguments cannot [Apel says] be tested without, in principle, positing a community of scholars who are capable of both intersubjective communication and reaching a consensus .... the *validity* of solitary thought is basically dependent upon the justification of verbal arguments in the actual community of argumentation."[68]

The fundamental difference between Apel's and Habermas's legitimative strategies lies in this: Apel draws his transcendental *a priori* rules (universally and necessarily binding on rational thought and argument – theoretical as well as practical) *from* the very nature of community life; whereas Habermas claims that the practice of social communication requires a progressive strengthening of universal constraints on rational participation. These constraints are apparently not *a priori* but pragmatically arrived at in the very process of reflecting on the ongoing objectives of such communication.

For the moment, this is precise enough. It explains the sense in which Habermas is an optimist but Apel is not. Apel appeals to the reflexive powers of transcendental reason working within the boundaries of the "communication community." (Apel means thereby to obviate noumena.) Habermas eschews all transcendental power but he cannot explain the legitimative resources that remain. (They are apparently at once pragmatic and necessary.)

I offer two provisional arguments on the legitimative issue. In accord with one, *if* Kant's general strategy (employing phenomenal reason in order to discover transcendentally necessary constraints constitutively binding within itself) fails to explain the strict necessity of what it claims to find, or fails to explain why the seeming necessity of what it finds should not be construed as an artifact of its own incompletely penetrable (or variably preformed) *phenomenal* conditions,[69] then it is not clear why Apel's new account should hold any more convincingly. The other argument concerns Habermas's treatment of a challenge Hans Albert had put to Apel, that, by an interesting irony, applies to Habermas's weakened theory of legitimative discourse only where it pretends to be the equal of Apel's. The upshot of these paired considerations is to segregate arguments from the *a priori* powers of reason and from the *a posteriori* powers of reasonableness, and to jeopardise, by that disjunction, the claims of both Apel and Habermas.

Albert is right, I think, in supposing that *if* one seeks "an absolute foundation" for knowledge or rational practice, then *any* concession to "fallibilism" (in the weak reading) will prove fatal.[70] *If* transcendental reasoning must yield such a foundation, then the best strategy for contesting Apel's extension (or replacement) of Kant's method becomes instantly clear; and, then, the impossibility of Habermas's securing anything like Kant's (or Apel's) finding by *a posteriori* means alone becomes even clearer.

Albert himself subscribes to the Popperian analogue of a thoroughgoing (Peircean) fallibilism. He claims the "classical epistemologists" (he includes Apel and Habermas), pursuing "an Archimedean point of knowledge" with respect to both "the *attainability* and the *decidability* of truth," subscribe to the "principle of sufficient reason" – which states: "always seek an adequate foundation – a sufficient justification – for all your convictions."[71] On Albert's assumption, transcendental arguments, arguments pursuing (but not assured of) "an absolute foundation" for *"everything"* (in the way of truth-claims), must resolve "the Münchhausen trilemma": that is, the need to choose between "an infinite regress," "a logical circle," and "the breaking off of the process [of justification]." "Since both an infinite regress and a circular argument seem clearly unacceptable," Albert suggests, "one is inclined to accept the third possibility." But that would involve "an arbitrary suspension of the principle of sufficient justification."[72]

On this, Habermas has the following to say, having already acknowledged that Kant's defense of the categorical imperative *is* doubtful – because it rests on a dubious "moral intuition" (a form of cognitivism) or because, by appealing to "the substantive normative concepts of autonomy and free will" (involving the conceivability of a noumenal order), it may well have "committed a *petitio principii*":

> I am not dramatizing the situation when I say that faced with the demand for a justification of the universal validity of the principle of universalization, cognitivisms are in trouble. The skeptic feels emboldened to recast his *doubts* about the possibility of justifying a universalist morality as an *assertion* that it is impossible to justify such a morality. Hans Albert took this tack with his *Treatise on Critical Reason* by applying to practical philosophy Popper's model of critical testing, which was developed for the philosophy of science and intended to take the place of traditional foundationalist and justificationist models. The attempt to justify moral principles with universal validity, according to Albert, ensnares the cognitivist in a "Münchhausen trilemma" in which he must choose between three equally unacceptable alternatives . . . . The status of this trilemma, however, is problematic. It arises only if one presupposes a *semantic concept of justification* that is oriented to a deductive relationship between

statements and based solely on the concept of logical inference. This deductive concept of justification is obviously too narrow for the exposition of the pragmatic relations between argumentative speech acts.[73]

I'm afraid Habermas is confused here, in spite of the fact that, beneath his countermove, there lurks a genuine discovery (which Apel isolates). For one thing, he misreads the force of Albert's charge (regardless of Albert's intention). He construes the point of the *third* option (of the trilemma) to be restricted somehow to the rules of ordinary deductive inference. But Albert's challenge is rightly directed to the epistemic powers of reason (whether theoretical or practical), not to the structure of any would-be (propositional) argument. Habermas's objection is simply beside the point.[74] Simply put: Albert is challenging the *assertion* of the "self-evident" or "self-authenticating" power of reason Apel and Habermas favor, *with respect to their own legitimative claims* – which range over *act* and *conduct* as well as inference! Surely, Habermas's demurrer is a conceptual howler: he fails to see that *he is asserting* that a certain pragmatic commitment is universally necessary at a certain critical point.[75]

But even if we conceded the pertinence of Apel's and Habermas's rejoinder to Albert, there would remain a *reductio* (related to Albert's argument) which neither Apel nor Habermas could possibly defuse. For all one would need to do would be to substitute an account of the "logic" of reference, predication, the use of concepts or the like for the logic of propositional argument: one would thereby outflank Apel's and Habermas's insistence on the import of a strong disjunction between theoretical and practical constraints. Plainly, the same communicative resources are implicated in theory and practice (I mention the pertinent details lightly in the next two chapters). Here, I advance the argument conditionally, but the argument itself is more than conditional. If reference, predication, the use of concepts cannot be supplied with epistemically firm, suitably determinate criterial rules – if we must fall back to the informal consensual tolerance of the effective linguistic practices of actual societies (beyond criterial resources) – then Apel's and Habermas's versions of the "first principle" of morality cannot be universally, necessarily, neutrally abstracted (by *a priori* or *a posteriori* means) from the vagaries of whatever contingent forms of communication may obtain. There is no neutral way of knowing or confirming *that* we understand one another, inter- or intrasocietally, by sharing the same criteria or concepts or speech-act practices. No one denies communicative success – in the "holist" sense. But no one can demonstrate that determinate invariances of a semantically explicit sort are normatively necessary and binding on all serious communication. There you have the insuperable lacuna in Apel's and Habermas's argument.

Still, Habermas is also in a way right: the legitimative question concerns "pragmatic relations between argumentative speech acts." *He* introduces (in order to dismiss) "the structure and status of the transcendental–pragmatic argument" in the form Apel and other theorists offer: for instance, theorists like A. J. Watt (influenced by Collingwood) and R. S. Peters, who invokes a principle of equality or "fairness" that cannot fail to remind us of both Putnam's and Rawls's moral intuitions.[76] What Habermas means to show (against Apel) is that, although "a transcendental–pragmatic justification of the moral principle is in fact possible ['possible' in something like Kant's sense] . . . this justification of discourse ethics [Habermas's and Apel's moral program] cannot have the status of an ultimate justification and . . . there is no need to claim this status for it."[77] This is meant to enable us to steer a middle course between the apriorists who claim that only "an ultimate justification" will do and the "skeptics" (Albert, the Popperians, and others who side with them) who claim that only "an ultimate justification" will do but that such a justification cannot be supplied. (Here, we return to Mackie once again.)

Watt argues *to* the "presuppositions of a mode of discourse" that he takes to yield invariant principles. Of this he says (Habermas quotes him):

> [We are] to accept the skeptical conclusion that these principles are not open to any proof, being presuppositions of reasoning rather than conclusions from it, but to go on to argue that commitment to them is rationally inescapable because they must, logically, be assumed if one is to engage in a mode of thought essential to any rational human life. The claim is not exactly that the principles are *true*, [but] a mistake is involved in repudiating them while continuing to use the form of thought and discourse in question.[78]

Here, Watt shows Habermas the way to accept Albert's objection and (Habermas believes) to outflank him at the same time. But Watt *is* an apriorist, after all. *He* holds that, whatever may be the contingent variety of discursive practices that obtain historically, *there are* universal principles "essential to any rational human life" that can be directly drawn from such variety. Habermas believes that *he* can discern such principles without denying the flux of discursive practices and without falling back to any apriorism. (This, by the way, is not strictly in accord with

Collingwood's line of argument. I take this to be the analogue of Putnam's argument about the *Grenzbegriff*.)

The claim is an intriguing one; but you can see that it is poised for self-destruction. (It catches up the line of argument Habermas objects to in Apel.) Habermas provisionally concedes that the skeptic (Albert) "can join the ranks . . . of the neo-Aristotelians and neo-Hegelians, who point out that discourse ethics does not represent much of a gain for the real concern of philosophical ethics, since discourse ethics offers at best an empty formalism whose practical consequences would even be disastrous." But then, he gamely goes on to insist – adopting the Hegelian thesis that "morality is always embedded in . . . ethical life (*Sittlichkeit*)" – that "discourse ethics is always subject to limitations [of determinate historical practice], though not limitations that can devalue its critical function or strengthen the skeptic in his role as an advocate of a counterenlightenment."[79]

What Habermas means is this: (1) there *are* universally necessary constraints on discourse ethics (and, presumably on the Peircean argument, on science as well); (2) such constraints cannot (and need not) be "derived" in the *a priori* or essentialist manner, on pain of cognitive privilege, or of claiming what has already been discredited in Kant (as by Apel), or of risking the formalism Hegel exposed in Kant, or of falling victim to Albert's trilemma, or the like; and (3) such constraints *can* be reclaimed, pragmatically, by testing "counterexamples" drawn from actual discourse – by demonstrating "that *there are no alternatives* to the presuppositions [the champion of discourse ethics] has made explicit."[80] There you have Habermas's boldest claim – a kind of First Philosophy by progressivist means.

You must also bear in mind, however, the following equivocation: that between (a) a "pragmatic" (rather than a formal) constraint on discourse such that discourse cannot be communicatively successful at all where the constraint is not operative (even if denied) and (b) a "pragmatic" constraint on discourse such that, although the constraint is not operatively essential to mere communicative success, it would be contrary to "rational" discourse to oppose it. I do not find the equivocation suitably resolved by either Apel or Habermas, and I do not believe either option makes much sense.

Furthermore, Habermas differs from Rawls (and Apel) in this: (1) he makes no preliminary posit of a liberal objective, he assumes he can draw his own version of such a doctrine ("discourse ethics"), as universally necessary, from slimmer resources; and (2) he means to avoid the instant universalized rule ("justice as fairness") Rawls proclaims, which would be aprioristic if it were not already merely ideological. He insists that his own provisionally necessary rules are always at risk in the next emergent phase of communicative life. In terms of a distinction already supplied (against Bernstein), Habermas argues ("fallibilistically") in a Deweyan way to a Peircean conclusion. Still, it is obvious that *a posteriori* reasoning cannot approximate to *a priori* powers.

What Habermas is bent on identifying are what he calls "performative contradictions" which are meant to explicate the following programmatic desideratum, viz.: "the identification of pragmatic presuppositions of argumentation that are inescapable and have a normative content."[81] Habermas offers little in his own voice in the way of explanation, but I think we shall find that we can work well enough with what he does say. For one thing, the formulation is meant to replace his earlier search for the lineaments of "an ideal speech situation." He still believes his earlier "intention" was "correct": that is, "the reconstruction of the general symmetry conditions that every competent speaker who believes he is engaging in an argumentation must presuppose as adequately fulfilled." This leads (he now believes) to various sets of "communication rules" at different levels of intervention- where enabling provisions are supplied for ruling "out all external or internal coercion other than the force of the better argument and thereby also neutraliz[ing] all motives other than that of the cooperative search for truth."[82] (We must bear in mind, of course, that "uncoerced" agreement can be discerned only relative to the "coercion" of one's *Sitten*. This is as true for the "optimisms" of Putnam, Rawls, Kuhn, Popper, and Habermas as it is for Peirce. The meaning of "coercion" has not yet been shown to be more than an artifact formed within our own enabling *Sitten*. I recall, here, Berlin's warning.)

The trouble is, the usual paradigms of "performative contradiction" are no more than hothouse cases or profoundly problematic. Apel, whom Habermas follows here, offers, as exemplars, the "denial" of the *cogito* and the self-refuting "arguments" of the skeptic.'[83] I don't deny that (as described) the Cartesian doubter and the Popperian skeptic "contradict" themselves "pragmatically"; but I see no reason to suppose that those famous puzzles need be construed in the fortunate way Apel foists on us.

Apel has indicated (in conversation) that he is entirely prepared to embrace Albert's trilemma when applied to arguments in propositional form; he claims it is ineffective against his analysis of the implications of communicative acts. Perhaps so. (That was the point of Habermas's demurrer against Albert.) But even rational practice (certainly, the theory of rational practice) entails propositional claims; and there, something akin to Albert's challenge would have scope. Apart from that, however, there are, as already remarked, linguistic and conceptual resources common to theoretical and practical reason – for instance, reference, predication, the use of concepts – that, it may be shown, cannot be sufficiently precised in Apel's and Habermas's way to support the claim of "pragmatic contradiction" as a discernibly universal constraint on communicative success. For one thing, both Apel and Habermas acknowledge that communication can succeed without conforming to their supposedly necessary normative conditions; and, for a second, normative constraints, like contradictions, obtain only in suitably interpreted instances open to interpretive dispute and change.

But, beyond these local objections (which are effective nevertheless), there lurks a deeper worry. Both Apel and Habermas mean to go beyond Kant's transcendental formalism: to embed a transcendental or a "transcendental–pragmatist" or "pragmatic" argument in the very practices of particular societies, to draw what is normatively and universally binding *from the sheer contingencies of historical practice*. Still, the strategy of drawing the *a priori* from the a *posteriori*, the modally necessary from the historically contingent, the universally binding from the phenomenally particular, the unconstructed from the constructed, is singularly baffling. I find no perspicuous account of this in Apel's or Habermas's argument and I cannot imagine how it could succeed. You must bear in mind that it represents a tendency that may be mapped as well in the exertions of Hegel, Marx, Dilthey, Peirce, Heidegger, Cassirer, Lukács, Horkheimer and Adorno, Gadamer, the later Wittgenstein, and Foucault at least. It represents the logically indigestible effort to unite and reconcile universalism and historicism under a form of modal necessity said to be neither transcendental in Kant's formal sense nor privileged in the foundational sense. To my knowledge, no one has been able to bring the two together compellingly.

Consider some of Habermas's would-be pragmatic rules. Habermas offers a list of "presuppositions of argumentation" developed by Robert Alexy, which he says operate on various levels of communication. (Alexy also addresses the "Münchhausen trilemma." He does so in a way congenial to Apel's and Habermas's outlook.[84]) The following is a fair specimen:

1.2 Every speaker who applies predicate F to object A must be prepared to apply F to all other objects resembling A in all relevant respects.[85]

Now, this is surely a vacuous rule; also, a perniciously misleading one. For, consider that to be properly eligible for "predicate F" means nothing more than to "resemble A in all relevant respects." But there is no reliable rule *for* determining when particular things resemble one another in "all relevant respects." There is no known algorithmic solution to the problem of predication or "real generals."[86] Either rule (1.2) has no ethical import at all or its import depends on ulterior normative resources that are nowhere supplied. But what of

2.1 Every speaker may assert only what he really believes.[87]

Surely, there is no way of ensuring the pragmatic necessity of (2.1), unless one falls back to something like Kant's view of pure practical reason. It may be an ingredient in some imagined "ideal speech situation"; but to say only that strengthens our sense of the profound difference between such a vision and the viability of actual discourse.

Alexy goes on – apparently Habermas approves:

3.1 Every subject with the competence to speak and act is allowed to take part in a discourse

and

3.2 Everyone is allowed to question any assertion whatever.[88]

Here, of courses the *aporia* that Rawls inadvertently concedes (while deliberately recognizing the fairness of Isaiah Berlin's "burden" on moral and political judgment) surfaces in a new and troubling guise. For, surely, (3.2) is preposterous in real-time terms and (3.1) is open to the worst possible abuse. (The numbering, I may say, is intended to convey the sense [drawn from Alexy] that Habermas has surveyed the principal runs of pertinent questions affecting the pragmatics of discourse.)[89] Alexy continues blithely enough; for instance, to

5.2.1 The moral rules that form the basis of the moral conceptions of the speakers must be able to withstand scrutiny in a critical, historical genesis;
5.2.2 The moral rules that form the basis of the moral conceptions of the speakers must be able to withstand the scrutiny of their individual history of emergence;

and

5.3   The factually given limits of realizability are to be observed.[90]

Rule (5.3) means that where debate has a practical payoff, one may have to act without having arrived at an entirely satisfactory solution. Of course! But the "rule" is no more than a reasonable companion to Berlin's dilemma. The other two rules presuppose that the "rational justification" of moral norms is possible and that the contingencies of history must be assessed and, where necessary, discounted. (None of this is explained or vindicated anywhere.)

This shows the drift of Habermas's entire argument. There are no stronger cases and there is no escape.

There are also no stronger Kantian programs to recover, unless one means to go completely apriorist.

PART II

The Theory of Practice

4

A Reckoning of Sorts on
Moral Philosophy

I

I have avoided up to now a certain nagging intuition but it is time to
bring it out of the philosophical closet. If the agents of moral and
political activity – human persons, selves, "subjects," ourselves – are
(not unlike artworks) socially constituted, "constructions" or "artifacts"
of different histories,[1] then it must strike you that the instruction of the
most influential moral theorists may be no more relevant to our own
reflections than the manuals of those authors who have codified and
explained our table manners. It is, of course, obvious that moral
philosophy nearly always invokes the high concerns of the "universal
man." But, on the assumption just broached, Castiglione's *Courtier* will
be no less dated than Aristotle's *Ethics*. Indeed, the fifteenth-century
humanist, Lorenzo Valla, criticizes Aristotle's *Ethics* on at least two
counts that are decidedly less minor than they at first appear: first,
because, in elevating contemplation to the highest of human activities,
the activity that belongs to the gods, Aristotle fails (Valla says) to
recognize that contemplation is itself learned, hence runs contrary to
divine activity; and second, because, in attributing to humans both
contemplation and political activity, Aristotle fails to consider the
significance of their potential collision. Naturally, Renaissance figures
construe what is historically local under Aristotelian and Platonist
universals. *But what if the whole idea were radically mistaken? Both*
learning and political activity, remember, suggest the transient and the
local: reference to the concerns of the "universal man" may be little
more than the partisan proposal of a neighborhood entrepreneur.

The important point is that the issue is rarely examined. The idea plays a sturdy role in the tradition that runs from Nietzsche to Foucault at least. Call that historicism, if we understand by the term the thesis (1) that there are no necessary ("modal") invariances in nature or thought; (2) that the world (a "flux") is not, as a result, altogether bereft of discernible, relatively stable structures; and (3) that the characteristic perceptual, rational and active powers of humans are historically and variably preformed as a consequence of their having first evolved as the linguistically and culturally apt agents they become ("selves") by internalizing the resources of their native society. If this picture is accurate, then the entire commitment of what I have called first- and second-tier theories is entirely off the mark. The Macedonian Aristotle and the Königsberger Kant would be little more than country figures who have made it in the city; and we, ranging through second- and third-tier moral philosophies, would have lost our way. (I am speaking, of course, of moral instruction, but also, in good measure, of philosophical reflections about how such instruction is conceptually possible.)

I am persuaded that some version of historicism is true, and that, for at least that reason, we must consult what I have called fourth-tier thinking. The startling fact is that one can hardly find it represented in the canonical literature. There is, I concede, something of an effort in recent English-language philosophy to accommodate the theme of history, if not historicity or historicism. I had broached the matter in scanning part of the bridge literature between second- and third-tier thinking that includes such figures as MacIntyre, Kuhn, Bernstein, and, more remotely, Rorty. The literature is a little ampler than that and includes, in addition, such figures as Charles Taylor and Michael Sandel, who hold more robust views about the role of history than does Rorty. And, of course, as soon as one includes Hegelian and Marxist sources, many more alternatives begin to make themselves felt – including the views of some who are actually more sympathetic to fourth-tier themes than those just mentioned: Dewey for instance, Marx, the early Frankfurt-Critical thinkers (but not Habermas), post-Heideggerean hermeneuts like Gadamer, and such figures as MacKinnon and Unger, whom I've mentioned in passing. I have also briefly remarked that the most promising third-tier theory may well be that of Sabina Lovibond's *Realism and Imagination in Ethics*[2] – because it attempts (almost alone) to incorporate, *via* Hegel and Wittgenstein, some form of historicism within the terms of (third-tier) analytic philosophy. But my entire argument up to this point has been to show that the principal strategies of first-, second-, and third-tier theories favoring cognitive privilege, invariant structures of human nature and reason, approximations to any of these, moral essentialism or moral realism, are entirely uncompelling, not especially responsive to legitimate challenge, and not demonstrably valid or necessary for our deliberations – for instance, as being such that their denial (as with the denial of Aristotle's metaphysics, say) would instantly produce formal or pragmatic contradiction or paradox.

The strategies of canonical moral philosophy, then, are largely occupied with what I earlier termed *modal invariance*, meaning by that that feature of any theory's being committed to binding norms in virtue of what holds necessarily of reality or theoretical or practical reason. Once you see matters thus, the entire tradition will be judged to have favored modal invariance almost without exception (in science, in cognitive settings in general, in moral matters, in logic and mathematics); and, even where, as I have just noted, history or historicism seems to have been awarded a measure of attention (as in MacIntyre and Taylor), some form of strong invariance has almost always been rescued from the contingencies of history, so that flux and relativism may be successfully eluded once again.

I mentioned the matter in speaking of Gadamer's insistence on the "classical" and MacIntyre's insistence on the fixed ordering of the goods of human nature – even if not the fixity of any actual human *telos*. (I shall come back to that in the company of Lovibond's third-tier strategy.) But I draw your attention to the fact that the neglect of history on the part of Rawls and Apel and Habermas is not really offset by the seemingly strong interest in history evinced by Gadamer, MacIntyre, Bernstein, Taylor, or similar-minded theorists.

This comes as a surprise, since the latter are on the whole pointedly opposed to the former. (Bernstein is decidedly ambiguous and equivocal.) What this means is this: either the latter are opposed to a particular doctrine (say, MacIntyre's view of liberalism) or they believe the former have not produced arguments compelling enough to ensure a second-tier victory. Roughly, the tradition's trajectory may be rather neatly summarized by isolating the theories of Aristotle and Kant at the point of first-tier paradigms and Lovibond's theory (and similar theories) at the end of third-tier thinking.

Remember: I was saying (in effect) that *if* human nature were, in some reasonably strong sense, historically constituted (historicized), then it would be very hard to show more than the marginal relevance (for our own concerns) of classical Greek and eighteenth-century German or British philosophy. I conceded that there were second- and third-tier theories that appeared to acknowledge the historicized nature of human sensibilities and rational powers (Gadamer's and MacIntyre's). But I found those strategies uncompelling, and I (now) anticipate that the same will be true of Lovibond's account. Furthermore, the very doctrine of modal invariance will prove (I'm sure) unnecessary and utterly unconvincing. I hasten to say, therefore, that, in construing the "self" as an "artifact" of history, I do not mean to construe human persons as fictions of any sort, or as lacking discernible structure, or such as to discount the relevance (for moral reflection) of their physical and biological endowment (the species-wide features of *Homo sapiens*). On the contrary, it is a way of drawing attention to the historical variability of human life and the conceptual implausibility of drawing up a universal morality from biological considerations alone or of pretending that cultural diversity may be counted on to yield normative invariances transparent enough to offset worries about historicity.

This was what made Habermas's and Apel's strategies so important to defeat. Neither took a historicized standpoint but each claimed to address the contingencies of history. Apel charged that a certain *a priori* paradox lay at the heart of every social practice that refused to abide by the pragmatic constraints he claimed to have unearthed. Historicity, therefore, was precluded at the very start from his thought-experiment: his argument would have made no sense if reason had not been invariant. But consider that even if one held that the principle of noncontradiction imposed invariant, inviolable, insuperable constraints on theoretical and practical reason, it would hardly follow that *any* would-be determinate contradiction could never be favorably defused by reinterpretation. Any supposed substantive contradiction – for instance, what was involved in adopting at once the corpuscular and wave theories of light *at a certain time in the history of physics* – was open to being reinterpreted (and was reinterpreted) so as to remove the offending contradiction. Hence, the bare uninterpreted "principle" can hardly be adequate for Apel's purpose. Admit that, and you defeat Apel at a stroke. (*A fortiori*, Habermas as well, for Habermas recovers the force of Apel's argument by weaker means.) It is only the interpreted specimens that count in Apel's thought-experiment; Apel cannot rightly suppose that *a priori* reason precludes the possibility of historically diverse ways of construing the world or human thought and practice or the appraisal of same.

Furthermore, if that be conceded, then, by a very small step, Aristotle's magisterial claim (regarding the principle of noncontradiction) – in *Metaphysics* Gamma – proves irrelevant to Apel's issue (as well as to his own). I shall come to that shortly – it's the general strategy that interests me here. Because, if Apel and Habermas fail, if Rawls is unresponsive, if MacIntyre fails for a related reason, then *Aristotle and Kant must also fail with regard to modal invariance*; and if they fail, then fourth-tier theories cannot be discounted and may well eclipse the entire tradition of first-, second-, and third-tier thinking; and if historicism proves coherent (as I believe it is), then, as I say, the moral theories of the past can hardly be reliable guides for legitimating what should count as the moral norms for our own lives. QED. (I hardly mean by that that civilized thinkers like Hume and Aristotle cannot possibly offer fruitful lines of moral speculation for our age. But they remain creatures of their own history. So do we all. Whatever proves useful in what they say is more a function of our own interests and inventive interpretations than of their timeless grasp of what is morally essential.)

I offer two eccentric clues in support of this line of reasoning. The first is drawn from a short paper by Hilary Putnam which partly concedes and then pretends to outflank the historicist thesis. Speaking of Hegel's great contribution, Putnam says, summarily: "Thinkers who accept the first Hegelian idea, that our conceptions of rationality are all historically conditioned, while rejecting the idea of an end (or even an ideal limit) to the process [the second idea], tend to become historical or cultural relativists."[3] You see, here, the point of Putnam's characteristic insistence on truth as a *Grenzbegriff*: relativism (Putnam believes) cannot be reconciled with the function of a *Grenzbegriff*.

There are two principal ways of offsetting Putnam's charge. (He plainly treats relativism as incoherent and unacceptable.)[4] For one thing, Putnam must explain why theorists like Gadamer, MacIntyre, Taylor, Bernstein, possibly even Kuhn, cannot consistently believe (as they do) that *they* are not relativists although they do not admit truth as a *Grenzbegriff*; for another, Putnam must explain why relativism cannot escape the charge of incoherence, as well as how *he* himself escapes his own charge. (He nowhere examines either matter.)

The first returns us to a second-tier strategy; the second, which I favor, leads us to the prospect of fourth-tier strategies. I see no evidence (and no argument) to confirm that either historicism or relativism need be incoherent. MacIntyre, for instance, clearly believes that, without appealing to a *Grenzbegriff*, we are still able to resolve our "epistemic crises" episodically, even where they implicate incommensurable doctrines and methodologies. I don't doubt that MacIntyre's argument is much too slack for his own purpose,[5] but that hardly confirms Putnam's charge. Furthermore, Putnam's admission that there *is* no principled demarcation between the "subjective" and the "objective" defeats the very presumption of a *Grenzebegriff*;[6] hence, if Putnam is right to make that concession, then he must be a relativist on his own grounds. But whether relativism is or is not a coherent option he nowhere helps us to decide.[7]

In effect, I claim that Putnam's and MacIntyre's arguments are rather similarly constructed and similarly flawed (in spite of appearances): one is cast in a Kantian-like idiom (favoring the *Grenzbegriff*); the other, in an Aristotelian-like idiom (favoring goods internal to a practice). But if we assume that what Putnam calls Hegel's first idea *is* what he and MacIntyre jointly concede, then, I say: (1) neither can escape historicism or relativism; (2) both ultimately reject historicity and relativism; and (3) there need be no disaster in yielding on either count.[8] (It is just here that Lovibond's strategy proves instructive.)

The second clue comes from Wittgenstein, from the notorious paragraph 201 of the *Investigations*:

> This was our paradox: no course of action could be determined by a rule, because every course of action can be made out to accord with the rule. The answer was: if everything can be made out to accord with the rule, then it can also be made out to conflict with it . . . . What this shows is that there is a way of grasping a rule which is *not an interpretation*, but which is exhibited in what we call "obeying the rule" and "going against it" in actual cases . . . . And hence also "obeying a rule" is a practice.[9]

Wittgenstein, as we know, had little interest in history and apparently no sympathy for historicism, although it may be that (against his own conviction) his concept of a *Lebensform* may be fairly reconciled with both.[10] (I believe it can.) In any case, I construe Wittgenstein's point to be that "following a rule" does not entail that "*there is* a rule that one follows": for, "obeying a rule" is an openended practice for which an actually formulated rule is no more than a reflexive (if reasonable) interpretation of the practice in question. (We need not deny that the rules of chess are constitutive of chess; but *there are no rules constitutive of life*.)

Now, if Wittgenstein's claim may be generalized (as seems reasonable), then, I submit, neither Putnam's notion of a *Grenzbegriff* (the "Kantian" escape from historicism and relativism) nor MacIntyre's notion of goods internal to a practice (the "Aristotelian" alternative) can possibly function in a criterially relevant way. We may *say* we are "guided" by (the *Grenzbegriff* of) truth or rationality, but there is no determinate rule of truth or rationality that we are, or could be, guided by; and we may say we are "pursuing" certain normative goods internal to our practices, but there *are* no such determinate goods that we pursue. Hence, there *is* no *rule* of reason by which moral incommensurabilities are ever rightly resolved; and there *is* no demarcation line between the "objective" and the "subjective" by which the disputed claims of science are ever resolved. The upshot is that both theoretical and practical reason, said to discern what is objectively true or rationally required, will be artifacts of historical life – which is of course the principal concession that fourth-tier theories require.

In Putnam's picture, since reason is denied any cognitive privilege, a *Grenzbegriff* will have to be a construct; but if it is, it cannot then be a regulative limit of any kind. In MacIntyre's picture, since the adjudicative powers by which moral incommensurabilities are to be resolved (whether "within" a tradition or "between" traditions) entail an artifactual redrawing of traditional boundaries, there can be no principled difference between what are to count as opposed traditions and what is to count as the right adjudicative power by which their difference may be resolved. (Here, Wittgenstein's notion of "following a rule" plays a decisive role.) The argument goes against MacIntyre's well-known brief:

> When rival moralities make competing and incompatible claims, there is always an issue at the level of moral philosophy concerning the ability of either to make good a claim to rational superiority over the other . . . . The history of morality-and-moral-philosophy is the history of successive challenges to some pre-existing moral order, a history in which the question of which power defeated the other in rational argument is always to be distinguished from the question of which party retained or gained moral and political hegemony.[11]

Surely, *if* MacIntyre rejects "ideal rationality" in favor of the historicist alternative,[12] he cannot then resolve the Wittgensteinian puzzle in a way that would ever confirm the objective "superiority" of one tradition over another; he would then never escape historicism or relativism.

I conclude, therefore, that MacIntyre's and Putnam's solutions to Putnam's puzzle fail.

II

Broadly speaking, there are three ways in which the moral theories of the past may be reasonably made relevant to the rigors of contemporary theory: (1) if we suppose that human nature or human reason exhibits a form of modal invariance that has normative significance; (2) if, whatever the diversity of cultural practice and moral theory may be, the best theories are adequately grounded in the biological dispositions of the race, even if they are not invariant in the sense of (1); or (3) if only certain lines of moral description and rationalization are clearly preferred through the entire span of moral philosophy. Hence, despite its opening line, the importance of the *Nicomachean Ethics* surely rests with considerations ranging over (2) and (3).

As I shall shortly show (and have already hinted), Aristotle's grip on modal invariance is unsatisfactory. It was perhaps for that reason that MacIntyre, as a thoroughly contemporary theorist, was willing to historicize Aristotle's account of the virtues; although, as I have also shown, MacIntyre finally retreats to some deeply buried (some supposed) safe invariance of reason. In any case, this may explain the difference between MacIntyre's use of Aristotle and Martha Nussbaum's: for MacIntyre initially presents a historicized strategy – the trouble is, it fails; whereas Nussbaum invokes little more than a literary analogy beween the *Ethics* and (for instance) Henry James's and Joseph Conrad's implied appraisals of the mores of very different ages.[13] Nussbaum nowhere explains the rationale for her analogies, and she offers no discussion of the relevance of history. On a favorable reading, she invokes Aristotle's invariances (however distantly); on an unfavorable reading, what she offers belongs in Castiglione's company.

The same is true, I daresay, of Hume's *Treatise*, except that Hume has no pretensions about modal invariance at all, and Hume's official philosophy (which he sets aside whenever he discusses moral matters) is a complete conceptual disaster. The reason, obviously, is that Hume *cannot* construct a viable theory of the self on the resources of his own empiricism; for neither epistemology nor moral philosophy makes any sense without an active, cognizing, and *persisting* agent. More than that, even the speculation about what the self is or how it functions – the entire doctrine of association – makes no sense on Hume's official theory.

That may explain why Hume recommends the pursuit of philosophy "in this careless manner" (as he says), for Hume is plainly aware of the full paradox of his own undertaking.[14] What is "careless" (or "carefree") is what, in spite of not being able to be resolved in empiricist terms, illuminates (for Hume) both science and morality – preeminently, the identity and nature of the self. Hume recovers a part of what (I earlier termed) the "existential" features of the self, in spite of the adequational cast of his official empiricism. It is just that feature of his work that confirms the continuing (the "careless") relevance of Hume's *Treatise* and Aristotle's *Ethics* (and Kant's *Foundations*), despite the mortal failings of each (with regard to item (1) of the tally given above).

Notice that that signifies that none of these three theorists can legitimate the most arresting parts of his own moral theory – on his own terms: not Aristotle or Kant, because *they* cannot ensure the invariances they invoke; not Hume, because Hume sets his own philosophy aside, to make whatever gains he can. In the terms I favor, confirming that much ensures the bankruptcy of first-tier theories and the plausibility (already argued) of preferring "existential" accounts over "adequational" ones. It also signifies a considerable gain in favor of fourth-tier theories. What I infer, therefore, is that approaching the end of our millennium, it is probably impossible to construct a plausible moral philosophy that is not substantially in debt to Hegel and Nietzsche; for it is Hegel and Nietzsche who set out the principal features of what a historicism applied to moral questions (fourth-tier questions) would be obliged to address.[15]

III

Turn, then, to Aristotle and Kant. What is needed is an analysis of the same gauge for each. But that would be an unequal labor if we restricted ourselves to their moral philosophies alone. For, apart from its opening line –

> Every art and every inquiry, and similarly every action and choice, is thought to aim at some good; and for this reason the good has rightly been declared to be that at which all things aim.[16]

– there is very little in the *Nicomachean Ethics* (and apparently even less in the *Eudemian Ethics*) that sustains an explicit search for modal invariances of any sort. You may say that Aristotle assumes the telic invariances the *Metaphysics* offers. Nussbaum makes no particular use of them, which, on the foregoing argument, confirms the reasonableness of classifying her account of James with Castiglione's text. If you deny or ignore the modal claim and its philosophical ramifications, then, however more gifted Aristotle was than Castiglione or Nussbaum, Aristotle's *Ethics* cannot be all that different, theoretically, from Theophrastus's gallery of characters or Nussbaum's appreciation of James's stories. By contrast, Kant could not be more explicit or singleminded about his complete preoccupation with the issue of modal invariance.

There is, in this respect, no detailed comparison to make between the *Ethics* and the *Foundations*. Of course, no one will seriously deny the relevance of the modal thesis in the *Ethics*. But the only parts of the text (apart from the passages about the unique powers of *nous*, which are admittedly exalted but also philosophically preposterous and of no help at all in moral matters) at which the thesis surfaces in a potentially serious way concern the relationship between *theoria* and *praxis*. There is clearly an essentialism in the *Ethics*, but it is so muted and so allusive that most commentators are content to affirm merely that ethics cannot be a science. The right analysis of the powers of practical reason, however, depends on the full relationship between theoretical and practical reason in all pertinent moral judgments: the use of a eudaimonistic model, for instance, is not sufficient in itself to ensure the bearing of modal invariance on moral judgment as such.

I have no interest in pursuing the matter in these restricted terms. There is a much more powerful – a briefer and a more direct – approach to Aristotle's metaphysics that overrides the legitimative force of whatever we may concede regarding Aristotle's adherence, in the *Ethics*, to normative invariances. The argument confirms the canny brevity of MacIntyre's and Nussbaum's use of Aristotle; but Aristotle's perceived importance in recent reviews of first- and second-tier thinking depends on the role of invariance in his entire philosophy.

Aristotle's master stroke – I mean the executive argument on which nearly everything of importance in his *oeuvre* depends – lies with the idea that if we deny that things have invariant natures or essences, we must contradict ourselves *somewhere* in discourse. By that denial, we violate (Aristotle thinks) either the principle of noncontradiction or the principle of excluded middle or both. Well, of course, if Aristotle is right in this, we had better not tamper with the realist reading of invariance, and we had better come to terms with its relevance in the *Ethics*. Also, it needs to be said, no stronger line of defense for invariance is possible than the one Aristotle offers, although you may well wonder whether simpler or more effective versions of it might be had. There cannot be a firmer defense, since (as Aristotle claims) denial straightway leads to contradiction.

There are a number of places where Aristotle advances the idea. For economy's sake, I select the following as being as true to his thesis as any brief passage is likely to be:

> But if not all things are relative [says Aristotle], but some exist in their own right, not everything that appears will be true; for that which appears appears to some one; so that he who says all things that appear are true, makes all things relative ... make[s] everything relative ... to thought and perception, so that nothing either has come to be or will be without some one's first thinking so. But if things have come to be or will be, evidently not all things will be relative to opinion.[17]

The argument is a complex one, though disarmingly worded. I cannot do full justice to it here. Still, we need only isolate its main thread. It is obviously directed against Protagoras, because Protagoras is said to have held (1) that we may give up invariance and fall back to changeable appearances; and (2) that what appears (to someone) *is* true (relative to his perception but not necessarily to another's). Aristotle says that that means that everything will be both true and false.[18] But that charge is clearly misleading. What Aristotle means is that the argument does "away with substance and essence": accidents (he says) must be the accidents of something (some substance) other than another accident; to construe all predication as holding only of appearances leads ineluctably to contradiction.[19] Speaking loosely, restricting ourselves to "appearances" is not tantamount to restricting ourselves to *the* "appearances *of things*" – hence, not tantamount to restricting ourselves to "accidents" in Aristotle's sense. There you have the point of the convergence of Plato's attack on Protagoras, in the *Theaetetus*, and Aristotle's, in *Metaphysics* Gamma. One way of putting the point (which, if I may risk saying so, suggests a convergence between Protagoras and the views of a mature Buddhist like Nāgārjuna) treats *denotata* and *predicabilia* as relationally and provisionally abstracted distinctions made within a logical space in which individual things need not be conceded to have fixed natures.[20]

Aristotle is right in what he says, of course, *if* one assumes "substance and essence" (in his sense). But why should we do so? *If* individual things (*ousiai*), now denied invariant natures, were to be viewed as artifacts constructed in accord with the data of "the phenomenal world," then there would no longer be grounds for the charge of inescapable contradiction. Aristotle's argument requires that the principles of noncontradiction and excluded middle be first reconciled, as a condition of right application (in morality as well as science), with his metaphysics of invariance. *But there is no modal necessity for doing that.*

By parity of reasoning, the law of excluded middle is easily opposed. It is plainly weaker in a formal sense than the law of noncontradiction, since its denial is not inherently contradictory on any familiar reading. It is certainly not modally necessary to adhere to excluded middle. (I suggest that relativism begins to gain a footing here. I cannot take up the issue just now, but I draw your attention to it. I'll not neglect it.) When Aristotle says that "a contrary is a privation of substance, that contradictories cannot belong to the same thing in the same respect,"[21] that (speaking of substances) "the understanding either affirms or denies every object of understanding or reason,"[22] he clearly links excluded middle to the same metaphysics he affirms in supporting noncontradiction. But *if* his metaphysical principle is not necessarily true (not true modally), then the entire argument collapses (as a modal claim), although we are at liberty to recycle any nonmodal part of Aristotle's theory we find useful. I remind you that I have already argued that the principle of noncontradiction is utterly vacuous unless interpreted – in the sense that no interpreted or substantive instance (more simply: no self-consistent substantive claim) *is* modally necessary (for instance, Aristotle's own metaphysical dictum).

Once we accept the falsity of the *modal* claim – for what is not necessarily true *is* false *as* a modal claim – Aristotle's entire system ceases to be conceptually binding: in moral philosophy, in metaphysics, in epistemology, in the philosophy of science, in logic itself. As a consequence, the *Nicomachean Ethics* cannot be the necessary model of all valid moral philosophies, *and cannot even be shown to be valid* when construed as harboring necessary moral principles. It comes as a surprise to see how straightforward the refutation is, and how that can be effected without citing a single word from the *Ethics*. And yet, for second- and third-tier purposes, the question of invariant norms is the single most important question the *Ethics* poses.

Recall, now, the opening line of the *Nicomachean Ethics*.[23] If it means (as indeed it does) that we must construe Aristotle's eudamonism as being in accord with norms internal to the human essence, then, no matter how much we suppose practical ethics to be occupied with particular contingencies and accidents, the entire undertaking will be tethered to invariances said to be discovered by some science (in Aristotle's sense of a science[24]) that knows the invariant nature of man. But if that is no longer possible, for the reasons just given, then *no* second-tier Aristotelian can be said to be doing more than drawing weak analogies between the structure of our own historical world and the classical world Aristotle limns. On that reading, we have (as yet) no demonstrable sense in which the *Ethics is* rationally or morally or prescriptively compelling. It *is* impressive, I don't deny. But it is only an ideology of sorts – in precisely the same sense in which, as I have already argued, Rawls is an attractive idealogue.

No one will be satisfied with my saying only this. But if *we* find the vision of the *Ethics* compelling, the short truth is that we simply find Aristotle's moral taste akin to ours. There's nothing more to say, unless stronger philosophical resources are at hand. I say there are no resources of the modal gauge Aristotle supposes. But you would be hard put to find the admission acknowledged by Aristotle's admirers.

IV

The argument against Kant is both easier and more difficult. It is certainly easier to begin with Kant's *Foundations of the Metaphysics of*

Morals than with the first *Critique*; it is also obvious that the objective of the *Foundations* is as opposed to the project of Aristotle's *Ethics* as any such tract could possibly be. But Kant's thought is notoriously intricate, and we must search for the right clue if we are to challenge his doctrine in a way that compares favorably with the argument against Aristotle. I begin naively, therefore – autobiographically, in fact: I simply note that I don't recognize in myself a "will" to act in accord with duty for duty's sake alone – in anything like the sense Kant advances. Am I mistaken in supposing that such a (pure) "will" is not "present" in me insofar as I am rational? Or am I corrupt or irrational in not recognizing that I am still morally bound by its commands? If the implied objection holds, then (I say) Kant's doctrine falls. The puzzle is how to show *that* such an autobiographical intuition cannot be rationally dislodged by Kant's arguments in the *Foundations*.

In the First Section of the *Foundations*, Kant makes the offhand observation: "It should not be thought that what is here required [a metaphysics of morals] is already present in the celebrated Wolff's propaedeutic to his moral philosophy, i.e., in what he calls universal practical philosophy, and that it is not an entirely new field that is to be opened."[25] So it is clear that if the modal claim Kant imposes on us depends "entirely" on the validity of his new argument (in the *Foundations*), I may perhaps be vindicated if that argument does not succeed. The incredible thing is that, singlehandedly, Kant seems to have invented (with the *Foundations*) a sense of duty – of acting solely from a sense of moral obligation, of acting on *a priori* grounds that bind practical reason categorically, "absolutely" – that "everyone" supposes must have been "there" in ordinary moral experience before *Kant* proposed the thesis. (Kant implicitly endorses the trick.) The question remains: does the argument succeed, and how can it be shown to do so?

I must cite, here, Bernard Williams's excellent objection to Kant's proposal. Williams draws attention to the fact that what Kant calls "moral laws" are "*notional laws*," that is, the fact that their force depends on what Kant conceives to be "the business of making [moral] rules."[26] He goes on to object that the test Kant prepares for us (conformity with the Categorical Imperative)

> is not a persuasive test for what you should reasonably do if you are not already concerned [say] with justice [or perhaps with other projects of Kant's divising]. Unless you are already disposed to take an impartial or moral point of view, you will see as highly unreasonable the proposal that the way to decide what to do is to ask what rules you would make if you had none of your actual advantages, or did not know what they were.[27]

I see a similarity here between Williams's and Wiggins's modes of argument.

It seems plain that Williams is addressing Rawls here (or perhaps Alan Gewirth) more than Kant, though he claims to be speaking of Kant; for Kant would certainly not admit that the force of his argument depended on whether "you were already disposed" to take a favorable view of acting from a sense of duty. (This explains the provisional irrelevance of my autobiographical remark.) Nevertheless, it leaves us with the puzzle of just how Kant intends to prove his case.

Williams's objections are very reasonable – even telling – except that they do not quite engage the principal claim. Williams sees what is required, of course, and doubts that what is required can be supplied. But he does not go far enough.[28]

In the First Section, Kant offers, by way of the following tally, a first pass at his own thesis:

> The first proposition of morality is that to have moral worth an action must be done from duty. The second proposition is: An action performed from duty does not have its moral worth in the purpose which is to be achieved through it but in the maxims by which it is determined. . . . The third principle is a consequence of the two preceding, I would express as follows: Duty is the necessity of an action executed from respect for law.[29]

Here, my complaint about the alien quality of Kant's claim may seem at least pertinent. For, now, one may ask: what is the sense of "necessity" that Kant invokes? I don't mean the *necessity* that *follows analytically* from embracing Kant's conception of moral worth; I mean the *necessity* that obliges us *to* adopt the notion in the first place.

The charge is this: Kant cannot successfully establish *that we are (unconditionally) bound by the necessity he alleges*. It's clear that Kant's notion of necessity is very different from Aristotle's. Frankly, Aristotle had confused the conceptual relationship between logical and metaphysical necessity; whereas Kant means to draw our attention to the necessity (in the moral context) *of* admitting the import of "the entirely new field" he introduces. He states this in a frontal way:

> Is it not of the utmost necessity to construct a pure moral philosophy, which is completely freed from everything which may be only empirical and thus belong to anthropology? That there must be such a philosophy is self-evident from the common idea of duty and moral laws. Everyone must admit that a law, if it is to hold morally, i.e., as a ground of obligation, must imply absolute necessity.[30]

(This catches up the trick of appearing to analyze a *prior* intuition shared by the general public, whereas it actually plants its own congenial anticipation among the philosophically impressionable.) There simply is no conceptual "duty" to admit any unconditionally overriding moral duty. You would be right, incidentally, to find in the passage cited a clue to the sense in which Husserl and Heidegger follow Kant in attempting to free ethical norms from mere anthropologism or psychologism. But, since Kant cannot make the case effectively, neither can Husserl or Heidegger. (Our interest here is primarily with the prospects of first-tier paradigms.)

The counterargument is deceptively simple: first of all, it affirms that, considering only ordinary views of "duty" (I am not sure in what sense "moral laws" are part of the "common idea" of morality), the denial of duties "imply[ing] absolute necessity" is *not* itself self-contradictory or paradoxical; second, it asks Kant to supply the precise sense in which, in whatever substantive respect he intends, *he* can demonstrate that the necessity he introduces is implicated (somehow: *not* analytically) in the ordinary view of duty or the common idea of morality. I see no demonstration lurking; but we are of course still at the First Section. It's at the Second Section that Kant springs his argument. We must go a little further.

The nerve of Kant's claim lies in the following:

> From what has been said it is clear that all moral concepts have their seat and origin entirely *a priori* in reason.
>
> But since moral laws should hold for every rational being as such, the principles must be derived from the universal concept of a rational being generally. In this manner all morals, which need anthropology for their application to men, must be completely developed first as pure philosophy, i.e., metaphysics, independently of anthropology (a thing which is easily done in such distinct fields of knowledge).
>
> Everything in nature works according to laws. Only a rational being has the capacity of acting according to the conception of laws, i.e., according to principles. This capacity is will. Since reason is required for the derivation of actions from laws, will is nothing else than practical reason.[31]

I have deliberately left unmentioned the capstone of Kant's theory. The reason is this: the argument embedded in what I have just cited is meant to convey the sense of moral necessity *by which* we first infer the categorical force of (that is, the necessity binding on us as a result of admitting) the "moral imperative." But the initial "metaphysical" constraint is supposed to be independently necessary: that is, *it* necessarily or rationally obliges us to admit the (further) necessity *of* the condition moral obligation imposes on us. There are two forms of necessity here:

one is the philosophical necessity to accept the categorical necessity of the "moral imperative"; the other is the entailed necessity of the "moral imperative" itself, once one faces the prospect of acting as a responsible agent. As Kant puts it: "the imperative of morality" is a "categorical imperative," "one which presents an action as itself objectively necessary, without regard to any other end."[32] So *we do not need* to consider the details of Kant's famous doctrine of the Categorical Imperative: *its* validity is a consequence of the necessity of the argument just cited. *It's the prior argument that fails.*

Consider, for one thing, that it is *not* demonstrably necessary that "everything in nature works according to laws." Causality and nomologicality do not entail one another. Van Fraassen, whom I've cited earlier, offers a perfectly coherent account of a natural world like our own, but one that lacks laws in the "modal" or strong realist sense. Secondly, if the objection just supplied were honored, then, with respect to the second citation (regarding "moral laws"), Kant could hardly advance his own claim except by *analytically defining* "a rational being" as one who acts "according to the conception of laws"; hence, he could never claim to have made a *metaphysical* discovery about merely human agents; he could never claim to have done *that a priori*. (The required argument would be an analogue of Aristotle's mistake in *Metaphysics* Gamma.) Thirdly, whatever Kant says (thereupon) about the Categorical Imperative – to bridge our acknowledging ourselves as rational beings and our recognizing the consequent necessity the Imperative imposes on us *qua* rational beings – is nothing but an analytic consequence of his original definition. (It's in *this* sense that Williams's objection acquires its greatest strength.) Finally, if we admit the first objection, we cannot ignore the fatal gap in supposing that any invariant, *a priori*, apodictic necessity *can* be compellingly drawn from non-analytic linkages between rationality (or freedom) and the universality inherent in the concept of a law. Kant needs a more robust metaphysics than he cares to admit. The strategy is a palpable failure.

Of course, as everyone knows, Kant's account of the Categorical Imperative draws on a strong "analogy" to the laws of nature – it relies on the supposed transcendental findings of the first *Critique*. The laws of nature are said to be universal; hence, the maxims by which we act "rationally" must (Kant says) be of the same formal sort as the laws of nature. In fact, Kant explicitly affirms:

> By analogy, then [with the universal laws of nature], the categorical imperative of duty can be expressed as follows: Act as though the maxim of your action were by your will to become a universal law of nature.[33]

This should mean only that the rules of practical reason are given a form analogous to that of natural laws; but Kant means more than that. My verdict, therefore, is that the modal argument utterly fails, although (as with Aristotle) we are entirely within our rights to salvage the Kantian formula (if we wish) – now, without the presumption (or any ground for same) of the invariance or unconditional force of moral reason itself. The Categorical Imperative (that is, its application in particular cases, under maxims) *cannot* "in the strict sense, command, i.e., present actions as practically necessary."[34] The rest of Kant's account cannot recover what is needed: it is never more than an explication of what Kant supposes is a successful argument.

Allow me an additional leap, therefore. Kant never rightly appreciated that his own constructivism was *not* modally necessary. The reason is clear from the preface to the second edition of the first *Critique* and from Kant's famous letter to Markus Herz (February 21, 1772), even though the formulation given in the Herz letter is superseded in the mature form of the *Critique*. The point is that Kant acknowledges in the revised preface that "though we cannot *know* [any] objects as things in themselves, we must yet be in a position at least to *think* them as things in themselves; otherwise we should be landed in the absurd conclusion that there can be appearance without anything that appears"; and, relative to this already complex matter, Kant adds the double thesis that "nothing in *a priori* knowledge can be ascribed to objects save what the thinking subject derives from itself [; and] pure reason, as far as the principles of its knowledge are concerned, is a quite separate self-subsistent unity, in which, as in an organized body, every member exists for every other, and all for the sake of each."[35]

The trouble with this reasoning is this. Kant is very clear that the concepts we employ to give form to what appears as our phenomenal world are not *abstracted* from "objects" experienced; they are innate or at least prior (which need not be the same as being innate) in "the thinking subject." That is the novelty of Kant's "Copernican revolution": "objects" are to be *compared* with our native (or "pure") concepts. Nevertheless, if we cannot know the "noumena" of which appearances are *thought* to be appearances, then we cannot know *what* (in the way of intelligible structure) *is* constructed by the "thinking subject"; and then, we cannot fill in with assurance what, precisely, is *a priori* and what is not *in* that construction. That is the essential challenge of the post-Kantian theme of the construction of the constructing subject – and, in particular, the historicized nature of that construction. I may perhaps suggest, here, that Kant anticipates the entire project of Husserl's phenomenology – and, therefore, in betraying the failure of his own

understanding, he exposes the failure of Husserl's as well.[36] The reason
is simply that Kant assumes (as Husserl does as well) that if we have the
capacity to reason, then reason *must be* autonomous in some sense,
utterly unaffected, in its proper functioning, by empirical input (even
though, according to Kant's argument, it cannot be set in motion, so to
say, except in the context of empirical considerations). But that is
nowhere demonstrated and may be reasonably thought to be a noumenal
presumption of some sort. To grasp that is to grasp as well the inherent
weakness of any strictly Husserlian moral philosophy.[37]

My shorthand summary of what is illicit in Kant's account is this:
Kant has no secure source of information about the possible (unsus-
pected) further forms of phenomenal experience beyond what he himself
posits, *if* (as he admits) he is confined to the phenomenal world itself.
(He is tempted to think of "pure reason" as a "separate self-subsistent
unity" – as is Husserl.) Thus, for example, he fails to grasp that *there is*
no necessary connection (analytic or synthetic) between causality and
nomologicality. What he ventures to assign to the (prior) *constructive*
powers of the "thinking subject" – as distinct from the *constructed*
features of the phenomenal world (*which. now, includes, indissolubly,
the empirical self*) – leads him (illicitly) to think he has discerned the
invariant structure *of* that "thinking subject" (constructive or constitut-
ing, *but not itself constructed*), whereas what he has actually done is
discern the strongest contingent regularities (thus far) of what (under the
same historicized horizon) he assigns as part of the necessary structure
of the "thinking subject" (*within the phenomenal world*).

Here, Kant arbitrarily distinguishes the process of "construction"
from what is constructed. To segregate, *in* the "constructed" phenomenal world, the (prior) work of the "subject" who constitutes that world
a world, is already to *deny* that *we are confined* in evidentiary terms *to*
the phenomenal world – as Kant orginally supposed. I have no doubt
that it catches up the general themes of early modern philosophy but it
also fails to protect itself from the valid criticism philosophy draws from
a later vantage – in particular, from admitting the historicized nature of
human thinking.

The problematic argument in the *Foundations* regarding the *a priori*
necessity of rationally endorsing the Categorical Imperative shows the
way to exposing the more general failure of Kant's strong claims about
the *a priori* conditions under which human knowledge is made "possible" at all. The best Kant can suppose is that we *can conjecture*,
empirically, about what might (for all we know) be the *a priori* condition
of our sciences and other inquiries. But to think along such lines would
be to drop the pretense of ever discerning the invariant structure *of* "the

thinking subject" and to opt instead for the contingencies of the social construction of the subject. Kant implicitly declines that option: it would defeat his purpose – it would lead us to treat the *a priori* as an artifact of contingent experience. (That, incidentally, is Foucault's formula.)[38] Kant is never tempted in that direction: "this system [of *a priori* conditions] will, as I hope [he says], maintain, throughout the future, this unchangeableness [its apriority]."[39] On the argument, it is no longer a viable option.

I have, therefore, by somewhat opposing strategies, now challenged the claims of modal necessity or invariance, in both Aristotle and Kant, with respect to the normative questions of morality and (more briefly) of knowledge and the world in general. Since I have also shown – or, perhaps better, sketched an argument by which to show – that contemporary Aristotelians and Kantians are not likely to recover the invariances Aristotle and Kant have forfeited, the question remains: what are the prospects of an objective morality and how are they related to the conditions of objective knowledge in general? Here, we arrive at the central puzzle of our age. The specimen views of the second- and third-tier thinkers I have already examined betray the extraordinary fact that we are still marking time with irrecoverable strategies. For it is obvious enough that the doctrines and strategies of such thinkers are among the most admired exemplars of current moral philosophy.

I have brought us to an apparent stalemate. There is some virtue in having done so. But we shall need a new beginning.

V

I have now traced, somewhat eccentrically, the principal fortunes of moral philosophy from first-tier thinking to very nearly the limits of third-tier thinking. The critical issue remains curiously constant: viz., whether there is a convincing sense in which we may legitimate moral norms as objectively binding. The lesson to be drawn is both radical and straightforward: (1) it is probably impossible to legitimate moral objectivity if we confine ourselves to the supposed invariances of reason and reality; but (2) it may be possible if we concede that "objectivity" and "rationality" are themselves artifacts of social consensus. The effect of making an adjustment from (1) to (2) would be considerable – unprecedented, I should say. For, if we abandoned modal invariance, we should effectively be abandoning as largely fruitless the principal canons and exemplars of the whole of moral philosophy. I say this lightly, but the verdict is genuinely startling. (I see little prospect of reversing it.)

There are many unexamined views, of course, that might still be trotted out; but it would no longer be unfair to anticipate that they, too, are likely to fail, for reasons closely linked to the weakness of Aristotle's and Kant's strategies (or of lesser paradigms, Hume's for instance, that explicitly avoid the pretense of modal invariance).

To be sure, the argument remains open and incomplete, but there is nothing untoward in that. The more radical lesson concerns what new strategies are made possible by shifting from the policies abandoned along the lines of (1) to experimenting with others that can be honored only under the terms of (2). All that clearly requires a fresh beginning, but it is also clear that the principal defect of the analytic canon had been its habit of favoring "adequational" accounts of the human subject over "existential" ones. A balance must be restored.

I offer only an inkling of how profound the changes are likely to be. The important thing is that our reflections can no longer be confined in the usual way to moral philosophy; its new resources will be drawn from puzzles that were never broached by canonical theories. After all, that was precisely what was betrayed by the work of the strongest third-tier theories. It was for this reason that I suggested taking a closer look at Lovibond's strategy, for Lovibond is nearly unique among the "moral realists" in attempting to incorporate certain strategic features of history and cultural life that, under a more favorable interpretation, might have encouraged speculations in accord with (2); nevertheless, in Lovibond's hands, all of these promising changes fall back to the failed policies exposed in accord with (1).

Before I turn to Lovibond, I want to mention, by way of anticipation, a small number of distinctions – theorems, as I shall call them – that a change in policy will permit us to explore effectively. I offer them in an informal way. They are noticeably not featured in the leading second- and third-tier theories, and they are deliberately left undeveloped. The most important will doubtless be the first, viz.: (1) *there is no principled difference between theoretical and practical reason.* On the defeat of Kant and Aristotle on the matter of modal invariance, theoretical reason can be no more than a form of practical reason; and practical reason cannot then be shown to have any aptitude at all for discerning necessarily invariant structures in thought or reality. You will have noticed that both Aristotle and Kant insist on a principled disjunction between theory and practice (although for entirely different reasons). Also (I remind you), no one can now seriously entertain Rawls's liberalism without invoking something like Kant's confidence in the invariant powers of (pure) practical reason; nor can anyone seriously entertain MacIntyre's "historicism" without invoking something like

Aristotle's confidence in the universal validity of what theoretical reason (*nous*) may be said to discern in the contingent (even opposed) truth-claims of rival claimants. Neither of these accounts addresses the issue directly, which is something of a scandal. But the lapse is barely noticed by those who, otherwise well informed, have been habituated to thinking in terms of the strategies now being dismantled.

Once you admit theorem (1), you cannot fail to admit as well what I shall call theorem (2) viz., *predication and, as a consequence, reference are, inherently, logically informal, in that there cannot be an invariant rule or criterion or algorithm or principle by which predicable similarities among, and the numerical identity of, actual things can be fixed.* Theorem (2) affects the prospects of discerning any would-be laws of nature, any forms of strict determinism or supervenience, as well as any would-be invariant moral norms – as, for instance, in questioning whether (say) abortion, suicide, euthanasia, and murder may be said to share the same morally condemnable features or not. I cannot possibly do justice to this complex matter here. I have explored it elsewhere,[40] and mean (here) merely to draw your attention to the fact that the fortunes of moral philosophy cannot fail to be fundamentally affected by the fortunes of theories that seem (at first) hardly relevant at all. In fact, I regard theorem (2) as the very keystone of fourth-tier theories!

For example, W. V. Quine's theory of denotation and reference (and the theory of predicables that it requires – which, I am bound to say, is nowhere made explicit in Quine's own work) is, though obviously influential in analytic epistemology, utterly incompatible with theorem (2).[41] It is nowhere defended and, on the argument intended, it cannot be. Nevertheless, the plausibility of Habermas's "Discourse Ethics" (as well as Rawls's notion of "the original position") presupposes (without explicit mention) some pointedly favorable resolution (along algorithmic lines) of the very issue of predicative similarity that Quine and other strong analysts invoke but never resolve. (Very few theorists make the connection.) I should also say that *that* – correctly understood – defeats both Mackie and Wiggins at a stroke.

Of course, I do not deny that reference and predication are ubiquitously successful in natural-language contexts. On the contrary, I insist on it. The question remains, however, what, precisely, does their success signify? The answer may be cast as theorem (3): *all "lingual" and linguistic activities are successful only in terms of the consensual life of actual societies – only in terms of the praxis of particular societies.* This is an even more complicated matter than the one broached in theorem (2). I had earlier offered an important clue about it, drawn from Wittgenstein, in terms of the notion of "following a rule." The shortest way to put the point (though it will need to be augmented) is to say that theorem (3) treats *savoir* (theoretical knowledge, or science, or the like) as an abstraction from *savoir-faire* (the practical competence, "know-how") with which we spontaneously extend habituated or institutionalized practices – notably, predication – to new instances and new contexts. In this sense, theorems (1)–(3) are corollaries of one another. Part of the sense of (3) may even be implicit in Aristotle's original notion of *praxis*. It is certainly the key sense Marx originally radicalizes in his own theory of *praxis* (which he directs against Aristotle).[42] Variants of the notion may be found in the work of Gadamer, Foucault, and Bourdieu at least. It is more than suggested in MacIntyre, for instance – which, as I have argued, is precisely what undermines MacIntyre's theory of the objective resolution of disputes between incommensurable traditions: because MacIntyre initially concedes the relevance of historicity and then attempts to extricate himself from the *praxis*-centered limitations of human reason that he acknowledges.

Perhaps a further clue may be drawn from Michael Sandel's well-known attack on Rawls's liberalism – that is, the attack on Rawls's notion of the powers of practical reason read in the "Kantian" manner. Sandel is sanguine about so-called "communitarian" obligations (directed against Rawls's doctrine); hence, Sandel does not subscribe to anything quite so attenuated as theorem (3). Nevertheless, what he offers is close to being the analytic analogue of the various collective and historicized themes I have just mentioned; what he says is also implicitly sympathetic with Lovibond's thesis and (therefore) with part of the "moral realist" movement; furthermore, what Sandel says is likely to be far more legible to English-language philosophers (just as Wittgenstein's notion of a *Lebensform* is) than the more complex (and controversial) variants that may be drawn from Hegelian or Heideggerean sources. But they point to the same widespread neglect. In any case, here is what Sandel says:

> To have character is to know that I move in a history I neither summon nor command, which carries consequences none the less for my choices and conduct. It draws me closer to some and more distant from others; it makes some aims more appropriate, others less so. As a self- interpreting being, I am able to reflect on my history and in this sense to distance myself from it, but the distance is always precarious and provisional; the point of reflection never finally secured outside the history itself. A person with character thus knows that he is implicated in various ways even as he reflects, and feels the moral weight of what he knows.[43]

You may gather from this that theorem (3) need not implicate (what I shall now call) theorem (4), viz., that *human selves, human reason.*

objectivity, the norms of theory and practice (truth and rightness or goodness, for instance) are contingent artifacts of historically diverse forms of enculturation. I have already suggested the plausibility of this strenuous theorem by demonstrating what is illicit in Kant's philosophy as well as the relevance of Hegel's constructivist account of the human subject.

The point is central, of course, to Hegel's critique of Kant's formalism: it marks the import, for instance, of Hegel's distinction between *Sittlichkeit* and *Moralität*.[44] So I am invoking Sandel's account chiefly for expository reasons that lead on to a historicized and constructivist account of selves. Its moral implications, I think, may be drawn into a clearer orbit by examining Lovibond's more developed theory (whether or not Sandel and Lovibond share the same moral values). Theorem (4) is a thesis MacIntyre appears to accept in criticizing Rawls – for instance, in speaking of the "inescapably historically and context-bound character which any set of principles of rationality, whether theoretical or practical, is bound to have."[45]

But MacIntyre, as I say, is not steadfast enough on the resolution of the question of moral objectivity. It is not merely the historicity of norms that is at stake, it is also the historicity and constructed nature of the powers of rationality by which particular norms spontaneously take form and change in the processes of societal life. MacIntyre insists on the historicity of reason; Sandel pretty well confines himself to the contingent authority of traditional norms (which, needless to say, he does not characterize as being "constructivist" in Rawls's sense).[46] I do not find, however, any sustained attention on Sandel's part to the "constructed" nature of reason or the constructivist function of history (in anything like the Hegelian sense). Rather, Sandel is at pains (quite properly, I should say) to show that Rawls's constructivism is neither really Kantian nor particularly favorable to the life of supposedly autonomous agents. So there is a considerable difference between MacIntyre's and Sandel's views, which helps to explain the difference (and the importance of the difference) between theorems (3) and (4). I endorse both theorems.

If this much may be taken for granted, we may press on to theorem (5), namely, that *the world of human culture. in which practical and theoretical norms obtain (as constitutively embedded in our practices), is as real as the physical world.* On my own account, cultural phenomena prove to be "embodied" in physical phenomena – as indissolubly complex and emergent there.[47] (The technical details of the metaphysics of culture need not concern us.) But I remind you that I invoked something very much like theorem (5) in order to explain the profound triviality of Wiggins's puzzle about the "meaning of life." If something like theorem (5) were admitted, then, as a matter of course, moral norms (in Hegel's sense of the *sittlich*) would have to be admitted as well, *in* admitting the reality of human selves and their world. That would not yet resolve Mackie's question, but it *would* show (as I have already argued) how naively Mackie has put his own question. Here, the argument joins hands with Sandel and MacIntyre.

Finally, if we review the force of these accumulating theorems, we may anticipate our being drawn to theorem (6) as well: viz., that *we are not bound by necessity to a bivalent logic.* Relativism proves to be conceptually viable and at times distinctly apt in moral matters; I had something like theorem (6) in mind in contesting Aristotle's modal invariance (in particular, his treatment of noncontradiction and excluded middle). I had also suggested earlier that, as in accommodating both the approval and condemnation of abortion, suicide, euthanasia, and the like, we should be well advised to invoke a relativistic logic. I cannot, of course, stop here to spell out what we may understand by a fully formed "relativistic logic." I have defined it elsewhere,[48] and I shall come to it later. For the moment, I mean only to interest you in conceptual resources that have been pretty well refused in the most important moral philosophies of our day (and more).

The theorems I have numbered are hardly more than a sample of the altered resources of fourth-tier thinking. They are not to be thought of as confirmed in any knockdown way, although they are clearly favored by the developing argument. They are not even sufficiently well-formed. But they do already expose the peculiarly narrow range of admissible strategies among canonical moral philosophies as well as the ease with which those same strategies may now be retired and replaced. I shall return to them, later, in a more pointed way. But, for the moment, I need to bring us as close as possible to the effective point at which the transition from third- to fourth-tier strategies will strike you as well-nigh irresistible.

VI

There is a final family of strategies that we must examine before bringing this particular reckoning to a close. Loosely put, the strategies in question are of the "moral realist" sort but they are now distinguished by the following ingenious adjustment: (1) moral norms and values are construed in realist terms because they are embedded in the *lebensformlich* or *sittlich* practices of a society (speaking with either Wittgenstein or

Hegel); (2) no particular member of any such society need explicitly *know* what those norms or values actually are, in order to exercise correctly an acquired aptitude (or "know-how") for conforming to them in practical life; (3) nevertheless, those norms and values can be determinately known; and (4) they and only they function at all prescriptively or categorically (in the sense that answers – or promises to answer – the legitimative question Mackie originally raised, even if *his* question was never really perspicuously posed). The point is – it is an important point – that, in admitting the realist standing of the human or cultural world, (1) Wiggins's question about the "meaning of life" may be trivially resolved; and (2) Mackie's charge about the "queerness" of moral norms (with respect to both first- and second-order discourse) may be shown to fail. Nevertheless, the defeat of Wiggins and Mackie *does not yet* satisfactorily answer the full question of moral legitimation. We must go another mile.

I turn back again, therefore, to the moral realists in order to make a fresh approach to Lovibond's theory.

I begin with Mark Platts. Platts offers a relatively early version of "the moral realist view": "if a moral judgment is true, [he says,] if it hits its target, that is so in virtue of an independently existing moral reality."[49] The explanation is intended to subvert Michael Dummett's "anti-realist"[50] doctrine with respect to both epistemology and the philosophy of science in general and moral philosophy in particular. (It misfires because it misses the realist intent of Dummett's anti-realism. But we may ignore the fact.)

Platts favors the precept, " 'These things can be so independently of our ability to tell'." In the moral world, the thesis comes to this (Platts's formula is rather strenuous):

"These things can be so independently of our desires" .... The realist treats evaluative judgments as descriptions of the world whose literal significance (viz. truth-conditions) make no reference, or generally make no reference, to human desires, needs, wants or interests. Such a view appears incompatible with a disjunction of two doctrines, one a dogma of moral philosophy ["that moral judgments, including evaluative moral judgments, always (or at least frequently) purport to give at least *prima facie* reasons for doing (or not doing) some possible, or already performed action, together with the claim that, when an agent has indeed performed some intentional action, his acceptance of some moral judgment, which may be an evaluative moral judgment, can have been his reason, his motivating reason, for doing it"], the other a dogma of philosophical psychology ["that any complete specification of even a *prima facie* reason for action must make reference to the potential agent's actual or possible desires (which) becomes the potential agent's own reason, a motivating reason for him, if he has, and recognizes himself to have, the desire specified in the antecedent of the conditional"].[51]

The elaboration of Platts's claim need not delay us. What Platts means is that, to preserve the objectivity of particular moral claims, we must suppose that that objectivity is independent of the desires of the claimant then and there but not, in any holist sense, independent of the human condition itself (which would make no sense). By this formula, Platts fixes the generic form of the moral realist's thesis: it could, of course, be elaborated in many different ways. For instance, John McDowell draws out the same theme in terms of a more or less Lockeian model of secondary qualities – thinking of "fearfulness" as a perceptual quality.[52] Sabina Lovibond draws it out instead in terms of a somewhat Hegelian-ized reading of Wittgenstein's notion of a "language game" within the human *Lebensform*. McDowell's model strikes me as too narrow for specifically moral questions, although, in McDowell's hands, it puts Mackie's original challenge in jeopardy. Lovibond's is more inventive and more promising. I introduce it in order to test whether third-tier strategies are (finally) sufficient for securing moral objectivity or whether we must (finally) go beyond all such strategies. I favor the latter verdict, but I want to draw it out from a careful analysis of what the strongest options are. For, if I am right, then a great deal of Western moral theory has simply gone astray – and nearly all of English-language moral theory with it.

There are some qualifications I may mention that will serve us well in what follows. Regarding one of these: Platts appears (to me) to read Wittgenstein in a way that Donald Davidson has developed. (I cannot be entirely sure of this, but the direct lineage hardly matters.) Platts's reading, I suggest, enters in an essential way into Lovibond's strategy and doctrine. It is, however, completely indefensible: I take it to defeat all the prospects of Lovibond's line of argument – as well, metonymic-ally, as all comparable arguments (for instance, Sandel's, MacIntyre's, Charles Taylor's), no matter how distantly related to hers they may be, so long as they invoke (by Hegelian or Marxist or Wittgensteinian or similar models), *as fully and objectively legitimated*, the embedded norms and values of collective social life. If such an argument were successfully mounted, we should be well on our way to what I have called fourth-tier strategies.

I can isolate the nerve of Lovibond's maneuver by isolating the nerve of Davidson's argument in a larger epistemological setting. I hope you will not mind the detour: I offer it as an economy. Here is what

Davidson has to say in clarifying his dictum that "belief is in its nature veridical":

> I urge that a correct understanding of the speech, beliefs, desires, intentions and other propositional attitudes of a person leads to the conclusion that most of a person's beliefs must be true, and so there is a legitimative presupposition that any one of them, if it coheres with most of the rest, is true.[53]

I cannot see any way to read this passage but as a howler, a simple instance of the fallacy of division. It might of course have been possible to treat Davidson's thesis as the claim that we must suppose that, in general, human belief accords with what is true regarding the independent world, that the very presumption of human rationality presupposes that much. But if that were offered as Davidson's claim, then, for one thing, no determinate consequences would follow regarding any particular realist claim and, for a second, the admission would be entirely compatible with the further thesis that, regarding particular claims, truth is always dependent on conceptual or interpretive *tertia*. The first conjecture goes contrary to what Davidson actually says, and the second is specifically ruled out by Davidson himself.

Wittgenstein appears to hold (more carefully) that there must be a considerable background of true beliefs embedded in our practices in order for any particular belief to be questioned; but, as far as I know, Wittgenstein never held that any determinate (or "distributed") belief or claim could ever appeal to that general truth as to a reliable presupposition for legitimating the likelihood that *it* was true.[54] Now, if I am right in this, I think I may claim to be justified in holding that Lovibond's important maneuver fails for a reason that, though not precisely the same as Davidson's, is closely enough linked to what it affirms. In short, Lovibond reads the import of Wittgenstein's "language games" in accord with Davidson's dictum! That hardly does justice to Wittgenstein and it cannot capture what is needed for moral legitimation. But the argument is quite strenuous and repays close attention. I shall go the extra mile with the moral realist in order to make the full turn toward fourth-tier strategies as convincing as possible.

A second qualification is purely verbal, but not unimportant for that reason. Among the "moral realists" – Wiggins, Platts, McDowell, and Lovibond particularly (Iris Murdoch and Philippa Foot as well) – "noncognitivism" is a pejorative term used to label views very much like Mackie's moral skepticism (emotivism, for instance) or certain empiricisms (*not* Hume's). As Lovibond explains:

Non-cognitivism, as its name announces, is the thesis that there is no such thing as moral cognition or knowledge ... there is no objective moral reality; consequently, as far as morals are concerned, there is nothing to know.[55]

No provision is made by the moral realists for the Kantian-like sense in which constructivists (like Kant and Rawls and Habermas) are also, technically, "noncognitivists" though not moral skeptics. We need to have the distinction in hand so as not to misinterpret what the moral realists are saying or to allow them to distort the tradition. Certainly, Lovibond misleads us if what she says entails that Kant would deny that one can *know* what is categorically required of any would-be moral maxims. The truth is, Lovibond perceives a way to construe Wiggins's thin (Moorian-like) intuitionism in collective terms – which she draws from Wittgenstein and Hegel – reading the mix, curiously enough, along Davidson's lines. Wiggins touches on a related possibility, but does not commit himself to it in any explicit way. Platts favors it, but not altogether consistently. And Davidson fancies that his own objectivism is adumbrated in Wittgenstein's account without his needing to yield to historicism. There are mistakes enough to go around.

The irony remains that Wittgenstein, whom a number of moral realists (notably, Lovibond) profess to follow, is no moral realist at all. He himself declares in the *Tractatus*,

> If there is any value that does have value, it must lie outside the whole sphere of what happens and is the case. For all that happens and is the case is accidental.
>
> So too it is impossible for there to be propositions of ethics. Propositions can express nothing that is higher. It is clear that ethics cannot be put into words.[56]

It is the same Wittgenstein who, in the well-known lecture on ethics, speculates:

> Now let us see what we could possibly mean by the expression, "*the* absolutely right road." I think it would be the road which *everybody* on seeing it would, *with logical necessity*, have to go, or be ashamed for not going. And similarly the *absolute good*, if it is a describable state of affairs, would be one which everybody, independent of his tastes and inclinations, would *necessarily* bring about or feel guilty for not bringing about. And I want to say that such a state of affairs is a chimera. No state of affairs

has, in itself, what I would like to call the coercive power of an absolute judge [God].[57]

Here, Wittgenstein introduces a version *of what* the moral realist would insist on and then, consistently, denies that it can be affirmed discursively. On Wittgenstein's view, the disposition to put all this discursively is both humanly natural *and* parasitic on a sense of something like a divine imperative: "If any proposition expresses just what I mean, it is: Good is what God orders."[58] (This suggests another reason for not discounting the "Kantian" form of noncognitivism. But let that pass.)

I confess I see little point to pursuing Wittgenstein's moral "theory" in any depth. It is marginally important both because it confirms that Wittgenstein was undoubtedly a (kind of) noncognitivist on Lovibond's somewhat overgenerous version of Wiggins's account (directed, originally, if you remember, against Richard Taylor's empiricism) and because it must have impressed both Wiggins and Lovibond with the natural (even essential) connection between the "meaning of life" issue and the prospects of moral realism. The moral realists deform Wittgenstein for their own purpose: doing that, I say, they invoke something that is akin to what (with respect to understanding language and discerning what is morally right) Davidson affirms in the influential passage already cited. Lovibond goes further: she Hegelianizes Wittgenstein – treating language games (within the human *Lebensform*) as *sittlich* (in something like Hegel's sense) – so that, on the convergent benefit of Davidson's and "Hegel's" arguments, *a quite determinate form of moral realism is finally vindicated.* Extraordinary! You see the reason for entertaining this new deflection. It is the best that third-tier thinking has invented. (It requires some tortured thinking, you must admit.) I shall give it the amplitude it deserves.

The fact is, Wiggins had begun his own account by citing a letter of Mozart's, in which a personal answer to the question of the meaning of life (one recommended to the human race) is naively given in terms of a divine purpose and divinely ordained human *telos* and sense of duty. Wiggins professes to "envy" Mozart's simplicity and takes note of the fact that our own world requires a more strenuous reading of moral realism, one deprived of rational access to God's plan, or moral teleologism. What he does not rightly see – what Platts and Lovibond more transparently fail to grasp – is that marking the distinction between any purely descriptive (*"sittlich"*) use of moral predicates and the supposedly unconditional, necessary, universal, independent, prescriptive use of moral predicates (*also sittlich*, in Hegel's account) must affect *unfavorably* any "moral realist's" attempt to enlist either Wittgensteinian

Lebensformen or a Hegelian *geistlich* reading of *Sitten* or a Hegelianized Wittgensteinian reading of language games (Lovibond's option) in the defense of the moral realist's doctrine. *There is no such defense*, because there is no conceivable way of ensuring that the descriptively *sittlich* entails the prescriptively *sittlich.* or of ensuring that what appears, within a form of life, as descriptively or prescriptively *sittlich.* conforms to an *independent* purposive moral order. That, of course, is what Platts had naively supposed realism required and could secure. The same conviction, more skillfully deployed, appears in both Wiggins and Lovibond.

When Wittgenstein says that "no state of affairs has, in itself . . . the coercive power of an absolute judge," he obviously means that nothing *sittlich could* possibly possess the requisite moral authority (the moral realist requires). In fact, he adds, "No description that I can think of would do to describe what I mean by absolute value [and] I would reject every significant description that anybody could possibly suggest, *ab initio*, on the ground of its significance . . . . [T]heir nonsensicality [is] their very essence."[59] (The thesis is, of course, Tractarian.)

Rush Rhees actually cites Wittgenstein as saying:

> Suppose you simply described the *Sitten und Gebräuche* (ways and customs) of various tribes: this would not be ethics . . . . Or suppose someone says, "One of the ethical systems must be the right one – or nearer to the right one." Well, suppose I say Christian ethics is the right one. Then I am making a judgment of value. It amounts to *adopting* Christian ethics. It is not like saying that one of these physical theories must be the right one. The way in which some reality corresponds – or conflicts – with a physical theory has no counterpart here.[60]

This shows decisively: (a) that Wittgenstein was not a moral realist; (b) that he regarded moral realism as untenable and inadequate to the needs of an authoritative prescriptivism; and (c) that Wittgenstein believed that (b) was entirely compatible with a profound sense of the meaningfulness of life. We are not of course confined to Wittgenstein's view. But the curious thing is that just that group of thinkers who have made so much of the linkage between the question of the meaning of life and moral inquiry's having point – Wiggins, Platts, Lovibond – have counted on making their thesis compelling in the context of a reading of Wittgenstein's *Lebensform*. The matter invites a closer look, but the short conclusion I wish to draw is that Lovibond has invented out of whole cloth the Wittgenstein she needs.

It is most extraordinary that, just when he concludes his defense of moral realism, Platts refers to precisely the materials in Wittgenstein's "Lecture on Ethics" that we have already noted. Nevertheless, drawing on those, he says, "When we consider perceptions of *moral* value, I think it clear that, if introspective phenomenology can be our guide, moral perceptions manifest a unity of such a kind that potential motivation is indeed internal to them." The theme may be traced in Wiggins (in opposing Taylor) and from there to Platts and Lovibond in a considerably altered form. It has its analogues in Habermas, Gadamer, Charles Taylor, Alasdair MacIntyre, and Richard Bernstein as well – all of whom are second-tier theorists. Platts himself transparently betrays Wiggins's inference: "It seems simply wrongheaded to think that one who sees the universe with wonder at its existence sees the same as one who just *notices* that it is there, differing only in some accompanying external response."[61] But he also deforms Wittgenstein's intention in a way that anticipates and prepares the ground for Lovibond's innovation.

VII

Turn, finally to Lovibond.

Lovibond begins with a seemingly unpromising remark of Wittgenstein's:

> *I*, L.W., believe, am sure, that my friend hasn't sawdust in his body or in his head, even though I have no direct evidence of my senses to the contrary. I am sure, by reason of what has been said to me, of what I have read, and of my experience. To have doubts about it would seem to me madness – of course, this is also in agreement with other people; but *I* agree with them.[62]

Lovibond's point is: first, that the passage shows "the transition from a philosophical to a participatory stance with respect to the language-game [any natural language game, the game of moral language for instance] – from describing it as a historical phenomenon, to joining it"; and second, that Wittgenstein's participation shows that asserting such a proposition (suitably, in a *sittlich* or *lebensformlich* context) ensures that the game or practice is objectively independent of any first-person source:

> once he [L.W.] has registered his disinclination to dissent [Lovibond explains], nothing remains to be done but to *assert* the proposition on which he and the rest of the world are in agreement; and that assertion

will not contain any reference to himself. The "I" of Wittgenstein's "declaration of trust" makes its appearance only to be "resolved" in the orderly process of the language-game, just as the "individuality of self-consciousness," according to Hegel, is resolved in universal Spirit.[63]

(You would be right to see an analogue here of Wiggins's repeated advice, "there is nothing else to think.")

There you have the briefest version of Lovibond's strategy for integrating (1) the objective independence of language and culture (from initially psychological or solipsistic sources) suitable for a realism of norms or values; (2) its characterization in *sittlich* terms suitable for natural cognizability or perception, again required for realism; (3) a model for linking the perceptual and motivational aspects of human life (the "outer" and the "inner," as Wiggins has it) suitable for favorably answering the question of the meaning of life (again in Wiggins's sense); and (4) a potential basis for developing an account of *normative authority* affecting cognitive, linguistic, and moral questions, which the Hegelian-like reading is meant to supply (and which Lovibond believes Wittgenstein illustrates). Item (1) supplies a conceptual ingredient that we had already noted was needed in order that moral discourse achieve conceptual parity with factual discourse; clearly, (1) will do, provided we construe the *sittlich* in its weaker sense: that is, in the sense in which it is purely descriptive of (the putative norms of) cultural life, *not* prescriptive or categorically binding or "authoritative" in the sense originally queried by Mackie. (It explains the mediating role of a realist theory of natural language – the hidden theme linking Hegel, Wittgenstein and Donald Davidson in the work of such authors as Wiggins, Lovibond, McDowell, and even Charles Taylor.)[64] Anything more – specifically, anything more that would be adequate for a full-fledged moral realism – would require a convincing account of (4) – what I have termed the Hegelian element (which catches up the equivocation on "sittlich").

We need not regard the systematic connections among (1)–(4) as more than a reconstruction of Lovibond's argument. She herself is admirably explicit:

Now the view of linguistic rules which we have been considering [she says] – the insight, namely, that obedience to a rule consists in conformity to a practice – is strongly reminiscent of the Hegelian concept of *Sittlichkeit*, or "concrete ethics." *Sittlich* obligation enjoins the individual to maintain, or recreate, an already existing social practice which, because of his personal contribution to the common task of maintaining it, is also the objective expression of his own identity . . . . The idea of an *obligation to sustain the institutions which embody a shared way of life* seems to characterize to perfection the way in which, according to Wittgenstein, we are governed by the rules of our language.[65]

I find these remarks extraordinarily close in spirit – and here and there in language – to Sandel's "communitarianism." Also, in opposition to Kant and the Kantian tradition (that includes Husserl and Heidegger in very different ways), the realist argument offered by Wiggins and Lovibond begins to provide a basis in English-language moral philosophy for an "anthropologized" account (*Weltanschauungsphilosophie*). This is the upshot of favoring conceptual models like those of Hegel's *Sitten* and Wittgenstein's *Lebensform*, though that has nothing (as yet) to do with resolving the problem of legitimation.

But Lovibond's argument is entirely mistaken – not merely in the textual sense of confusing Wittgenstein's account with Hegel's, but in the deeper sense that the line of argument offered cannot possibly achieve its objective. (Here, Davidson's fallacy seems relevant.) For the weaker sense of *sittlich*, the one from which moral, linguistic, and epistemic *authority* is to be drawn, is at once merely holist, incapable of supporting distributed claims, and in any case never grounded in a cognitive way. Furthermore, the *rules* of such practices are never actually formulable, objectively closed, or fixed over a run of instances; and, in Wittgenstein's account, they literally cannot be violated. (This again conveys the meaning of "following a rule.") The moral realist (Lovibond, now) insists on rules, criteria, cognitive principles keyed to the holist practices that apparently enable us to determine which particular claims and commitments conform with a given practice and which do not. But there *are* no such rules and there can be none. That is the whole point of Wittgenstein's texts (chiefly collected against G. E. Moore) of what has been issued as *On Certainty*.

Lovibond's most sanguine version of the *sittlich* – the Hegelianized reading of Wittgensteinian language games – appears in the following remark: "Our proposed theory of ethics [she says] is a realist theory in that it asserts the existence of *intellectual authority-relations* in the realm of morals, whereas non-cognitivism denies these."[66] What, however, are these "intellectual authority-relations"? They must be (1) actually present in given practices; (2) discernible there by virtue of an exercise of a natural aptitude for understanding the practices of one's society; and (3) capable of yielding prescriptive or categorical or authoritative criteria and norms for a wide range of determinate judgments and commitments (relative to our *Lebensform*). But how can we distinguish between the true function of the *sittlich* – between mere conformity with social practices (in the descriptive sense) and submission to the consensual "authority" of a society functioning prescriptively? Lovibond never satisfactorily addresses the question, although she clearly worries about the contrast between conservative and liberal prescriptives.[67] Without an answer, we cannot even be sure that her theory *is* a form of moral realism.

There are several places where Lovibond offers something of an answer. For instance, in the following: "To recognize that there may be moral truths which transcend one's awareness is to submit one's moral judgment to further correction by the 'pull toward objectivity'; it is an act of submission to intellectual authority in the sphere of morals."[68] But the would-be explanation is a strange one. First of all, she draws the notion of a "pull toward objectivity" from W. V. Quine,[69] whose suggestion she finds "highly reminiscent of Wittgenstein's account of the role of coercion in language-teaching."[70] Yet the only possible sense in which Quine's theory might be said to resemble Wittgenstein's (in the *Investigations*), must be one in which our training in science, language, mutual understanding, and the like is radically holistic and subject to what Quine calls "radical indeterminacy."[71] That would hardly serve Lovibond's purpose. On the contrary, Quine is an opponent of *any* realism by which a determinate "metaphysics" could be said to be objectively implicated in his sort of holism. Quine would have *no* interest at all in the criterial role of *Sitten* (linguistic or moral) that Lovibond requires; he would surely repudiate any such use *of* the "pull toward objectivity." Again, unless Lovibond reads Wittgenstein along the lines of Davidson's fallacy, it would be more than doubtful that Wittgenstein would ever have favored the claim she advances. It runs completely contrary to his known views on ethics.

Furthermore, when she speaks of the possibility of "moral truths which transcend one's awareness," she draws on Platts's deliberate extension (to moral discourse) of Davidson's use of the Tarskian conception of truth. This is a rather complex matter in its own right, much of which does not directly concern us.[72] But Platts holds that "The realist claims that (S_n) [that is, the sentence, or the suitable use of the sentence, 'An object α satisfies "is courageous" if, and only if, α is courageous'] expresses something knowledge of which would ensure, assuming competence of the usage of at least some of the rest of the language, competence in the usage of the expression designated." It is with regard to the use of this model that Platts says that the linguistic competence in question can be had by a speaker even if it is beyond that speaker's present recognitional capacities to recognize particular instantiations of courageousness; and this competence, this grasp upon the concept of courage, can persist through, can transcend, changes in the speaker's recognitional capacities, including such changes brought about by changes in the speaker's beliefs about the grounds of his recognitional capacities, his changing *conceptions* of courage.[73]

Now, Platts's view is (thus far) a perfectly reasonable one: think only of a child growing up in his own culture. But his thesis has nothing to do with legitimating the prescriptive sense of the *sittlich*. If it is to hold in the stronger (realist) sense intended, then Platts would need to supply an argument that bears on more than the weaker sense of the *sittlich*. He does not do so.[74] But that means that Lovibond relies on a model that is patently (even essentially) defective in the respect wanted.

Only the Hegelian maneuver remains – apart from a flat appeal to some form of intuitionism, essentialism, teleologism, natural law doctrine, or the like, alternatives that are ruled out by the initial rejection (agreed to by all hands) of all forms of cognitive privilege.

We must be careful not to caricature Lovibond's position. She *is* a moral realist, of course, but she means to make the best case: not *for* realism but for a liberalized conception of values *within* the realist pale, *once we establish realism itself*. There is, therefore, a decisive lacuna in her account.

On the critical question, she says only that "empiricism is rejected as soon as we get the idea that there is no external authority to validate the norms of judgment and argument enforced within a linguistic community."[75] That is her gloss on Wittgenstein's "manifesto": "No empiricism and yet realism in philosophy, that is the hardest thing."[76] The supreme irony of Lovibond's entire strategy lies with the fact that the "Hegelian" requirement (the prescriptive function of the *sittlich*) is already exemplified in the Humean treatment of aesthetic taste. For it is Lovibond's thesis that Hume realized that "there is [there *is*] a standard of correctness to which we can appeal, the opinion of the *qualified judge*, who is a person possessing delicate and unprejudiced powers of perception."[77] Yes, of course, there *is* such a judge, or, more persuasively, there are indefinitely many judges apt in the benign (but inconclusive) *lebensformlich* sense – that is, the sense that has absolutely nothing to do with confirming the *morally (or aesthetically) prescriptive*. It shows only that apt members of a society living within a *sittlich* or *lebensformlich* space are (and must to some extent be) aware of the (descriptively) operative norms of their world: that *is* Wittgenstein's *holist* point, but it is hardly enough for Lovibond's purpose.

The argument is not that the norms are independent or exist independently of our practices; the argument wanted is that they must be able to be shown to be independently valid *in* the prescriptive sense, that is, independent of their merely being consensually ("descriptively") supported. Here, finally, Lovibond acknowledges a fatal difference between science and morality:

> I suggest, [she says,] that the reason it makes sense to suppose we might all be wrong about a question of astrophysics is that *observation*, whose deliverances are "more or less immediate," might at some time or other *show* that we were. This [however] is not what it is like for a community to change its mind about a moral issue – or, normatively, to attain to a deeper moral insight. The reason . . . is that changes in collective moral outlook – as in individual moral outlook – tend on the whole to happen slowly, by contrast with the immediacy of changes in what we all believe about the physical world . . . . In connection with moral judgment, we do not have the idea of *fresh evidence* which, when it came to light, would prompt a uniform and immediate reassignment of truth-values to sentences on the part of competent speakers. That idea "belongs to" our concept of the physical world, but not to our (possible) concept of the moral world.[78]

This is partly right in the most exact sense. But it completely subverts the realist's account of the prescriptive or categorical force of moral values beyond any merely *sittlich* sense that accords with Wittgenstein's holism. There is no pertinent conceptual connection between the *rate* at which beliefs change in science and morality and the supposed objectivity of factual science and normative morality. Furthermore, the admission that we lack a use for the "idea of fresh evidence" in moral matters that parallels its use in science is more likely to support the skeptic's original charge than the problematic "Hegelianized" reading Lovibond recommends.

Lovibond is surely right that "it is only as a member of some community that I exist as a moral being."[79] But that merely sets the puzzle, it hardly solves it. I take it to signify the exhaustion of all the known strategies of the third-tier sort. For, quite apart from the local failings of Lovibond's arguments, her strategy transforms our sense of the question of moral objectivity. The lesson to be savored is a double one: first, that there *is* no conceptual problem regarding the "meaning of life"; and, second, that there *is* no *initial* conceptual problem regarding the realist standing of the moral norms and values that belong (holistically) to our form of life. The only problem there is – and that remains a serious problem – concerns legitimating the "prescriptive" or "categorical" or "authoritative" objectivity *of* those moral norms and values that we read distributively. *That* is the moral analogue of Davidson's mistake.

I admit the difficulty of the task that remains. But I also claim that it has been made very much easier to fulfil, since we recognize (through Lovibond's failed effort) that it cannot be completed in any of the standard ways that have now been collected in the forms of first-, second-, and third-tier thinking. That's all! To grasp the verdict is to grasp the need to turn to the entirely different strategies of fourth-tier thinking. But that requires a fresh beginning.

5

Life without Principles

I

I have singled out Aristotle and Kant as the great exemplars of the two master visions of moral philosophy. I have taken a liberty in doing so, of course, since there are many lines of theory that are neither Aristotelian nor Kantian. But I trust it will be clear that most if not all of the alternative options are either unpromising from the start (moral intuitionism, for instance, because it invents a special and privileged cognitive faculty)[1] or make no serious pretense about their having any demonstrably universal or necessary or lawlike or rationally obligatory bearing on determining what, finally, is morally right or good (Hume, for instance, though, obviously, equivocally).[2] But I have also shown that both visions suffer from the same mortal weakness – the inability to prove that there are any modal invariances at all; *a fortiori*, the inability (according to their own lights) to specify invariances pertinent to confirming the conditions of moral objectivity. Roughly, what I have said is that, failing in that, moral philosophies, particularly those I have called second-tier theories (the views of thinkers like Rawls, Gewirth, Apel, Habermas, Sandel, Taylor, MacIntyre, Gadamer, Lovibond, MacKinnon, Dworkin), whether or not they explore third-tier questions as well, devolve into *moral ideologies* – by which I merely mean (in a nonderogatory sense) that those philosophies convey substantive convictions about what *is* morally prescriptive or "authoritative" or categorically binding but without advancing satisfactory legitimative grounds for same. On this argument, the whole of Western moral philosophy never entirely escapes being ideological.

I see no harm in admitting that. On the contrary, an essential part of the legitimative undertaking of what I am calling fourth-tier strategies may still be said to be occupied with explaining how (what are, frankly) moral ideologies may be shown to yield objectively valid findings in something like the prescriptive sense at issue – and what that should mean in the way of altering our legitimative notions. I put it to you that none of the principal theories belonging to the large company I have been canvassing even admits this possibility. Where, particularly in English-language philosophy, the full failure of canonical legitimation is admitted – notoriously, in Richard Rorty's work, ranging over general epistemology as well as moral and political philosophy[3] – philosophy itself is summarily dismissed for that reason alone. This is the essential policy of what Jean-François Lyotard has called postmodernism[4] (which Lyotard himself does not ultimately favor). I trust it will be clear that postmodernism is a *petitio*, a *non sequitur*, and (I should insist) a completely incoherent policy. The reason is simply this: it makes no sense to admit that these or those beliefs, statements, judgments, commitments, and the like are true or right or correct or justified, without conceding that it also makes sense to indicate (to be able to explain) the legitimative grounds on which the first may be shown to be such. This is nothing but a reminder of what, in the local setting of moral disputes, Mackie rightly distinguished as first- and second-order questions. (The trouble, of course, with Mackie was that he did not consider that the skeptical questions he put to canonical moral theory applied with equal force to epistemology: he therefore undercut his skepticism.) In any case, Rorty's postmodernism is little more than an incoherent analogue of Mackie's ill-formed skepticism.

But if Aristotle's and Kant's claims about modal invariance in moral matters fail, then we are bound to ask ourselves what, in addition, in a philosophically serious sense, *is* even relevant (in *their* work) regarding the viable grounds on which moral objectivity may be legitimated. The surprising answer is: not much! On the admission of their failure to secure modal invariance (essentialism in Aristotle's account, rational necessity in Kant's), Aristotle's *Ethics* dwindles to a very skillful summary of a version of the moral and political ideology of the Greek *polis*, well on its way (as Aristotle certainly knew) to being completely eclipsed by the consequences of Alexander's imperial vision; Kant's *Foundations* proves even less relevant to legitimative concerns, since, in a way, there is nothing else to Kant's theory but the argument for adopting the legitimative option he puts forward.

Now, what is most instructive about the failure of both Aristotle's and Kant's undertakings in this respect is caught up in the thesis already cited from Lovibond: "It is only as a member of some community that I exist as a moral being."[5] The same thesis, sometimes almost identically worded, appears in Sandel, in MacIntyre, in Charles Taylor, and in Gadamer – to confine ourselves to figures featured in these pages. I have suggested that this single theme is the conceptual fulcrum on which the difference between third- and fourth-tier theories may be sorted. Read in a way that is (still) neutral as between such theories, this single thesis, properly construed, leads directly to our completely discounting (1) the need to "solve" Wiggins's puzzle about the "meaning of life" and (2) the need to vindicate a realist account of moral norms and values as strong as that intended (and thought to be required) by the "moral realist's" failed strategy for meeting Mackie's challenge. That is part of what I have been at pains to show. Both adjustments prove to be trivially entailed by a plausible reading of Lovibond's dictum.

That much of the counterargument is captured at a stroke by admitting that moral matters – all human concerns, in fact – arise in and only in a *sittlich* or *lebensformlich* world. (I regard that as a gloss on Lovibond's remark.) What, however, I wish to add to this quite reasonable adjustment is this: second- and third-tier theorists either never consider the inherent historicity of what is *sittlich* or *lebensformlich* (remember: Wittgenstein had almost no philosophical interest in the historical) or, if they do, they fall back (at least implicitly) to some ahistorical invariance meant to help us escape the supposed dangers of relativism, anarchism, irrationalism, sheer ideology, in accepting the constraints of historicism. That, in different ways, is patent in Habermas and Gadamer – and, notably, in their published disagreement. It is also for this reason that I characterized Lovibond, Sandel, and even MacIntyre as, ultimately, second-tier thinkers.

Fourth-tier theories are, by contrast, wedded to some form of historicism. In virtue of that, they cannot fail to have been influenced by Hegel – if (to be philosophically sensible) to admit that much is still entirely compatible with rejecting Hegel's own absolute idealism, historical teleologism, and forms of modal necessity applied to history. I should say that, in English-language philosophy, John Dewey's pragmatism shows the coherence of such an option – though perhaps not much more.[6] The most radical possibilities of the Hegelian option – *sans* Hegel, that is, what may be called Nietzscheanized possibilities – surely belong to Michel Foucault.[7] These two figures (Nietzsche and Foucault) help to fix the parameters of Hegel's influence; although, in my own opinion, the single most important theme in Hegel (apart from Hegel's own extraordinary work) is to be found in Marx's (admittedly fragmentary and often tendentious) clarification of what we should mean by *praxis* in a historicized world. For, once Aristotle (who, of course, introduces the notion of *praxis*) and Kant (who, of course, produces an insoluble paradox for the moral use of reason) are seen to fail on the matter of modal invariance, Marx's insights regarding *praxis* help us to understand the inseparability of theoretical and practical reason. I anticipate, therefore, that, in accepting (at least provisionally) the coherence of fourth-tier thinking, we grasp (1) the equivocal import of Lovibond's dictum, as between third- and fourth-tier options, and (2) the inescapability of conceding that, *if* legitimative questions are still to be honored (against the skeptic and the postmodernist), then *moral legitimation is the legitimation of moral ideologies.* QED.

The supreme clue is offered by Hegel himself. Hegel is a devastating critic of Kant's formalism. But, more than that (if I may say "more"), his critique of Kant ramifies through all the "Kantian" formalisms of our time – Rawls's, Gewirth's, Apel's, and Habermas's (and the formalisms of all those who follow the lead of these theorists, which constitute a not negligible part of the whole of current moral philosophy). Here, then, is the most famous passage (that addresses arguments from the second *Critique*) in which Hegel defeats Kant out of hand:

> I ask [testing the Kantian criterion] whether my maxim to increase my fortune by any and all safe means can hold good as a universal practical law in the case where appropriating a deposit entrusted to me has appeared to be such a means; the content of this law would be that "anyone may deny having received a deposit for which there is no proof." This question is then decided by itself, "because such a principle as a law would destroy itself since the result would be that no deposits would exist." But where is the contradiction if there were no deposits? . . .
>
> If the specification of property in general be posited, then we can construct the tautological statement: property is property and nothing else. And this tautological production is the legislation of the practical reason; property, if property *is*, must be property. But if we posit the opposite, negation of property, then the legislation of this same practical reason produces the tautology: non-property is non-property. If property is not to be, then whatever claims to be property must be cancelled. But the aim is to prove precisely that property must be; the sole thing at issue is what lies outside the capacity of this practical legislation of pure reason, namely, to decide which of the opposed specific things must be lawful. But pure reason demands that this shall have been done beforehand, and that one of the opposed specific things shall be presupposed, and only then can pure reason perform its more superfluous legislating.[8]

This is a wickedly businesslike refutation of Kant. There can be no recovery, in the plain sense that the supposed rule of reason cannot possibly establish *that* the practices we are judging must be in place or "lawful" as opposed to any alternative practice, equally self-consistent, that might (in its turn) morally preclude the first. For example, we could never, on Kantian grounds, prefer or reject slavery or abortion (or even suicide), although Kant might not agree. One can also easily see in Hegel's argument a possible basis for Marx's thesis that private property is theft.

But Hegel's argument goes very deep, well beyond the local convenience of defeating Kant. Rightly understood, I think it confirms (though I have no grounds for believing Hegel would agree) that: (1) moral legitimation is the legitimation of moral ideologies; (2) reference and predication (*a fortiori*, the confirmation of truth) are inherently historicized and function only informally within the *sittlich* practices of actual societies; (3) theoretical reason is a form of *praxis*; and (4) moral legitimation (*a fortiori*, the validity of moral claims) cannot but be relativistic.

These are startlingly powerful – and provocative – claims. (I do not say they are confirmed here.) You will appreciate, of course, that they go some distance toward redeeming the theorems I merely sketched in the preceding chapter. They are also characteristic of what I am promoting as fourth-tier theories. I need to remind you as well that nearly the whole of Western moral philosophy has avoided or actually rejected every one of the claims collected here as items (1)–(4): that is what I meant, earlier, in characterizing fourth-tier thinking as "radical." It was for this reason that I tried to show how theorists like Gadamer, Sandel, MacIntyre, and Lovibond fall back from the brink of adopting options of the fourth-tier sort, all the while they are obviously attracted to some form of what is *sittlich* in the historicist sense.

I draw all this from Hegel – shorn of Hegel's extravagances – although I am not persuaded that a proper reading of Hegel's philosophy of history would not support my view. It does not matter, and it would be extraordinarily difficult to show that the textual argument must go one way or another. I say instead that the failure of second- and third-tier thinking has brought us to a point at which my last set of claims – (1)–(4) – appear to yield the most promising legitimative strategies we are likely to recover, that have not yet been sufficiently explored and that may yield as well a plausible interpretation of the point of Hegel's critique of Kant.

You must see the point of Hegel's critique as, also, an enormous compliment to the boldness of Kant's argument. For what it means is that Kant risked his entire thesis on the likelihood that the purely formal grounds provided by the Categorical Imperative would weed out all would-be "rational" policies that the usual interests of moral communities would favor weeding out, without ever requiring *any* argumentatively relevant admission of the substantive content of those policies.

Extraordinary! What Hegel shows is that the formal possibilities are much wider than what any adherent of Kant's strategy may have supposed, so that, even on contractual matters, which offer the best prospects for a defense of Kant's conception, there are always resources enough to show that Kant's solutions lack a decisive premise for precluding the reverse of the maxims Kant was disposed to endorse – disjunctively. What Hegel showed was that Kant had placed too great a burden on a purely formal criterion. Kant meant to accommodate all manner of human interests, provided only that those interests could be reasonably represented – in the way of a "rational" defense – before the bar of the Categorical Imperative. In this, he may be supposed to be the supreme defender of moral pluralism. The trouble is that, in the hands of an ingenious tactician, the Kantian test might conceivably be made to endorse a policy of "anything goes." (I should also say that, although they deplore Kant's formalism, Apel and Habermas seem to me to be every bit as formalist as Kant. This is noteworthy, since the novelty of their respective approaches has it that the necessity or universality of moral principles must be drawn from the actual practices of living societies. I cannot see that they conform with their own injunction.)

Before leaving the larger matter, however, which may be clear enough, I should like to demonstrate the stunning accuracy of Hegel's charge, by bringing it to bear, without adjustment, on a central thesis of Habermas's "Discourse Ethics," written nearly two hundred years later. First of all, Habermas himself opposes Apel's "transcendental-pragmatic justification" of a Kantian-like ethics of "argumentation," largely because he anticipates difficulties in any apriorism. He says it is "even too weak to counter the consistent skeptic's opposition to *any* kind of rational ethics." But, secondly, he himself is quite sanguine about legitimating "the principle of universalization" *a posteriori*, "which alone enables us [he says] to reach agreement through argumentation on practical questions."[9] Habermas then introduces two principles: one (U), a "rule of argumentation" or "principle of universalization," and another (D), the "principle of discourse ethics" which he means to recommend. The formulations go as follows:

(U) *All* affected can accept the consequences and the side effects its [that is, "every valid norm's"] *general* observance can be anticipated to have for the satisfaction of *everyone's* interests (and these consequences are preferred to those of known alternative possibilities for regulation).

(D) Only those norms can claim to be valid that meet (or could meet) with the approval of all affected in their capacity *as participants in a practical discourse*.[10]

Apart from the question of how one could ever test whether (U) made any sense at all or was viable or testable, or whether (D) could ever be shown to conform with (U), one can see at once that whether any claim in accord with (U) or (D) or both *was valid* would presuppose that the actual "interests" of "all [those] affected" were *already* in place (were actually taken for granted) and were such that they could be reconciled with the interests of all others pertinently affected. But that clearly runs up against Hegel's argument – and for any number of reasons. I mention only three: for one, Habermas's program could not distinguish in principle between the ethical admissibility of supporting or opposing property in Hegel's example; and, for another, it could not justify choosing between the one or the other claim (incompatible between themselves) on the basis of (D). *If* we insisted that (D) must conform with (U), and if we admitted that (U) precludes Hegel's case, then of course (U) would itself be a substantive moral principle – which would be contrary to Habermas's intent – and arbitrary in any case. (Habermas seems not to have thought of this: it is the analogue of Rawls's inability to accommodate Berlin's dictum about the inevitable sacrifice of goods.) So Habermas's rather ambitious program – to which I may say many are drawn at the present time – collapses at its very inception, and for reasons that Habermas must surely have been aware of.

The third consideration is very much more complicated than the other two. I take it to be quite important – devastating, in fact, when rightly understood – but hardly easy to vindicate. I regard it as Hegelian in inspiration, *if* we understand Hegel's sense of history to preclude any conceptual scheme that, at any time, incorporates every arguably pertinent point of view (the "interests of all" or "all affected," as Habermas is fond of saying). I take MacKinnon (as a feminist) to have pressed the point, though more in a Marxist spirit than a Hegelian; and I associate the theme particularly (in very different ways) with Derrida's deconstructions, Foucault's genealogies, and Levinas's ineffabilities. At any rate, Habermas's formulation of (D) addresses only "all affected *in their capacity as* participants in a [particular] practical discourse." But what of those who are precluded from participating *but not* by way of being explicitly assigned a deprived role "*in* a practical discourse"?

Lyotard may be the best-known discussant of this matter, having introduced the idea of a *différend*. But in drawing attention to Lyotard's usage, I frankly want to distance myself from his rather extravagant way of putting things. He does characterize the *différend* as a term of art in a perspicuous way, and I am happy to invoke it:

A case of differend between two parties [he says] takes place when the "regulation" of the conflict that opposes them is done in the idiom of one of the parties while the wrong suffered by the other is not signified in the idiom.[11]

Lyotard gives the example of a worker's being obliged to treat his own labor (in the law) as a commodity traded by way of a contract. The point is, if Lyotard is right, then there cannot be an end to *différends*: systematic moral and political discourse will always invoke them; but if that is so, then the appeal to "universalizability" (or, in the more usual idiom, "universality") cannot fail to be exploitative, cannot overcome the condition everywhere, and where it overcomes a particular *différend* it cannot be supposed that, in doing that, we are "progressing" toward their final elimination. Habermas nowhere addresses the matter.

This, I should say, is the theme of a deliberately constructive "postmodernist" morality. I associate it particularly with the theme of the "Others" (*l'Autrui*) offered by Emmanuel Levinas and fleshed out more fully by Zygmunt Bauman. I mention the fact because, both in Lyotard and Bauman, you will find some convergences with my own line of argument against "modernist" moral philosophies – for instance, Habermas's appeal to a universalised criterion. But I reject both Levinas's ineffabilist reading of the Other (which affects both Lyotard's and Bauman's accounts) as well as any presumption of "finding" a moral ground inherent in that ineffable condition. These maneuvers are incoherent and little more than insinuations of ideological privilege.[12] But I appreciate the humanity of their protest.

II

I can think of no more than one conceptual picture that perspicuously fits all the arguments up to this point that is viable and coherent and plausible in its own terms. That picture (I say) directs us in a natural way to enlist fourth-tier strategies. The conception is this – I add it to the tally already mentioned because it is clearly the central theme of the "Hegelian turn": (5) persons – human selves, agents, "subjects" – are socially constituted ("constructed") as artifacts of the historically diverse and changing processes of an enabling form of enculturation. This is a very controversial and difficult doctrine. But what I want to emphasize, which bears decisively on the narrow concerns of moral philosophy (as well, of course, as on the larger issues of epistemology, the philosophy of science, logic, and the arts and criticism), is that selves are "artifactual" in at least the sense that, whatever their biology, their conceptual powers – especially linguistic but also "lingual," those that presuppose language but are not specifically exercized in speech or the like – are a function of, and function in and only in, the context of the *lebensformlich* practices of this or that (enabling) society. To show that (5) holds would help enormously to explain, for instance, why reference and predication are forms of *praxis*, why theoretical and practical reason are inseparable, why Aristotelian essentialism and Kantian rationality are indefensible, why legitimation must be the legitimation of ideologies, and why, as a consequence, *there are no modally necessary principles in moral matters* – as, indeed, there are (also) none in epistemology or the philosophy of science.

It may be helpful to remind you, here, that this was the implicit basis on which I argued earlier that Putnam's appeal to truth as a *Grenzbegriff* (very much as with rationality, for Apel and Habermas and, indeed, for Putnam again) could not be reconciled with Putnam's "internal realism" or, independently, with anything short of a retreat to cognitive privilege or First Philosophy. But I also need to guard against an easy misreading of item (5). Let me simply say that I do not construe the artifactual (the socially constituted) as fictional in any way and I do not deny that the cultural complexities of personal life are inseparable from the biological resources in which they emerge. But I also do not see how the "self" can be "naturalized" (or reduced, biologically) if selves *are* culturally emergent.

Once you admit historicism as conceptually viable and a possible basis for legitimative efforts in morality (as in science and cognitive matters at large), you cannot fail to grasp the profound incompatibility of historicism and universalize (whether the latter is exemplified in the form favored in Aristotle's essentialism or in Kant's model of maxims said to be capable of functioning as universal laws of nature). Gadamer, I think, is among the clearest on this matter, particularly in his well-known dispute with Habermas. There is some irony in this, because, for one thing, as I say, Gadamer tries (and fails) to escape the upshot of his own (crypto-essentialist) argument,[13] and because, for a second, perhaps more interestingly, the quarrel between Gadamer and Habermas is, if you think about it carefully, a quarrel between two branches of the same Kantian tradition: the one (Habermas's) centered in the first *Critique*; the other (Gadamer's) centered in the hermeneutic tradition drawn from the third *Critique* and eventually historicized through Dilthey and Heidegger.[14]

Gadamer's intended lesson comes in two steps. In the first, he identifies the grounds for repudiating any presumption of a neutral faculty of practical reason by the use of which the universal validation of morally enlightened norms of conduct is supposed to be assured:

> The overcoming of all prejudices [*Vorurteil*], this global demand of the enlightenment, [he says] will prove to be itself [an unjustified] prejudice, the removal of which opens the way to an appropriate understanding of our finitude, which dominates not only our humanity, but also our historical consciousness.... If this is true, then the idea of an absolute reason is impossible for historical humanity. Reason exists for us only in concrete, historical terms, i.e. it is not its own master, but remains constantly dependent on the given circumstances in which it operates.[15]

In the second step, Gadamer rehabilitates the cognitive and directive contribution of "prejudice" [*Vorurteil*] thus construed, and links it to a source of deeper "authority" that takes priority over the presumptions of "neutral" reason:

> History does not belong to us, but we belong to it ... [and so] the real consequence of the enlightenment is different [from what it proclaims]: namely, the subjection of all authority to reason [which is itself prejudiced against "legitimate prejudices, if we want to do justice to man's finite, historical mode of being"].[16]

Gadamer means by the "authority" of history and tradition the effective formative processes of a society by which we, as linguistically apt selves, are *first* made apt for all those activities that are usually collected as the exercise of theoretical and practical reason. This is not always clear in Gadamer: sometimes, it is true, "tradition" is meant not merely in the holistic sense in which specifically human life is lived in the "medium" of social traditions, but also in the determinate sense in which "traditional" answers to moral and political questions are, effectively, the right answers. Needless to say, the latter is always arbitrary – or undefended; Gadamer never affirms it in so many words, but it lurks in his account of the "classical."

I draw three important findings from Gadamer's account: first, that reason is an artifact of history, preformed in a variable way by the horizonal saliencies of one history or another; second (though Gadamer does not address the matter directly), that, as a consequence, our discursive powers (preeminently, reference and predication) function as they do only in terms of the "concrete, historical" habits of thought that are actually operative socially – which is what I mean by *praxis*; and, third, that, in the sense intended in the preceding two findings, we ourselves are artifacts of an enculturing history. (The summary is clearly Hegelian.)

Objectivity, therefore, is a construct of history; neutrality, a construct of prejudice. "Reason" cannot completely fathom its own competence; it has a changing history and inescapably reflects the tacit perspective (or "horizon") of that history. History and tradition play no criterial role of any kind. The "authority" of tradition is purely formative (and holist). It is, so to say, the medium of distinctly human life: "we stand always within tradition," Gadamer says, "and this is no objectifying process, i.e., we do not conceive of what tradition says as something other, something alien";[17] "the abstract antithesis between history and knowledge must be discarded";[18] and therefore "it is senseless to speak of a perfect knowledge of history, and for this reason it is not possible to speak of an object in itself towards which its research is directed."[19] The cognitive fates of science and morality converge here. There is no Hegelian-like *telos* to the whole of human history; there is no changeless *archē* of Aristotle's sort; there is no neutral power of practical reason such as Kant supposes.

Grant all that, and you see at once the importance of the quarrel between Habermas and Gadamer and the inherent untenability of Habermas's position. The quarrel concerns the supposed objectivity and neutrality of reason – its "universality," as Habermas and Apel are fond of saying. But Habermas concedes that *reason is a historically formed, historically emergent, competence*. At a stroke, therefore, the neutrality of reason is put at insuperable risk: *not* the very idea of neutrality or objectivity when viewed as a reasonable (constructive) *posit* matching our best (constructive) conjectures about science and morality, but only as a supposedly antonomous, original source for such neutrality. If you grasp the point, you cannot fail to see that it cuts against Rawls and MacIntyre with equal ease.

The quarrel between Habermas and Gadamer has a certain slack quality, however, that threatens to be interminable and unhelpful. I have no wish to fuel it further. But I am afraid that if I do not provide fair specimens of their opposed views, you may not see the full hopelessness of Habermas's "Kantian" claim or the nearly complete lack of interest on Gadamer's part to recover what is to count (*now*), under the "hermeneutic" conditions imposed, as the marks of objective rigor in judgment. The point is this: once reason is acknowledged to be historically constituted – whatever we take to be our cognitive and active competences – we must abandon all second- and third-tier strategies. Fourth-tier legitimation will then be seen to be the legitimation of ideologies; but, more than that, it will be seen to be a form of ideology itself: the legitimation of legitimation. There's a paradox there, but I believe it to be benign.

In any case, here is Habermas's fatal concession:

Moral universalism is a *historical result*. It arose, with Rousseau and Kant, in the midst of a specific society that possessed corresponding features. The last two or three centuries have witnessed the emergence, after a long see-sawing struggle, of a *directed* trend toward the realization of basic rights. This process has led to, shall we cautiously say, a less and less selective reading and utilization of the universalistic meaning that fundamental-rights norms have; it testifies to the "existence of reason," if only in bits and pieces. Without these fragmentary realizations, the moral intuitions that discourse ethics conceptualizes would never have proliferated the way they did. To be sure, the gradual embodiment of moral principles in concrete forms of life is not something that can safely be left to Hegel's absolute spirit. Rather, it is chiefly a function of collective efforts and sacrifices made by sociopolitical movements.[20]

I now add, without further comment, a well-known remark of Gadamer's, which, in effect, makes explicit the consequence of *Habermas's* concession to historicity (to hermeneutics, in effect):

> We say ... that understanding and misunderstanding take place between I and thou. But the formulation "I and thou" already betrays an enormous alienation. There is nothing like an "I and thou" at all [that is, primordially, invariantly] – there is neither the I nor the thou as isolated, substantial realities. I may say "thou" and I may refer to myself over against a thou, but a common understanding [*Verständigung*] always precedes these situations [an actual tradition that we share, that we emerge within, that actually forms us and mediates our understanding][21]

My sense is that the secret doctrine – the one that dies so slowly but is hardly noticed – in both continental European thought and in Anglo-American thought – the one that controls the fate of the entire dispute, is the single notion that *there must, necessarily be a neutral language into which all intelligible languages may be translated – because an "intelligible" language is a "translatable" language!* The argument is a palpable *non sequitur*. For how can we possibly demonstrate that what, within the (incompletely fathomable) horizon of society A, is regarded as a translation of utterances generated within B – or, for that matter, is so regarded by the apt bilinguals of A and B – *is* neutral in any sense other than the sense in which neutrality is itself a consensual artifact plausibly idealized by the speakers of A (or the speakers of A and B)?

Habermas's claim may be permitted to stand, therefore – though not its conclusion, namely, that "the trait that all traditional languages have in common and that guarantees their transcendental unity [is] the fact that in principle they can all be translated into one another."[22] There is, however, no sense as yet (and no demonstration supporting the sense) that Habermas has discovered a modal invariance (a "transcendental unity") of any sort. I remind you that when Rawls argues about the reflection of rational agents in "the original position," he is committing himself, in speaking of "reason," to an analogue of Habermas's thesis.

I also find no difference in this regard between Habermas's claim and the one Donald Davidson has made so famous in his attack on plural "conceptual schemes."[23] There, Davidson explicitly says, arguing against the conceivability of plural conceptual schemes (the analytic counterpart of Gadamer's notions of prejudice and horizonality), that:

> The failure of intertranslatability is a necessary condition for difference in conceptual schemes; the common relation to experience or the evidence is what is supposed to make sense of the claim that it is languages or schemes that are under consideration where translation fails. It is essential to this idea [Davidson insists] that there be something neutral and common that lies outside all schemes.[24]

Davidson means that the advocates of plural conceptual schemes (Kuhn, Feyerabend, Whorf) contradict themselves and, in any case, support an incoherent thesis: because, for one thing, they presuppose (and yet deny) a neutral "something" in merely formulating their own claims; and, for another, the very idea of "a difference of conceptual schemes" makes no sense apart from admitting a neutral "something" in virtue of which that difference may be said to be (thus) identifiable (and hence defeated).

But Davidson's argument, like Habermas's, is a *non sequitur* and a *petitio*. In fact, it is the same argument. First of all, we have no operative criterion of translat*ability* – or translatability into a neutral language. Second, failure of translat*ation* does not signify a failure of translatability. Third, it is not true (as Davidson claims) that a "failure of intertranslatability is [in principle] a necessary condition for difference in conceptual schemes." On the contrary, "different" or "incommensurable" schemes may well be translatable; certainly incommensurable "schemes" are intelligible – *a fortiori*, translatable *qua* incommensurable, *a fortiori*, paraphrasable in commensurable terms even if initially incommensurable.[25]

And, fourthly, the very success of translation and the determination of both incommensurability and a "difference in conceptual schemes" are themselves artifacts of discursive practice in precisely the sense in which objectivity and neutrality are. They cannot claim any independent privilege. Davidson's objection is a complete non-starter.

I can put the counterargument even more compellingly: for, even if we concede, with Davidson, that there must be a "neutral something" presupposed in merely admitting "a difference in conceptual scheme," it hardly follows that, *in* judging that there is a difference in conceptual scheme, we must be invoking *that* "neutral something" to confirm that difference. No, the operative criterion may be no more than an artifact (*not* demonstrably neutral, therefore) *of* our consensual judgment. Wherever substantive claims of neutrality or objectivity are at stake – in science or morality – the burden of proof obviously falls to the partisans of neutrality. Not to put too fine a point on it: in their very different ways, Habermas and Rawls and MacIntyre claim a march on rationality that they cannot rightly defend. They cannot do better than Davidson here!

III

I must balance the account on the "Aristotelian" side. Remember: I am trying to establish the plausibility of invoking fourth-tier strategies – which is to say, strategies that admit the historicity of thinking, the social construction of selves, the inseparability of theoretical and practical reason as specifications of *praxis*, the indemonstrability of our occupying a neutral stance or possessing a neutral language suited to science and/or morality, and the viability of relativism. All that is now beginning to come into focus. I argue in favor of fourth-tier thinking by way of demonstrating the utter collapse of second- and third-tier thinking, the obvious coherence and viability of fourth-tier strategies, and the evidence that late third-tier thinkers have skirted the prospects of historicism but pulled back too quickly and without justification.

I have also shown (on the Aristotelian side) that MacIntyre's treatment of reason in resolving incommensurabilities at points of crisis between rival "traditions" never quite explains how objectivity is actually confirmed. For example, there are incommensurable, as well as incompatible, accounts of the defensibility of abortion and euthanasia in American society today: how might we show that one or another rival tradition was indeed *rationally superior* to its rivals? It is difficult to see how *any* argument (on the grounds so far supplied) could possibly be advanced that would not be either plainly partisan or plainly arbitrary (in the way of claiming some cognitive or rational privilege) or plainly opportunistic (in claiming a certain preferable congruity with the "preferred" tradition). If reason were an artifact of history, as MacIntyre affirms, then it would seem to be too parochial for the task; and if it were equal to the task, then either it would not be an artifact of history or else the puzzles

posed by incommensurable (as well as incompatible) traditions would
be so elementary that it would hardly matter which it was. I find neither
of these last possibilities entirely convincing.

MacIntyre genuinely tries to steer a middle course between sheer
historicism and sheer universalism. I have no doubt that such a course is
possible, but I cannot see how it can fail to be anything but partisan.
That would not be a defect in itself, for there is no reason why an
ideologue might not prefer to hold a position that was maximally
coherent and supple and even challenging to its strongest opponents. But
MacIntyre obviously believes, along the lines Thomas Aquinas develops
in the *Summa* and elsewhere, that his middle course (not a policy of
compromise) is on to the truth of the matter; that is, in the same sense in
which Aquinas tries to discern *the truth* "through an overall work of
dialectical construction" that "summon[s] up" what must provisionally
pass as the truth "internal" to the "scheme of concepts and beliefs" that
mark off, say, the rival Aristotelian and Augustinian "traditions" (that
Aquinas actually sought to reconcile).[26] MacIntyre believes that espous-
ing the historicity of reason is not incompatible with "truth" being a
final "outcome" at the end of "an essentially incompleted debate."[27]
How so? you ask. Here is MacIntyre's answer:

> In the construction of any demonstrative science we both argue *from* what
> we take, often rightly, to be subordinate truths *to* first principles (*Com-
> mentary on the Ethics*, loc. cit), as well as from first principles *to*
> subordinate truths (*Commentary on Boethius' De Trinitate*, Qu. VI, 1 and
> 3). And in this work of coming to understand which premises it is that
> state what is the case *per se*, in such a way as to function as first principles,
> we continually deepen our apprehension of the content of these first
> principles and correct those misapprehensions into which everyone tends
> to fall.[28]

What this means, frankly, is that *there is a unique truth about things per
se*; that uttering that truth requires grasping "first principles" and truths
appropriately "subordinate" to them, despite the fact that *we* are forever
caught in an unending debate aspiring in that direction but characteristically deflected by the historicity of our particular mode of reasoning.

It needs to be said that an uncompromising historicism regarding
reason cannot but be incompatible with claims about truth "*per se*" and
"first principles" under which what is true *per se* may be known to be
such. The theory of truth (*a fortiori*, the theory of rationality that can
capture truth) that I have just cited is quite different from the theory
with which MacIntyre opens *Whose Justice? Which Rationality?* What
MacIntyre says at the beginning of that account is this:

Acknowledgement of the diversity of traditions of enquiry, each with its own specific mode of rational justification, does not entail that the differences between rival and incompatible traditions cannot be rationally resolved.[29]

True enough. But this second citation *is* incompatible with the rational resolution of differences in accord with the terms of the first. There cannot be any operative sense in which (1) first principles, truth *per se*, can be invoked in historicized inquiry, or in which (2) historicized inquiry can, meaningfully, be said to approach, by increments, to what is true *per se* or what would be true under the appropriate first principles and pertinent "subordinate" truths. There is a lacuna in MacIntyre's argument: I believe it to be incoherent.

I have already shown that Aristotle's system of first principles and subordinate truths offered in *Metaphysics* Gamma fails, because Aristotle cannot demonstrate that the denial of the modal invariance he affirms necessarily leads to self-contradiction. MacIntyre makes no effort (in this or anything like this sense) to demonstrate that there are (or must be) first principles that historicized inquiry can (come to) know or reasonably assume. I insist, therefore, that historicism is incompatible with the admission of first principles; hence, that MacIntyre is not genuinely committed to the historicism he appears to espouse. There must be a deep equivocation in MacIntyre's seemingly straightforward dictum, viz.: "rationality itself, whether theoretical or practical, is a concept with a history" – that is, rationality is always historically formed and effective only in settings that take due account of the original setting in which it was formed as it was.[30] The genuinely historicized reading of MacIntyre's formula is pretty close to a definition of *praxis*; the other signifies a very clever reinterpretation of apparent historicity ultimately reconciled with a Thomist (or Thomistic-Aristotelian) recovery of *nous* and the doctrine of the modal invariance of reality. You must bear in mind that the denial of modal invariance (what I call the doctrine of the flux) is not itself affirmed as a form of modal invariance. It is a philosophical "bet," a pragmatic, negative conjecture to the effect that no such invariance *will be* successfully sustained. The denial that there must be "first principles" is similarly a "bet": it is not a first principle.[31]

There is a cognate weakness on the side of the doctrine of virtue. The countermove that is in sympathy with historicism is plain enough. If the virtues and their proper order among themselves were local to particular traditions, then moral assessments of one tradition made in terms of the model favored by another would be no more than completely partisan; and if there were a universal model of the virtues, then, equally plainly, essentialism would be entailed. So MacIntyre finds himself confronted – in the preface and first pages of *After Virtue*, for instance – with the need to strike a middle course (MacIntyre's kind of middle course) between historicism and essentialism. He says there that what struck him was the fact that

> the nature of moral community and moral judgment in distinctively modern societies was such that it was no longer possible to appeal to moral criteria in a way that had been possible in other times and places – and that this was a moral calamity! But to *what* [he asks in print] could I be appealing, if my own analysis was correct?[32]

You must see how carefully this is worded. The solution MacIntyre seeks is one that will be "correct," but such a solution will involve, he adds, some "*what*" that *cannot* be drawn from the apparent data or resources of most "distinctively modern societies" – which (of course) only baffle what, "in other times and places," *once* enabled us to grasp the moral truth! Once you appreciate MacIntyre's candor, you cannot be surprised when, on the very next page of the same preface, he says flat out – reflecting (in the sixties and seventies) on "the question of the basis for the moral rejection of Stalinism" – that

> The conclusion which I reached and which is embodied in this book – although Marxism itself is only a marginal preoccupation – is that Marxism's moral defects and failures arise from the extent in which it, like liberal individualism, embodies the *ethos* of the distinctively modern and modernizing world, and that nothing less than a rejection of a large part of that *ethos* will provide us with a rationally and morally defensible standpoint from which to judge and to act – and in terms of which to evaluate various rival and heterogeneous moral schemes which compete for our allegiance.[33]

The heart of MacIntyre's argument is clear enough, the anticipated link between what comes "after virtue" – "in other times" and in our own chaotic times – and the recovery of a first philosophy hospitable (but "rationally and morally" correct nevertheless) to our historicized rivalries. In a word: what we have here is MacIntyre's statement of *his* "original position" – the mate of Rawls's. The clue is elementary: the judgment about how to begin is already characterized as "a rationally and morally defensible standpoint." So reason cannot be an artifact of history, whatever MacIntyre may have been led to say, later, in the book's sequel. The competence of "reason" (here invoked) must be invariantly suited to the first principles on which morality depends; for "moral philosophy" is not "an independent and isolable area of enquiry.[34]

To be perfectly frank, my reading of this is that MacIntyre cannot possibly have succeeded philosophically, but *has* succeeded ideologically in reclaiming the Thomistic version of Aristotle's powerful conception (scattered through the *Nicomachean Ethics*, the *Politics*, and the *De Motu Animalium*) by a melding of "first philosophy" and historicism that permits him to attenuate, if not actually to bypass, Aristotle's own essentialism. He reclaims the *telos* of human nature in terms of a supreme *archē*, by way of a dialectical contest embedded in the plural *sittlich* regularities of our rival histories. In this, if I may say so, MacIntyre "improves" on Gadamer (the Gadamer who himself recovers the "classical" from the scatter of historicity) by not leaving matters in a mysterious and unexplained state. He appears before us, therefore, as a kind of Hegelian reader of Aristotle.

I think you will find this confirmed in the final page of *After Virtue*, where MacIntyre considers (for a new beginning) "the reconciliation of biblical theology and Aristotelianism" in terms of Aquinas's doctrine that "only a life constituted in key part by obedience to law could be such as to exhibit fully those virtues without which human beings cannot achieve their *telos*."[35] I have no doubt, for instance, that this Thomistic confidence in what must now be called the *science* of ethics (in a sense akin to Aristotle's notion of a science) is just what must have provoked Martha Nussbaum's strong objection to MacIntyre's reading of Aristotle.[36] She was right, of course, to remind us that Aristotle did not regard ethics as a science; but the issue between MacIntyre and Nussbaum is surely more than textual. Her own extraordinarily relaxed analogies between Aristotle and, say, Henry James more than risk the historicized irrelevance I have already said threatens *any* Aristotelian theory shorn of essentialist assurances. Nevertheless, what MacIntyre claims is certainly premature (as philosophy), although it is by this time quite conventional as ideology.

Turn, then, to MacIntyre's theory of virtue.

MacIntyre catches up the idea of a moral *telos* once again:

> Unless there is [he says] a *telos* which transcends the limited goods of practices by constituting the good of a whole human life, the good of a human life conceived as a unity, it will *both* be the case that a certain subversive arbitrariness will invade the moral life *and* that we shall be unable to specify the context of certain virtues adequately. These two considerations are reinforced by a third: that there is at least one virtue recognised by the tradition which cannot be specified at all except with

reference to the wholeness of a human life – the virtue of integrity or constancy.[37]

In a way, I agree with MacIntyre and in a way I do not. I agree that, thinking along "Aristotelian" lines but not along "Kantian" lines, the absence of a human *telos* will threaten to "invade the moral life" with a "certain subversive arbitrariness"; but I do not agree that the denial of a human *telos* leads inevitably to moral "arbitrariness" or to a "subversive arbitrariness" in either a pared-down Aristotelian or Kantian line of speculation, or, indeed, in the fourth-tier mode of thinking I am recommending. Also, apart from that, to insist on the point is surely a blackmail argument, especially as MacIntyre's own speculation nowhere demonstrates *that* there is a human *telos* or *that* contemporary moral life is a "calamity." (I have no wish to defend Stalinism or Nazism, for instance, but I should like to know which age did not generate its own moral horrors – consistent with its technological capacity and our sensibilities?)

I say it is impossible to demonstrate that human existence or human nature has a true *telos*, that that is precluded by any constructivist account of the human self (including the doctrine MacIntyre favors in admitting the historical formation of the many forms of rationality). It is also precluded by any historicism. I do not infer from that that historicism makes a virtue-oriented morality impossible or "arbitrary." Historicized morality may seem arbitrary, I don't deny, to anyone who, like MacIntyre, believes in a human *telos* and in first principles that permit us to capture what is true and correct (in the way of a moral science). I say only that that conjecture is itself arbitrary – philosophically – though certainly not, for that reason, ideologically unviable.

I agree with MacIntyre that "every moral philosophy has some particular sociology as its counterpart."[38] But I take that to mean that Aristotle's original conception of *praxis* is indemonstrable and that a human *praxis* is nothing if not historicized. When MacIntyre speaks of "the tradition of the virtues," he means two things: first, a tradition (like the Aristotelian or the Thomist) that may be confirmed sociologically; and, second, that *that* historically promising tradition appears, dialectically, best placed to lead us to approximate to the truth about the human condition! That is the reason (as I understand it) that MacIntyre invites us to consider the "history of [the] transformation [of that most promising tradition, in the modern world]; for we shall only understand the tradition of the virtues fully [he says] if we understand to what kinds of degeneration it has proved liable."[39] Extraordinary!

I am aware of only one line of theorizing about language that attempts to show that the very idea of classification (somehow) entails a telic element – that, rightly developed, would recover the human *telos*. The idea is a caricature of the themes of the Socratic *elenchus* in Plato's early dialogues (where the assurance wanted is plainly lacking). It appeared in a relatively prominent way in an argument of Stuart Hampshire's. Hampshire claimed that "the notion of goodness . . . necessarily enters into every kind of discourse in which statements can be made"; so that

> We necessarily have the idea of "more or less a so-and-so" as part of the procedure of classification itself, and therefore as intrinsic to any use of language in thought and in speech.[40]

The plain fact is, Hampshire neglected to distinguish between "being good as a recognizable specimen of a so-and-so" and "being good in the way in which a so-and-so may be good." That remarkable oversight led Hampshire to suppose that, however attenuated, virtues (or functions: remember Plato!) form part of the natural classification of things or, more pointedly, part of the *natures* of things themselves. But the argument is a bust: first, because the idea of "a good so-and-so" is not entailed in the idea of "a so-and-so"; and, second, because (as I imagine Socrates knew) not everything is such that it makes sense to say that, by consulting its "nature," one can discover what *its* appropriate virtue is. Baboons are not good "by nature," although sheepdogs are – in a sense that obviously turns victory into defeat. By the same token, human beings have no telic nature, though shepherds "do."[41]

Now, the bearing of all this on MacIntyre's theory is plain. For, what it confirms is that the idea of a virtue cannot be shown to be entailed in the idea of what it is to be a human being, and that the idea of what the true virtue of human existence or human nature is is not internal to the idea of human existence or human nature itself – *because human selves have no essential nature, are only what they are historically formed to be or to be capable of making of themselves*. (In a way, this *is* the Nietzschean and Foucauldian theme.) Foucault has been credited with opposing every invented ontology that makes the world favorably disposed *ontologically* to any supposed human purpose and interest – *a fortiori*, favorably disposed to our essentialist ontologies of ourselves as well.[42] I should say that MacIntyre falls rather easily under the scope of that complaint.

I am lingering over MacIntyre's theory because it is, in my opinion, the most challenging late-"Aristotelian" exemplar that we are likely to find, that avoids a frontal acceptance of essentialism and that tries to reconcile an Aristotelian strategy with historicism. I say that it ultimately fails – in a knockdown way – but it is, also, the only exemplar that manages to unite a theory of "reason" (at once theoretical and practical) with a theory of virtue. I regard it, therefore, together with Lovibond's argument, as betraying the incapacity or unwillingness of all third-tier theories that admit the historicity of reason and tradition to go on to a full-blown reliance on fourth-tier strategies. (Habermas's argument is very nearly the only prominent specimen on the "Kantian" side that risks the historicity of reason. It does that only timidly, but Habermas's quarrel with Gadamer shows very clearly that the "Kantians" cannot really afford to admit the full artifactuality of reason.)

It is essential, from my perspective, that MacIntyre elects to read Aristotle in accord with Aquinas, although I concede that it might be very difficult otherwise to avoid the imminent relativism of the historicist option. I see Gadamer and Lovibond as having invented alternative maneuvers, but their failure is even more transparent than MacIntyre's. In any case, MacIntyre makes a welcome effort to explain how we should understand a virtue-centered morality under historicized conditions. I need to pursue this issue before bringing my account of MacIntyre to a close. Be patient, please.

The single most important feature of MacIntyre's account of the virtues and their relationship to institutional practices lies with the fact that that account *looks* entirely neutral and straightforward but is not. It may seem ungenerous to say so in advance of giving MacIntyre an inning. But I have already laid out a great deal of MacIntyre's theory, and what still needs to be said can be very much shortened (you will see) by my warning you (in advance) of its particular tendentiousness. What MacIntyre says about the virtues does recover the ancient policy of bringing society at large (the *polis*, in the Greek world) into harmony with the condition of human existence (the *psyche*, in Plato and Aristotle). I should myself insist on that, although it does not affect the assessment of MacIntyre's thesis. Here is its principal premiss:

> By a "practice" I am going to mean [MacIntyre says] any coherent and complex form of socially established cooperative human activity through which goods internal to the form of activity are realized in the course of trying to achieve those standards of excellence which are appropriate to, and partially definitive of, that form of activity, with the result that human powers to achieve excellence, and human concepts of the ends and goods involved, are systematically extended.[43]

MacIntyre adds at once – fatefully, as it turns out – that he is concerned only with "internal," not "external" goods: that is, with such goods (as he pointedly says) as "can only be identified and recognized by the experience of participating in the practice in question. Those who lack the relevant experience are incompetent thereby as judges of internal goods."[44]

> A practice [he goes on] involves standards of excellence and obedience to rules as well as the achievement of goods. To enter into a practice is to accept the authority of those standards and the inadequacy of my own performance as judged by them. It is to subject my own attitudes, choices, preferences and tastes to the standards which currently and partially define the practice. . . . In the realm of practices the authority of both goods and standards operates in such a way as to rule out all subjectivist and emotivist analyses of judgment.[45]

Hence, finally: "A virtue is an acquired human quality the possession and exercise of which tends to enable us to achieve those goods which are internal to practices and the lack of which effectively prevents us from achieving any such goods."[46]

If you look carefully at these remarks, you will see that the virtues are defined in terms of goods internal to institutional practices and that the practices pertinent to moral review (as far as virtues are concerned) are limited to those that are at least "partially defined" by them. That means that MacIntyre does *not* include within the scope of his theory *any practices for which goods and virtues can only be specified as externally imposed on them* (by whatever theoretical means we choose). That is extraordinary, partly because, whatever may have been true in the past – for instance, for the periods MacIntyre favors (however disputably) – modern and contemporary institutions tend *not* to be definable by goods "internal" to themselves; they tend not to be such, therefore, that virtues could be defined by way of goods internal to given practices. Possibly, the game of chess might meet MacIntyre's model, certainly not a modern market economy. Does that mean that the market betrays the "kinds of degeneration" MacIntyre has warned us about? Apart from that, it's clear that MacIntyre's theory of virtue cannot be disjoined from his account of the human *telos* and moral principles already noted. The additional warning about those who have not participated in the requisite practices rings a little hollow, since it begs the question of just *what* is morally at stake. In short, the notion that the virtues are (1) internal to a practice and (2) conformable with the human *telos* strips historicism of its essential charge – reduces history to a play of ("Aristotelian") appearances that confirm our constant nature.

IV

Nothing more need be said about MacIntyre's model. It pretends to be hospitable to historicism but it is not. Everything that may now be added is bound to be colored by its ulterior commitment to the ahistorical invariances it acknowledges but never defends. I believe that this explains MacIntyre's peculiarly sanguine treatment of incompatible and incommensurable traditions. Of course, it also exposes in a serendipitous way Rawls's naivety, since Rawls makes no proper provision for the diversity of "reason." MacIntyre admits the obvious about diversity, but he mutes its force through his overriding loyalty to St Thomas. His concern with the catalogue of virtues also threatens (for related reasons) the continued relevance of Hume's immensely appealing *Treatise*, for how can we now be sure that Hume's account of eighteenth-century sensibilities can have much to do with twentieth-century moral concerns or with those of admittedly alien societies? One has only to scan what, in the *Treatise*, Hume terms "natural virtues" to realize that they are inseparable from the eighteenth-century *praxis* Hume was reviewing (meekness, moderation, clemency, frugality, for instance).[47]

There's the important lesson to be drawn from MacIntyre as well – against MacIntyre's own use of it. What it suggests, what I believe is true but cannot stop to demonstrate,[48] is that the legitimation of morality is the legitimation of moral ideologies, because neither practical reason nor virtue nor any comparably large theme of moral theory is meaningful apart from the historical *praxis* in which it arises and has its primary application.

To concede the point is to raise anew the enormously baffling unanswered question of what *is* "common" and what accounts for what is "common" in the repeated – valid – use of the same general predicates. It is to acknowledge, of course, nothing less than the bothersome conundrum behind the ancient doctrine of "universals." What I say is that the solution to that puzzle is inseparable from the right assessment of the compared resources of third- and fourth-tier thinking. Grant that predication is inexplicable apart from the *praxis* of a linguistically apt society: you cannot then deny that "reason" (whether theoretical or practical) is an artifact of history. Grant that, and Rawls, Habermas, and MacIntyre are defeated at a stroke: that is, defeated in their presumption, however differently deployed, of an essential invariance on which moral objectivity rightly depends. So the stakes are immense – and risked on an issue the full relevance of which is almost never perceived.

Ironically, the theme is strengthened by Martha Nussbaum, who (rightly) opposes MacIntyre's arch reading of Aristotle; her own scruple, however, tends to confirm the increasingly marginal relevance of Aristotle's *Ethics* in much the same sense in which historicizing Hume affects the relevance of Hume.

Following a general recommendation offered by G. E. L. Owen,[49] Nussbaum maintains that Aristotle, speaking of *phainomena*,

> will be describing the world as it appears to, as it is experienced by, observers who are members of our kind. . . . The *phainomena* are drawn [she says] from Aristotle's own linguistic community and from several other civilized communities known to him to have recognizably similar general conditions of life, though with different particular institutions.

It is true that, for Aristotle, "the human being . . . is the only living creature who has experience of the good and bad, the just and unjust, and the other ethical concepts with which [the *Politics*] deals; in consequence only the human being has the capacity to express these conceptions in speech."[50] But if ethics is not a science, and if, in any case, we are not prepared to subscribe to Aristotle's notion of a science, then the net effect of Nussbaum's adjustment is to strengthen our sense of the marginal relevance of Aristotle's normative views: both because the virtues and the other normative notions will then be historicized and because our own predicative distinctions and Aristotle's regarding these same notions will be embedded in their own historical *praxis* – in which they function first and have their proper meaning.

This is not to deny that we do (and must) generalize over different runs of phenomena. It is only to draw attention to the problematic nature of doing that – especially regarding *sittlich* and legitimative distinctions that bear on the normative. (That is what I had in mind in reserving judgment on Mackie's insouciant skepticism.)

In any case, the concession utterly undermines the point of Nussbaum's analogies between Aristotle and, say, Henry James. For if what I have just said is true, then it is hard to see how reference to Aristotle's *Ethics* can serve to confirm the validity of James's moral assessment of a society entirely different from those societies that Aristotle examines; and if James's judgment rests on its own resources (as Aristotle's does), then we had better have before us James's moral theory before we assess the match in ways that go beyond the merely textual. But that is never rightly supplied.[51]

Nussbaum cites the *Ethics* (1141b): "Practical wisdom is not concerned with universals only; it must also recognize particulars, for it is practical, and practice concerns particulars." Ethics "should not [she says] even *try* for [the] precision [of the natural sciences, that is, their final deductive closure]": the *phainomena* of ethics are marked by "mutability, indeterminacy, particularity" in such a way that subsumption under universal principles is not really possible.[52] Nussbaum believes she is paraphrasing Aristotle's meaning. If so, then the emphasis in both Aristotle and Nussbaum is on the peculiar features of the *practical* (as opposed to the theoretical or scientific); whereas it seems to me that the emphasis should rather be on *predicables* as such. Nussbaum herself says, glossing Aristotle: "Practical wisdom . . . uses rules only as summaries and guides; it must itself be flexible, ready for surprise, prepared to see, resourceful as improvization."[53] Yes, of course, but *that* leaves completely unexamined Aristotle's presumption that, *in their proper place*, universals *are* fixed and determinate.

Most of those, in fact, who take satisfaction in insisting that ethics is not a science are also inclined to insist that the sciences *are* sciences in a sense akin to what Aristotle affirms. I oppose the idea: I say it cannot be defended. My point is that *there is no known argument by which the invariance of universals can be assured and assuredly known*. That adverse finding would be required, of course, by any consistent historicism; but historicism itself would be greatly strengthened by its independent validity. The issue is a vexed one: nothing less – as I say – than the entire question of what we should mean by general predicates ("red," "round," "hirsute," "loved," "just"). I cannot do full justice to it, but I mean to sketch how it can be resolved and what its resolution signifies.

The trick is this: *if* what makes general predicates genuinely general is their conforming with or corresponding to some *real common predicables* (so-called universals) that inhere independently in the world (whether separately or not), then Aristotle's (and Nussbaum's) emphasis is the right one. But if, as I believe, it is impossible to supply any evidence (1) to show that there are such universals or (2) to show that there must be such universals if there are "real generals"[54] (shared properties), then, of course, two decisive findings will fall out at once: one, that all those moral theorists (and more) who insist on the normative invariances of reason or the invariances of real norms or first principles (Habermas and MacIntyre, say) will have no grounds at all for their particular doctrines; the other, that historicism itself becomes instantly more plausible, possibly even inescapable, *on* admitting the first.

There you have the deeper connection between the notion of *praxis* and the fate of third- and fourth-tier strategies. For my present purpose, it is enough to draw your attention to the fact that the theory of universals is *utterly useless* (epistemically) because it is impossible to prise predicates and predicables apart; although it is not unreasonable to hold that there *are* "real generals," even lawlike generals, and that not all predicates correspond to such predicables.[55] For, on any viable theory, "real generals" cannot be, and cannot be shown to be, anything but artifacts of our consensual practice.

I believe this to be the single most important theme in Wittgenstein's *Investigations* and *On Certainty* – formulated (by Wittgenstein) in terms that happen to ignore the historical dimension of societal life but that remain compatible with historicity nevertheless. I know of no more compelling approach to the analysis of general predicates than Wittgenstein's. On the one hand, there *must be* "real generals"; otherwise, the spontaneous fluency of natural-language discourse (and science) would be impossible. On the other hand, we cannot meaningfully claim that there *are* real universals, because predication makes no sense if it is not cognitively construed, and universals (on any testable view: *a fortiori*, leaving aside Aristotle's view of the powers of *nous)* are incapable of being demonstrably discerned. The only possible resolution requires that "real generals" be confirmed in and only in our linguistic and lingual acts. But *that* is tantamount to denying a principled distinction between theoretical and practical reason and to yielding in the direction of a historicized *praxis* and the artifactual diversity of reason.

The great quarrel about universals will hardly be put to rest by this thin maneuver. I agree. You may even complain: "You are nothing but a nominalist or a conceptualist." But that misses the most important point. On the argument I am advancing, *there are no universals*. There are no predicative *tertia*. So the ancient choice between nominalism, conceptualism, and realism no longer arises. That is the point of Wittgenstein's innovation and economy.[56]

The problem of universals devolves into the problem of "real generals," that is, the problem of how general predicates function in the fluent way they do in natural-language discourse – servicing truth-claims in science and morality. There *must be* "real generals" *because there is no truth-bearing discourse without* "*them*"! But there *are* no "generals"; none *exist*. It doesn't matter (at this point in the argument) how you explain "real generals," so long as you admit (1) that "real generals" no longer implicate universals; and (2) that no explanation that will work can presuppose a principled disjunction between language and world – *because to deny that would be to reinstate the mediating role of universals!* I have my own solution to offer, but this is not the place to argue for it. I say only that there can be no principled difference between our "languaged world" and our "worlded language" – or (I say) language and world can be sorted only within the terms of that "symbiosis."[57] The result is that real generality is Unsensual (in Wittgenstein's sense) – that is, *not criterial*, that is, *on* the model (already introduced) of "following a rule." That is what undermines Habermas and MacIntyre.

Predication is a cognitive competence, but there is no straightforwardly epistemic resolution of its puzzle – the smooth and spontaneous extension of general terms, in natural-language use, from known exemplars to new instances. What, in effect, Wittgenstein makes clear is that the confirmation of predicative claims, like the confirmation of binding moral norms, depends on (but not criterially) the consensual tolerance of a society's *lebensformlich* practices. Criterial matters, at whatever point of critical or legitimative reflection we may favor, can never completely escape the logically and epistemically informal feature of our *lebensformlich* or *sittlich* habits. That means that theorists like MacIntyre, Habermas, and Rawls are secretly committed (very possibly unwittingly) to some form of the theory of Forms. That, ultimately, is what historicism opposes.

With these distinctions in hand, you will find in Nussbaum a certain telltale confusion regarding reference and predication – or, particular things and their properties – that runs through most of the casual slippage of moral theory that would bring to bear on the assessment of *our* society what, say, Aristotle or Hobbes or Hume or Henry James says about the societies each considers. Remember: Nussbaum was explaining the sense in which, according to Aristotle, practical reason cannot function in the way of a science.

Aristotle's point concerns the universal invariance of the *predicative* regularities of a bona fide science; *practical* questions (Aristotle says – Nussbaum concurring) concern the *particular* – which is to say, not anything that has to do with predicative issues as such but only the extension of what general predicates rightly apply to. The failure of ethics to be a science does not entail that the "particular" lacks general properties. *Nothing does that*! It is only that the particulars ethics addresses (as opposed to the particulars the sciences address) do not form a suitable class of instances, a class that answers to a covering law or an essence. Nussbaum observes, correctly, that Aristotle is drawing attention to the comparative scope of ethical and scientific generalization; but she sometimes slips (or seems to slip) – construes what Aristotle says here to signify instead the absence of general properties as such. (That, of course, would be incoherent.)

Thus, for example, she says: "Aristotle suggests that the concrete ethical case may simply contain some ultimately particular and non-repeatable elements. He says that such cases do not fall under any *technē* or precept, implying that in their very nature they are not, or not simply repeatable." *But there are no "repeatable particulars."* What is "repeatable" – or, better, iterable in the way of predication – *is the use of the same predicate in discourse about different particulars.* What Nussbaum concludes, however, is that "in love and friendship features of shared history and family relatedness that are not even in principle repeatable are permitted to bear serious ethical weight."[58] But that is flatly incoherent.

What she obviously means (but does not quite say) is that the "repeatable" (general) properties observed in the context of love and friendship are not "repeatable" *in accord with* (able to be subsumed under) a scientific law. The equivocation is not meant to undermine Aristotle (although, as I have argued, Aristotle's modal invariances cannot be confirmed). What it draws attention to instead is, first, the problematic nature of *any* would-be laws or principles or norms or rules that pretend to rest on invariant universals rather than on consensually constructed generals;[59] and, second, the increasingly marginalized relevance of applying norms or principles drawn from the *praxis* of one society to the moral concerns of another. Here, Nussbaum's discussion of the moral power of James's fiction cannot fail to be at risk – philosophically. What I suggest is that she does not quite grasp the weakness of her strategy because she is not clear about the predicative puzzle. It lies at the heart of historicism, the theory of *praxis* and the constructed nature of human reason and human selves.

I can afford only a little more space for the confirming evidence drawn from Nussbaum's treatment of James, but the detour is worth the labor and the patience. You must bear in mind Aristotle's warning (in the *Ethics*):

> All law is universal; but about some things it is not possible for a universal statement to be correct. Then in those matters in which it is necessary to speak universally, but not possible to do so correctly, the law takes the usual case, though without ignoring the possibility of missing the mark.[60]

The point of Aristotle's warning is indeed that law, like science, "is universal" (necessary and exceptionless) despite the fact that the application of law to practical matters characteristically involves what cannot possibly support a "universal statement" (but may support a "general" statement).

Aristotle does not relinquish, for that reason, the truth of universal law or universal science; but *Nussbaum* fails to show that *James* invokes universal laws (or universal moral principles), or that there *are* universal laws or principles that Aristotle and James share or could share, or that she herself can confirm such laws or moral principles in justifying her bringing Aristotle and James together in the way she does:

> To juxtapose Aristotle and James [she says] is not to deny that in many salient features their conceptions of reasoning are not identical. They have relevantly different conceptions of consciousness, of the nature and taxonomy of the emotions, and all of this should be borne in mind. And yet the convergence of sympathies is more striking than these differences; nor is the convergence merely fortuitous. For one thing, numerous lines of influence connect James with Aristotle – from his own direct reading to indirect philosophical and literary influence of many kinds. But it is more important still to point out that if in fact, as I have suggested, this conception truly answers to deep human intuitions about practical reason, intuitions that recur in much, though not exactly, the same form across differences of time and place, then it is no surprise that two perceptive writers about practical reason should independently converge upon them. The problems of choosing well have a remarkable persistence; convergence on a good response requires less explanation than convergence in error.[61]

But you will not find the evidence, in Nussbaum, of the common human essence or the valid universal laws and principles that James and Aristotle share. She skirts the issue.

Nussbaum does say straight out that Henry James's novels explicate Aristotle's treatment and conception of practical reason (or better: "practical wisdom"): "if we want to know more about the content of the Aristotelian way of choosing, and why it is good, we cannot do better than to turn to [James's novels, where] the Aristotelian view is appropriately embodied."[62] She cannot offer more than similarities in their categories of description and analysis (regarding emotion and imagination, for instance); but she claims that James's novels "embody" the Aristotelian conception of practical reason – and that is neither demonstrated nor demonstrable (either in the sense that James subscribed to Aristotle's theory or in the sense that Aristotle's theory is true).

Hilary Putnam has observed, about Nussbaum's "Aristotelian" reading of James's *The Golden Bowl*, that her "view is in danger of collapsing into 'an empty situation morality' in which everything is 'a matter of trade-offs'."[63] The point, of course, is that, without Nussbaum's possessing invariant principles, the comparison between Aristotle and James on treating "literature as moral philosophy" cannot fail to confuse similarities in descriptive technique or theme with similarities in moral philosophy. You can see for yourself the validity of the charge by weighing some sample remarks (of Nussbaum's) regarding James's treatment of Maggie Verver in *The Golden Bowl*. (I shall not belabor the point.) After mentioning some episodes in Verver's life, Nussbaum summarizes the "Aristotelian" import of James's treatment thus:

> In ethical terms, what [the episodes mentioned mean] is that the perceiver [Verver] brings to the new situation a history of general conceptions and commitments, and a host of past obligations and affiliations (some general, some particular), all of which contribute to and help to constitute her evolving conceptions of good living. . . . Perception, we might say, is a process of loving conversation between rules and concrete responses, general conceptions and unique cases, in which the general articulates the particular and is in turn further articulated by it. The particular is constituted out of features both repeatable and nonrepeatable; it is outlined by the structure of general terms, and it also contains the unique images of those we love.[64]

I believe Nussbaum never attempts a firmer comparison (than this) between Aristotle and James. Also, the citation reminds us of the problematic nature of the "repeatable" and Nussbaum's conceptual perseveration on the "nonrepeatable."

V

I shall resist adding the evidence confirming the ubiquity of the presumption of moral invariance under conditions of historical, fictional, and ideological contingency. I trust I have made a fair case for one finding of exceptional importance – which nearly everyone refuses to admit – viz.: that *there are no demonstrably valid moral principles*, if by a principle one means an exceptionless normative rule (that is not tautological) legitimated by reference to some modal invariance or necessity of reason or reality. Grant that all known arguments to the contrary fail, you cannot then deny that, if it obtains, *moral objectivity is the objectivity of moral ideologies*. I do not draw from that the skeptic's conclusion. On the contrary, the history of moral philosophy has gone completely wrong (I suggest) because it has never endorsed this verdict or shown how one may escape it.

Having come this far, however, and anticipating now the end of the argument, I should like to round out the account with a few small observations and a distinction of fresh importance. First of all, I cite, for the record only, what is probably the most entrenched aprioristic insistence on invariance that one is likely to find anywhere among contemporary moral theories of the Kantian stripe. I have touched on it before; but now that we know that contemporary Aristotelians have failed to recover Aristotle's sort of modal invariance, it may be useful to have in hand an actual text (of the Kantian sort) with which to conjure – particularly as Rawls and Habermas have proved so coy in the defense of their respective Kantian programs. Here, then, without comment, is Karl-Otto Apel's well-known statement of his own *a priori* moral principle, which he calls "the principle of a dialectics . . . of idealism and materialism" (by which he means the rationale for extracting an ideal or "utopian" principle from every "material" or historical *praxis*):

> Anyone who engages in argument automatically presupposes two things; first, a *real communication community* whose member he has himself become through a process of socialization, and second, an *ideal communication community* that would basically be capable of adequately understanding the meaning of his arguments and judging their truth in a definitive manner. What is remarkable and dialectical about this situation, however, is that, to some extent, the ideal community is presupposed and even counterfactually anticipated *in* the real one, namely, as a real possibility of the real society, although the person who engages in argument is aware that (in most cases) the real community, including himself, is far removed from being similar to the ideal community. But, by virtue of its transcendental structure, argumentation is left no choice other than to face this both desperate and hopeful situation.[65]

Secondly, again without sustained comment, I should like to cite a counterpart statement (regarding scientific explanation) offered by Wesley Salmon, to remind you that arguments in moral philosophy and the philosophy of science are often surprisingly similar. I had mentioned Salmon before, but what I wish to emphasize here is that the appeal to modal invariance in science is just as much an undefended *a priori* assumption as it is in moral matters. Salmon distinguishes three models of explanation in the physical sciences, which he associates with Laplace's original conception; although he himself is hospitable to causal explanations that are inherently indeterministic.[66] He favors what he calls the "ontic conception" of explanation, which he summarizes in this way: "to explain an event is to exhibit it as occupying its (nomologically necessary) place in the discernible patterns of the world."[67] The use of the expression "nomologically necessary" signifies that the "ontic conception" entails the "modal conception" (of explanation), which may also function as an independent model. According to the "modal conception," Salmon says, "there is a relation of *nomological necessity* between [explanandum and explanans]."[68] In this sense, "nomological necessity" is not any sort of "logical" necessity; here, explanation need not, as such, be taken to be an argument. For this reason, Salmon identifies a third model, the "epistemic conception," which regards necessity in terms of the logic of argument; here, Salmon speaks of "nomic expectability."[69]

What is especially of interest to us is that Salmon traces all three conceptions to Aristotle's *Posterior Analytics* (71b 14–16), to the dictum "The proper object of unqualified scientific knowledge is something which cannot be other than it is." Salmon supports the "ontic conception" but he does not do so in the strong modal sense in which (as already remarked) Aristotle argues in *Metaphysics Gamma*. (That is, he does not offer an argument *for* modal necessity that is itself modally necessary.)[70] The trouble is, Salmon has already linked the "ontic" conception to "nomological necessity"; hence, it is difficult to see in what sense explanation is supposed to assign (in a valid way) some particular explanandum "its nomologically necessary place *in* the discernible patterns of the world." I have no wish to generate extraneous puzzles at this late hour, but only to identify the *a priori* element in Salmon's account. You see, therefore, that the argument I have been mounting against the canons of moral philosophy should rightly be applied as well in the philosophy of science. But I shall forego the effort here.[71]

The "fresh distinction" I promised at the start of this section I can now produce without ceremony. Once moral necessity is rejected, in the sense in which it is explicit in Aristotle, in Apel, in Salmon, and implicit in Rawls, in Habermas, in MacIntyre, in Nussbaum, *there is no longer any demonstrable necessity for hewing exclusively to a bivalent logic.* I offer two corollaries: for one, there is no known argument that shows that a many-valued logic is inherently paradoxical, self-defeating, inconsistent, or self-contradictory; and, for a second, there is no known argument that shows that a bivalent and a many-valued logic are incompatible, if the scope of each is operationally segregated from that of the other and provided with relevance constraints.

I should argue that the choice of a "logic" (which may be informally construed) is itself a contingent matter that depends on our analysis of what a given domain of inquiry requires or is able to support or favors in the way of conceptual felicity. If you concede, for instance, that, although moral claims and judgments take truth-values (or truth-like values), it is arguable that a particular act of suicide or a particular euthanasian act may be validly defended and also validly condemned in the same circumstances – without contradiction and without falling back to "appearances" or the like (the pluralist's option) and without thereby being unable to offer pertinent or telling reasons for each such judgment – then it may be said that bivalence should there be set aside (or "bracketed") and a "relativistic logic" put in its place. I am not saying that a many-valued logic is a relativistic logic, but I do say that a relativistic logic is a many-valued logic – one, in fact, that differs from other such logics in being willing to validate certain claims and judgments (properly segregated) that, on a bivalent logic but not now, would be incompatible or contradictory. I see no paradox there.

The paradigm for a relativistic logic is easily provided in the context of literary and art criticism: for instance, in the proliferating interpretations of *Hamlet*, where one is unwilling to deny that two expert interpretations, incompatible with one another but compatible with the text, may be judged reasonable or plausible (where "reasonable" and "plausible" are truth-like values in some many-valued run of alethic values); where, that is, the alternative interpretations may, *now*, be jointly affirmed without contradiction. I should say that such interpretations were, on a suitable logic, *incongruent* (and thus valid) even though incompatible or contradictory on a bivalent logic. Clearly, they could not be jointly true.[72] (That is what distinguishes relativism from pluralism. For pluralism regards seemingly incompatible interpretations as *true* when read as collecting the admissible "appearances" of the same text, whereas relativism would not. Relativism retires the bivalent use of "true" and construes selected incompatible interpretations as "plausible" or "apt" or the like in accord with a many-valued set of truth- or truth-like values that permit "incongruent" judgments to count as valid. Clearly, the distinction between pluralism and relativism must go beyond any purely formal choice between alternative truth-value schemes to theories about the ontic nature of different sectors of the world. The two accounts are not equivalent.)

The point, here, is that, for cognate reasons – for reasons that bear on (1) the indemonstrability of any doctrine of moral invariance or necessity, (2) the ideological aspect of practical life, and (3) the implications of historicism and cultural *praxis* – a relativistic logic is likely to be particularly useful in moral disputes. Many suppose that relativism is a form of skepticism or anarchism or even nihilism, and that, in any case, it cannot help but be incoherent. I know of no argument that demonstrates that it is impossible to formulate a pertinent form of relativism that is self-consistent.

I offer the following as a set of consistent constraints on the alethic values of a relativistic logic: (1) it is not a three-valued logic that merely adds a third value ("indeterminate") to what would otherwise be a two-valued logic; (2) it is a logic that treats truth and falsity asymmetrically, so that claims may be shown to be false without being able to be shown to be true; (3) it is a logic that refuses to treat "true" relationally, as "true-in-*L*" (for different languages) or "true-in-*W*" (for different "worlds") or "true-for-*X*" (for different subjects), or the like; (4) it is a logic that supplies additional, possibly graded truth-values (for instance, "plausible" or "apt" or "reasonable" or the like) in place of truth; (5) it is a logic that is compatible with a bivalent logic, if only suitably segregated and provided with relevance constraints; and (6) it is a logic that admits questions of consistency, noncontradiction, relevance, and the like.[73] Thus, *if*, in demonstrating that a would-be interpretation of *Hamlet* is falsified by the text, one trivially affirms (by straightforward negation) what is true of the text (what interpretation must then concede), then, of course, one straightforwardly invokes bivalence again. But doing that is not tantamount to disallowing a relativistic assessment of the interpretations themselves and is not incompatible with such an assessment. It is true that our "logic" is extremely informal and piecemeal as a result, but that (I say) is in the nature of the world. Let our sanguine logics beware.

Beyond these constraints, I freely admit that relativistic *claims* must be located in some epistemic and ontic space; alethic considerations are never enough. Put that way, relativistic *claims*, like all truth-claims, are (trivially) "relativized" to whatever is admitted as pertinent evidence. The trick is that, in relativistic contexts, no uniquely legitimated criterion can be convincingly supplied for testing (epistemically) the neutral and objective validity of competing claims. I have (you may remember) traced the failure to vindicate truth as a *Grenzbegriff* in Putnam (and, in effect, in Quine and Davidson and Rorty as well). What that means is that pluralism (a pluralistic form of realism that pretends to capture the way the "independent" world is) is, ultimately, no different from a realism that refuses to admit such a pluralized realism: both pretend to a minimal form of epistemic neutrality that neither can satisfactorily ensure. (That, as I see matters, is the futile point of the entirely unsecured contest between Putnam and Davidson.) Relativism insists on the lesson. Hence, relativism never admits any Archimedean point in our deliberations – in principle or in practice. It is for that reason that it allows "incongruent" judgments to stand as valid, whether in science or morality, within a constructed and historicized world.

The argument is very tidy now. The trouble is, it is entirely formal – uninterpreted in moral terms. I agree. There's little point to an extended analysis of moral objectivity if all that results is a picture that, however coherent and self-consistent, has no particular bearing on the resolution of serious moral disputes. I have, of course, a conceptual picture to offer. But I could not expect it to be hospitably received if readers were committed to a belief that, one way or another, an objective morality must be based on a principle in accord with some discerned form of modal necessity, or that a bivalent logic was modally necessary in some sense, or both. In this spirit, the fundamental claim and argument I originally had in mind has now been brought into clear view. There are no moral principles, I say, just as there are no laws of nature or rules of thought. Or, whatever we offer in the way of principles or laws or rules are artifactual posits formed within a changing *praxis*. It's the modal claim that fails, *not* the sense of "indicative" regularities. We risk no conceptual resources, therefore, that the canon dares claim – except the indemonstrable presumption of modal invariance itself. "Principles" are no more than the idealized "necessities" of the observed *sittlich* regularities of our world (or invented "improvements" of same). They are the instruments of effective ideology.[74]

Epilogue

A Second-best Morality

I

I am of the opinion that there is no evidence in Plato's Dialogues that Plato ever supposed he had mastered the Forms. I believe the theory of Forms is indemonstrable, a certain variant of the doctrine of modal invariance futilely committed to resolving the essential problems of human knowledge and rational behavior. There are in the Dialogues two periods, I think, in which Plato's spokesman does not invoke the use of the Forms: the first is the period of the early Dialogues in which Socrates introduces his elenchic method; the second is the period in which the search for the Forms is set aside as unsatisfactory or unfulfilled and in which, nevertheless, moral, scientific, educational, and religious questions are permitted to press in on us and are deemed answerable. What very few readers of the Dialogues bother to consider or explain is the question of just what sort of conceptual rigor remains – in either period; that is, in the absence of a knowledge of the Forms. We ought to find, say, that we ourselves are in the same logical space as Plato's spokesman since we too have put the enchantment of modal invariance aside.

In Plato, the first period culminated in the *Republic*, or at least in that part of it that leads us to speculate about what a knowledge of the Forms might be thought to supply. The point is that we approach the question by way of dialectical strategies that no one pretends command the requisite knowledge. The second period is marked by the *Statesman*, in which the discourse admits failure at mastering the Forms but carries on in a rationally disciplined investigation anyway. It is in the *Statesman* that Plato introduces the idea of a "second-best state." It signifies what we judge to be best for ourselves, (1) given our conjectures of what the best state would be like under the tutelage of the Forms, which of course we know we lack, and (2) given our assumptions about the epistemic resources that remain, knowing that they too are only conjectured to be apt in the way we suppose they are.

Plato is there describing the human condition, namely, that our inquiries appear to be directed to no more than a "second-best" science and a "second-best" morality. On that reading, *objectivity* is a "second-best" conjecture. I find the suggestion convincing and extremely witty. Apel and MacIntyre, for instance, are creatures of a second-best world who (preposterously) claim to have captured an important part of the world of Forms. The rest of us cannot possibly confirm, by our second-best lights, that they have done what they say they have done. Yet we claim to have discerned their failure to have demonstrated how to escape our second-best condition. Shorn of the grandeur of the Dialogues, that is precisely what I mean by affirming that a moral objectivity is the objectivity of moral ideologies. It's a remark confined to the Cave.

For all the verbiage of the *Statesman*, the joke is never entirely lost – and is certainly worth repeating:

> There is only one constitution in the true sense [the Stranger says] – the one we have described. For the rest of them owe their very preservation to their following a code of laws enacted for this true state and a strict adherence to a rule which we admit to be desirable though it falls short of the ideal. (297d)

About the "true state," we must admit (so the joke goes) that, although "statesmanship is a form of knowledge [we are] unable as yet to say precisely what form of knowledge it is" (292c)! Furthermore, it is clear that the entire business of government by law is under a cloud, since the "true" art would not need to be bound by laws (even if it employed them), and in any case there may not actually be a "specific art of nurture of *human beings*" (276b).[1] If this gives a fair sense of Plato's irony – and I see no reason to suppose it is farther from the lesson of the Dialogues than any other – then the conclusion I've drawn (from my own argument) I dare extend to Plato's argument: namely, that objectivity is an artifact of our "second-best" vision and that our best conjectures about what to count as objectively valid (in moral matters) cannot fail to accord with a relativistic logic. Under the circumstances, any other conclusion would presuppose something like a knowledge of the Forms.

I am not interested in textual analysis here. It hardly matters what people believe about Plato's intended lesson. If, indeed, he meant to be guided by the Forms, then he failed miserably, as all first-, second-, and third-tier theorists must. The really significant point is that it is well-nigh impossible to mention a single important moral philosopher of the Western world who has conceded the findings I've just drawn from the denial of modal invariance and necessity and has then gone on to characterize the problem of moral objectivity as the problem of *the conditions of the objectivity of moral ideology.* On the textual matter, there's reason to think Plato himself was exploring, through the elenchic rigor of the early Dialogues and the definitional strategies of the later ones gathered around the *Statesman* and the *Sophist,* what we should judge to be normatively "objective" despite our lack of mastery of the Forms.

As I see things, there is no dearth of conviction about what should count as the "best" morality. That is just what my first- and second-tier theories never fail to exhibit. My suggestion is we abandon the idea that we can ever resolve that issue – the question of which of these *is* the best morality or what is closer (than any other) to being the best. All such conjectures are projected under conditions conceptually weaker than what is canonically supposed to be needed (and available) for the task. Admitting that, we should consider only what to count as our "second-best" conjectures – under second-best resources. Those are the only resources we have. Under the circumstances, there cannot be a uniquely valid resolution. Limited in that way, we cannot but be well served by a relativistic logic. But to confirm even that degree of rigor would be to confirm, as in the two periods of the Dialogues mentioned, *that* we may indeed proceed – vigorously – without the Forms, without privilege, without modal invariance, but under our second-best powers. Very few are willing to trust such a policy.

I take Plato's joke to be just that: the exposé of the transparent pretense that the second-best state is, objectively, the best approximation to the ideal state when the "ideal state" is itself a conjecture under "second-best" conditions! The best we can do is judge what to take to be the best of our second-best conjectures when measured against one another and guided by our blind conjectures about the "best" morality. *We ourselves never exit from the limits of our second-best resources – and we know it.*

The whole of the argument comes to this: that a second-best morality is one that (1) eschews all presumptions of epistemic privilege and modal invariance; (2) treats all findings of validity, objectivity, legitimation, reasonableness, and the like as artifacts reflexively formed under the terms of (1); (3) construes our cognitive and rational competence applied to the disputes of (2) as themselves variably formed in accord with our

Sitten or *Lebensformen* (which we cannot completely fathom); (4) admits that we too are changeably constituted by our changing cultural history; (5) concedes that we alter ourselves, in exercising our cognitive and rational powers; (6) recognizes that, as a consequence, all our conjectures about ideal and second-best moralities are horizonally limited; (7) infers that our referential and predicative powers are effective only in continuous extension from the consensual usage of our own society's *praxis*; (8) infers, as a consequence, that a relativistic logic is better suited to our inquiries than an exclusively bivalent one; and (9) further infers that unconditional moral prescriptives, categorical obligations, and practical constraints that are overriding *sans phrase* cannot rightly be confirmed.

I take (1)–(9) to define pretty well what I mean by the dictum, moral objectivity is the objectivity of moral ideologies: that is, moralities that are *praxis*-centered, historicized, opposed to any strongly (epistemically) construed disjunction between first- and second-order powers, incapable of yielding first principles, hospitable to "incongruent" alternatives – in a word, second-best, judged by our "second-best" lights.

II

The question remains: what might such a morality look like? Of course, I can only offer a candidate view, knowing full well that other proposals incompatible with mine may pass muster equally well. This means, of course, that a conflict of moralities cannot be evidence, as such, of the failure of moral philosophy itself. That is already decidedly heterodox. It shows that certain familiar presumptions – the universalisms favored by my first- and second-tier theorists – already violate conditions (1)–(9). If so, then to adopt those conditions as conditions of fair debate is to have displaced hitherto canonical views about what moral objectivity comes to. I emphasize the point, because it is what I had in mind in urging fourth-tier strategies and because I anticipate that others who may wish to travel with me for a while may come to demur on a substantive matter and then complain that I have violated what *they* take to be the plain conditions of objectivity and rationality and neutrality and universality and the rest. I admit others may play by other rules – or better, that there are no rules to play by.

The single most important consequence of admitting all this is that it will make sense to scale back what we should regard as the decisive marks of an adequate or passable or minimal morality. For instance, I have already acknowledged that a strict universalism of Rawls's or Habermas's or MacIntyre's sort cannot be counted on. No change of rules will change that. If so, then there may be many events in the human world that continue to have moral significance but can no longer be easily condemned in the usual way they now are. Thus, our "failure" to resolve the question whether suicide is permissible or rightly condemned as such need not count as a mark of philosophical failure; and a particular suicide may be thought to be validly judged in "incongruent" ways – without ever conceding that "anything goes." There you have two samples of how far I depart from canonical theories (and moral policies). You may well ask: if that is so, what is the point of an "objective morality?" The answer would similarly have to be scaled back from what canonical philosophies regularly suppose a responsive answer would be like. That's no more than a by-benefit of our having learned that the tradition was simply wrong to have supposed it could ever exceed its own second-best conjectures. That was the point, for instance, of challenging Mackie's view of what legitimation would entail. You begin to see, therefore, the bite of these very bland reflections.

But I must still explain the force of my fourth-tier strategies. Roughly, (1) they search out the most commanding "best" moralities of the tradition, particularly those second-tier theories (like Rawls's and Habermas's and MacIntyre's) that are honored in that way, or else the dominant ideologies of our *sittlich* practices (like liberalism, capitalism, the traditional morality of one religion or another); (2) they then set about deliberately constructing a second-best morality keyed to the same enabling *Sitten*, that may be shown, dialectically, to avoid the presumptions of privilege or invariance of the other, that are conceptually sparer, that are equally capable of enlisting the natural and spontaneous conviction of a viable society, that are demonstrably more *generous* conceptually, that are competitively comprehensive, supple, coherent, plausibly applied, that are not incompatible with known facts or admitted norms that are still endorsed, that rest on selected features of human life that are not themselves construed as intrinsically moral, essential, teleologically invariant, or the like, and that are capable of systematizing a second-best morality; and (3) they are concerned to decide only whether a particular second-best candidate is, on relativistic grounds, as valid, "objectively," as the "best" moralities with which they must compete and other possible replacements. In this sense, the objectivity of a second-best morality is no more than a second-best objectivity! But then, reclaiming Plato's joke, there *is* no objectivity beyond that.

You may be surprised to discover how easy it is to construct a whole flock of second-best alternatives to any of the grand visions of our second-tier theories or (even more obviously) any of the reigning ideologies of the day. Nearly all are defended (and defeated) by presumptions of privilege and modal invariance. In any case, the nerve of a fourth-tier strategy is to mate, by matching, the best features of any "best" morality in a way that pertinently alters, supersedes, or discards any of those "best" features – in conceptually sparer, more generous, less tendentious ways than the ways that hold among the "best" moralities. There is no need, therefore, to invent an entire system of morality from ground zero. On the argument, we cannot even begin to theorize in a practical way unless we come to terms with the *Sitten* of an actual society. We need not invent an imaginary world for a set of "second-best" laws: we already *have* the world to which our actual laws apply. If I am right in this, then in the same sense in which (against Wiggins) the question of the meaning of life was shown to be trivial, the question of the (minimal) objectivity of morality is entirely straightforward – though neither trivial nor privileged. Legitimation belongs to the real world of human activity, and that "world" is as real as the natural "world." Doubtless, there are as many "second-best" ways of construing the reality of nature and culture as there are of construing the reality of the moral world. This, too, confirms the conceptual linkage between moral philosophy and the philosophy of science.[2] (What Mackie had failed to grasp was the fact that his own worry about the "queerness" of moral norms applies with equal force to the norms of truth and intelligibility: knowledge is no less queer than goodness.) To concede that theoretical reason is a form of practical reason is to concede that all discourse has an intrinsically directive or prescriptive function, in the sense that what is said is already shaped by and bears on human interests and cannot fail to be interpreted and integrated in accord with the rational projects of those who inquire. It is true that moral discourse often makes this (directive) function linguistically explicit (as in saying, "You ought to pay your debt by the end of the week"); but, then, matter-of-fact statements often work in the same way, however inexplicitly (as in saying, "The sun ought to rise before 7 today," spoken to someone whose interests are likely to be affected by the news). Wiggins was wrong to think that differences in such a local feature of language somehow had a decisive bearing on the legitimative prospects of moral realism.

All right. We've cleared away the preliminaries. But the preliminaries are nearly all we need. I shall now add a sketch of a second-best morality that I personally find reasonable and appealing. It has the virtue of introducing a minimal conception, one that can be reconciled with many an ampler vision and that suggests the sense in which moral concerns may have to be assigned a more modest role in the economy of things

than canonical theories usually admit. That now seems sensible if, on
the argument being favored, we are confined to second-best options and
if those options risk being incongruent along a wide front of disputes. At
the same time, we ourselves cannot expect to escape playing a partisan
role in many such disputes. I say again I have always been impressed
with the clearsightedness of Sophocles and Aeschylus in recognizing that
moral seriousness usually entails irreconcilable convictions of reasonable
validity, and even the need for war between them, and that the sheer
discovery of what is right and wrong cannot possibly be the sole
overriding concern of creatures like ourselves.

My sense is that it is probably more important that we remain –
beyond our constructed moralities – *public witnesses* of the entire history
of what, given our sensibilities, strikes us as the details of man's
inhumanity to man, or human suffering, or justice and its absence. That
capacity, after all, is the ultimate resource from which our best second-
best moralities are generated. Being a witness – in Sophocles's sense – is
not, as such, I assure you, a moral role or indeed a passive role. If we
cannot appeal to privilege or invariance, and if our moral ideologies
change and diverge in the extraordinary way they do, so that people, in
good conscience, take opposing sides on important questions of admitted
moral concern, then it will be impossible to construct *any* valid morality
if we cannot draw on widespread (but by no means universal) sensibilities that are somewhat favored biologically (without being either necessary or essential to human nature in any way), and that may be enlisted
in constructing a systematic moral vision that can rightly claim a measure
of objectivity of the second-best sort.

Two corollaries suggest themselves: one, that every viable morality
incorporates one or another such sensibility widespread and spontaneous
enough to sustain it; the other, that nothing that human beings exhibit
in this way can ever be said, convincingly, to be contrary to (human)
nature. These are very modest corollaries indeed; but, I put it to you,
they are already incompatible with nearly the entire run of the most
insistent of the world's political and religious claims. I find myself
comforted by that, since it can hardly be denied that the most monstrous
crimes the race has ever (been judged to have) perpetrated are the work
of the partisans of "right principles" and privileged revelation.

Once you have these distinctions in mind, you may consider the
following reflections, which are meant to introduce a moral vision that,
as I say, I find compelling and as far from being arbitrary as any I can
imagine. I offer two suggestions about certain key sensibilities that (1)
are not specifically moral in nature, (2) are as ubiquitous across the
range of human history as one might name, (3) are very often featured

in moralities that pretend to be "good" or "best" on privileged grounds, (4) provide a plausible basis, therefore, on which to construct a second-best morality, and (5) need not (that is, the morality so constructed) be construed as binding in a categorical or unconditional way.

Remember: the assessment is entirely dialectical and meant to be compared with the ideologies of our own age. If legitimation cannot claim privilege, then moral theory cannot legitimate anything like the unconditional force of moral obligation the Kantian tradition favors or anything like the necessary, essentialist pretensions the Aristotelian tradition favors. But that, precisely, is where (as I say) moral philosophy has gone completely wrong. I mention the point again, because philosophical habits die slowly and opponents of my recommendation are likely to insist (quite rightly) that I cannot satisfy the usual requirements the canon has insisted on.

Now for my suggestions. I shall match an invented (second-best) moral norm with a form of human sensibility of the sort I've mentioned. I concede that many may refuse the norms I offer. That hardly invalidates the objectivity of the conception I advance. On the contrary, I hold that all moralities are of the same sort. For example, I find the sensibility manifested by a great many – when, quite recently, the starvation of the Somali people became evident – a very promising basis for a moral vision that might compete favorably with any known morality believed valid in its own right. Nevertheless, many who were moved at that time by the Somali starvation did not believe that any of us were actually morally obliged to come to their aid. I acknowledge the *logical* weakness of the picture I am constructing, but I claim that nothing stronger could possibly be legitimated. That of course is what I mean by rejecting moral "principles." But what I am offering is no more than a clue to what would count as a defensible theory.

I have in mind two invented norms: one I shall call *summum malum*; the other, *minimum bonum*. My idea is this. A second-best morality ordered in accord with these two norms could, I submit, be effectively defended (as valid) against any actual socially entrenched morality. The virtue of these two norms lies with their drawing on certain natural sensibilities that do not exceed conditions (1)–(5) tallied a moment ago. To meet such conditions is, in effect, to be not arbitrary, to be eligible in a *sittlich* sense, and to succeed in a competitive way in establishing good second-best credentials. It is of no consequence (logically, hardly morally) that others may elect other second-best moralities. I anticipate that they will. Universalizability (in moral matters) is an entirely formal consideration bound to consistency and coherence of one kind or another. Universality (in moral matters), taken in the sense of some real or necessary or essential or lawlike uniformity of reason or nature, is, as I have already made clear, utterly indemonstrable and unnecessary. I claim only that my specimen norms may be made to rest on sensibilities sufficiently widespread, genuine, closely enough associated with what motivates actual moral codes around the world, so as to be not noticeably arbitrary or favored for suspicious reasons, and (therefore) extremely difficult to disconfirm. That's all! Second-best objectivity is an objectivity of competing ideologies dialectically tested along the lines I have suggested or of others that are similar.

Morality is perhaps no more than a living practice the normative rationale for which has been made as little arbitrary as possible, as generous as possible (both logically and practically), as humanely motivated as possible, as free of obviously untenable claims as possible, and as capable as possible of being reconciled with the independent second-best conjectures of others and with pertinent ideologies. I see nothing, or very little, more that can be claimed, and I insist that the considerations mentioned are not moral considerations themselves.

About *summum malum*, let me say this.[3] If human beings are moved at all by the suffering of others, they are most affected – in as uniform a way as one can find – by the most extreme and prolonged suffering of whole populations or relatively large groups, under circumstances that they cannot control or much mitigate (whether because of natural events or because of the acts of other peoples) regarding whatever are generally recognized to be salient prudential needs and human interests: for instance, those having to do with disease, hunger, starvation, death and bodily harm, pain and incapacitation, torture, loss of security and the means of acting to secure prudential needs, plagues, earthquakes, droughts, floods, the destruction of the resources of social solidarity, incarceration, enslavement, concentration camps, annihilation, the disorganization of family life, and the like. I am only interested in the fact that such a sensibility is genuinely widespread, deeply and spontaneously felt, among all the peoples of the earth. It does not need to be uniform, and it does not need to be universal, and it is not as such a moral sensibility. It has obvious animal sources, and it motivates a wide range of moralities. I draw no consequences from its bare admission, regarding right and wrong. If I did, then, of course, I should be cheating – appealing to some kind of natural norm. I insist, rather, that we *construct* a morality *on* such a sensibility (or, where such a morality already obtains in the *sittlich* way, we may construe it as a reasonable construction).

More than that, once the sensibility is theoretically isolated *and* the constructed norm, *summum malum*, provisionally legitimated in terms of the connection just given, then it becomes possible to enlarge the norm's scope in ways that are logically and practically *more generous* or less arbitrary or dubious. For instance, we may apply the notion to smaller groups, to lesser harms, along additional lines of prudential concern. Anv steps of these sorts are, *pro tanto*, steps toward confirming the objective standing of our (second-best) construction. I insist on the informality of this way of building a morality. There are no substantive arguments necessary for the validity of such a schema. Any would-be moral practice more or less in accord with such a norm can claim a measure of second-best objectivity. I see no way to fault it, and I see no way to make the relevant appraisals more precise.

About *minimum bonum*, let me say this. If human beings have any conception of the prudential needs and interests of themselves, they are bound to have a very clear sense of what would be needed for the survival and moderate well-being of the newly born among them, and they would have a focused and sustained interest in providing for such needs. However scaled back the picture of those needs and interests may be, however relativized to the resources and technologies of particular peoples, every society should have formulated a minimal standard of what to provide for the general well-being of its children. That is the motivation for the constructed norm I call *minimum bonum*. There's no question of getting it right or wrong. But no society can have resolved (through its *praxis)* Wiggins's question regarding the meaning of life without also having formulated some viable norm of *minimum bonum*. Again, once such a norm is in place, the same considerations of reducing arbitrariness and dubious motivation and of increasing generosity of scope (mentioned in regard to *summum malum)* will hold as well here.

I am certain there are other possibilities of these sorts that might be coopted in as plausible a way as the two I've favored. (There is, I feel, a certain symmetry and amplitude in the choice I've made.) In any case, you must bear in mind that the objective validity that is wanted is itself constructed, second-best, judged in accord with a relativistic logic. Remember: on the argument, there is no other way to proceed. I think what strikes the eye is how extraordinarily straightforward and uncomplicated the strategy proves to be. I don't mean by that that there are no serious complications that may confront my model. I mean only that whatever complications may arise will do so within a framework that is not likely to be put into doubt as a result – or to be more controversial that what it replaces or qualifies. I have already rationalized its informality, its openendedness, its "incongruity" with models and norms advocated by others. A conflict of moralities is bound to arise, and is not itself evidence of a lack of validity or objective standing. On the contrary, on my argument, no society that finds itself driven to *summum malum* or the loss of *minimum bonum* can be convincingly faulted (in a bivalent sense) if, even at the cost of war or the further production of *summum malum*, it acts to improve its prudential resources and powers in the vicinity of such changes. It is for reasons of this sort that I reject the constraints of universality and the insistence on categorical obligation. You may find my model too concessive, but that is also its strength and plausibility.

I have two final proposals to make. Let me introduce a third norm, which I shall call *nullum malum*. Imagine a *sittlich* morality already in place. I am prepared to honor the idea that, in general, there is a prima facie obligation favoring conformity to a society's traditional norms. Both MacIntyre and Gadamer are right to mention this. I insist, however, that no such conformity can be justified unconditionally, and I can imagine all sorts of grounds on which one might rightly claim to be justified in refusing to comply or rightly claim to be relieved of the obligation. (I should want to make room, for instance, for Nietzsche's contempt for conventional morality.) But even within an established tradition, moral doubts and stalemates sometimes occur – because particular *sittlich* norms become outmoded or because insistence on them produces seriously unwanted consequences or because their rationales are obviously privileged. Particularly where such norms entrench views tending to define the proper function or essential nature of mankind, it would be a mark of the "generosity" I introduced earlier, in connection with *summum malum* and *minimum bonum*, to abandon or modify the troublesome norm: to declare *nullum malum*, where *malum* obtained before.

This is particularly pertinent in complex contemporary societies – for instance, with regard to suicide, euthanasia, abortion, marriage, divorce, contraception, homosexuality, racial and ethnic and sexual differences, and the like. *Nullum malum* is a kind of "meta-norm" regarding (selectively) releasing a society from its own prior *sittlich* norms under conditions of historical change. I have it on hearsay, for instance, that, in Poland, the Catholic hierarchy is attempting to restore a ban on divorce. It cannot be offered as a *moral* ban, on second-best grounds; and there are no better grounds to be claimed or rationally defended. I take it to be arbitrary, ungenerous, and merely ideological. In the limit, *nullum malum* may be needed to justify moral and political revolution where the inflexibilities of a society's *Sitten* make another course effectively impossible. But then, the affirmation of *nullum malum* is already an instrument of *sittlich* change.

Let me add another "meta-norm": *adaequatio*. Remember: I am construing the sensibilities that yield *summum malum*, *minimum bonum*, and *nullum malum* as moral norms as posited in terms of dispositions that hold in a salient way over substantial populations, particularly over populations that share a form of life (always acknowledging that Wittgenstein did not favor a pluralized sense of his notion or a historicized reading of it). *Adaequatio* I construe as a sense of "collective" judgment (that is, judgment aggregated over a population, that is or is in the process of being entrenched as part of its ideology) that assesses and remembers (and is motivated by its perception of) discrepancies between its level of life and its standing with regard to *summum malum*, the accessibility of *minimum bonum*, and the causal responsibility of other peoples with regard to the comparative enlargement or reduction of such discrepancies – or, the same with regard to the sympathetic assessment of the history of other peoples. Many familiar forms of "moral" conviction regarding retribution, justice, just war, the application of international law, and the responsibilities of nations toward one another are grounded in something like the sensibility I call *adaequatio*.

If you allow the addition, you see at once why Rawls's notion of justice and Kantian and utilitarian notions of universality are nearly useless. For *adaequatio* is essentially historicized and ideological. In recent years, you will find a rather bleak manifestation of it in the Bosnian war and a very modestly promising version of it in the UN relief effort in Somalia. *Adaequatio*, then, is the sense of determining in causal terms a significant rise or fall in meeting the perceived requirements of *summum malum* or *minimum bonum* (or the like) due to the intervention of other peoples *and* the appraisal of that causal connection and response to same construed in terms of justice on both sides – distributive, retributive, or similarly cast. *Adaequatio* is the measure of what is perceived to be an appropriate fit between the (assigned) causal responsibility for such changes in the state of *summum malum* or *minimum bonum* (or the like) and the justification of an affected people's response to same. One begins to see, here, pertinent considerations bearing on the prospects of an objective (a second-best) morality that academic theorists almost never bother to invoke. In my opinion, views on the admissibility of *adaequatio* are closely linked to the preference of an "adequational" or "existential" conception of the self.

This brings me to the end of my account. What I have offered is no more than a paradigm of how to apply fourth-tier strategies critically – against actual *sittlich* practices and salient moral theories. If my strategy proves reasonable, we should have to concede that a parallel strategy would apply to the sciences as well. Also, it would entail a considerably lowered estimate of the conceptual competence of moral philosophy – which is not at all the same as judging the importance of moral philosophy itself. (I think its importance would actually be enhanced.)

The purpose of the entire argument of this book was, of course, to support the claim that all the canonical theories of the Western tradition are seriously flawed and bound to yield in the direction of fourth-tier thinking. My best thought is that if indeed moral philosophy cannot but be a second-best undertaking, then there can be no principled objection to a policy of *nullum malum* or *adaequatio* or other ways of increasing "generosity" and "relevance" and reducing "arbitrariness" in the manner sketched.

Furthermore, if that is so, then, as I say, the entire question of moral principles and moral criteria cannot, logically, be firmer than the conditions under which predication can be shown to be sustainably objective. But then, there *is* no algorithmic resource by which general predicates can be validly extended to new instances. The matter is inseparable from the consensual tolerance of the linguistic and discriminative practices of actual societies. There, consensus is nothing like algorithmic. On the contrary, predication in natural languages proceeds analogically, case-by-case. "Principles," therefore, cannot but be abstracted rules of thumb subject to the vagaries of social history.

Many will flinch at the consequence for moral matters; but the point is, the finding we are forced to concede here is *not* moral in any sense derived from particular normative convictions and it is *not* due in any way to advocating relativism. On the contrary, the prospects of relativism are antecedently enhanced by the implications of the predicative question. That is the reason *nullum malum* and *adaequatio* cannot fail to be logically informal. But I must stop here. I must invite objections to my proposal before going further.

Notes

Prologue: A Sense of the Issue

1 See Thomas S. Kuhn, *The Structure of Scientific Revolutions*, 2nd edn (Chicago: University of Chicago Press, 1970); also, Joseph Margolis, "The Meaning of Thomas Kuhn's 'Different Worlds'," in Kostas Gavroglu *et al.* (eds) *Science. Mind and Art* (Dordrecht: Kluwer, 1995).

2 See Paul Feyerabend, *Against Method* (London: Verso, 1975); see also Paul Feyerabend, *Killing Time* (Chicago: University of Chicago Press, 1995).

3 See John Earman, "Carnap, Kuhn, and The Philosophy of Scientific Methodology," in Paul Horwich (ed.) *World Change: Thomas Kuhn and the Nature of Science* (Cambridge: MIT Press, 1993).

4 See Imre Lakatos, "Falsification and the Methodology of Scientific Research Programmes," *Philosophical Papers*, Vol I (Cambridge: Cambridge University Press, 1978).

5 See J. L. Mackie, *Ethics: Inventing Right and Wrong* (Harmondsworth: Penguin, 1977).

6 See Hans-Georg Gadamer, "The Universality of the Hermeneutical Problem," *Philosophical Hermeneutics*, trans. and ed. David E. Linge (Berkeley: University of California Press, 1976); also, Joseph Margolis, *Interpretation Radical But Not Unruly: The New Problem of the Arts and History* (Berkeley: University of California Press, 1995), ch. 7.

7 See Hans-Georg Gadamer, *Truth and Method*, trans. from 2nd edn Garrett Barden and John Cumming (New York: Seabury Press, 1975), pp. 253–8

8 See Newton Garver, "Naturalism and Transcendentality: The Case of 'Form of Life'," in Souren Teghrarian (ed.) *Wittgenstein and Contemporary Philosophy* (Bristol: Thoemmes Press, 1994).

9 This counts particularly against such theorists as Lovibond and Boyd. See Sabina Lovibond, *Realism and Imagination in Ethics* (Minneapolis: University of Minnesota Press, 1983); and Richard N. Boyd, "How to be a Moral Realist," in Geoffrey Sayre-McCord (ed.) *Essays in Moral Realism* (Ithaca: Cornell University Press, 1988).

10 See Richard Rorty, "Private Irony and Liberal Hope," *Contingency, Irony, and Solidarity* (Cambridge: Cambridge University Press, 1989).

11 See Richard Rorty, *Philosophy and the Mirror of Nature* (Princeton: Princeton University Press, 1979).

12 See Michel Foucault, "Nietzsche, Genealogy, History," *Language, Counter-Memory, Practice: Selected Essays and Interviews*, ed. Donald F. Bouchard, trans. Donald F. Bouchard and Sherry Simon (Ithaca: Cornell University Press, 1977).

13 For a fuller account – on which I rely here – see Joseph Margolis, *The Flux of History and the Flux of Science* (Berkeley: University of California Press, 1993).

14 Further regarding relativism, see Joseph Margolis, *The Truth about Relativism* (Oxford: Basil Blackwell, 1991).

15 I find Marx's usurpation of Aristotle's term *praxis* a very good exemplar of how the countermove should go, without necessarily subscribing to Marx's theory of human history. See, for an explanation, Joseph Margolis, "Praxis and Meaning: Marx's Species Being and Aristotle's Political Animal," in George F. McCarthy (ed.) *Marx and Aristotle: Nineteenth-Century German Social Thought and Classical Antiquity* (Savage, MD: Rowman and Littlefield, 1992). See, also, Karel Kosík, *Dialectics of the Concrete: A Study on Problems of Man and World*, trans. Karel Kovanda and James Schmidt (Dordrecht: D. Reidel, 1976).

16 Which is what Foucault means by the "historical *a priori*." See Michel Foucault, *The Order of Things*, trans. (New York: Vintage, 1970), ch. 10; and *The Archaeology of Knowledge*, trans. A. M. Sheridan Smith (New York: Harper and Row, 1972), Pt. III, ch. 1.

17 After completing the draft of the entire manuscript, it occurred to me that I should perhaps identify several essays regarding the sciences that strike me as particularly congruent with my general thesis, without yet entailing any substantive agreement or disagreement on particular issues. It would help to highlight the boldness of recent overviews of science in contrast to the stubborn conservatism of moral theories. So I scanned – rather late in the day – Bruno Latour, *We Have Never Been Modern*, trans. Catherine Porter (Cambridge: Harvard University Press, 1993), which, on the basis of earlier work, I rather suspected would emphasise the link between science and politics in a historicized way. Latour offers some extraordinarily interesting support for the general orientation I have in mind. I am happy to mention his book as an example of a growing trend. See, also, Donna J. Haraway, *Simians, Cyborgs and Women: The Reinvention of Nature* (New York: Routledge, 1991). Of work more narrowly in accord with the work of

analytic philosophies of science, I should mention Ian Hacking, *Representing and Intervening* (Cambridge: Cambridge University Press, 1983), noting as well that, in a more recent book, Hacking makes the constructivism, the historicity, and the relation between science and morality (or politics) more palpable. See Ian Hacking, *Rewriting the Soul: Multiple Personality and the Science of Memory* (Princeton: Princeton University Press, 1995). My own sense – it is no more than an impression – is that the principal modern source of this general line of thinking may well be Nietzsche.

Chapter 1: Adequational and Existential Strategies

1 John Rawls, *Political Liberalism* (New York: Columbia University Press, 1991), p. 92.
2 Ibid.
3 Cambridge: Harvard University Press, 1970. See, particularly, ch. 3.
4 See, Rawls, *Political Liberalism*, particularly section II.
5 For a sense of the historical sources of Rawls's equivocation in analyzing human reason, see Stephen E. Toulmin, *Cosmopolis: The Hidden Agenda of Modernism* (New York: Free Press, 1990).
6 For a sense of these developments see Peter Rylton, *Russell, Idealism, and the Emergence of Analytic Philosophy* (Oxford: Clarendon, 1990), particularly Pt. 2; and A. J. Ayer, *Russell and Moore: The Analytical Heritage* (Cambridge: Harvard University Press, 1971).
7 Rawls, *Political Liberalism*, p. 91.
8 Ibid., p. 27; italics added.
9 Ibid., pp. 3–4, 7.
10 Rawls, *A Theory of Justice*, p. 140.
11 Ibid., pp. 140–1.
12 Rawls, *Political Liberalism*, pp. 110–12.
13 Ibid., p. 111
14 Ibid., pp. 91–2.
15 See Rawls, *A Theory of Justice*, pp. 456–8; also, pp. 119–22.
16 See Immanuel Kant, *Foundations of the Metaphysics of Morals*, trans. (slightly revised) Lewis White Beck (New York: Liberal Arts Press, 1959).
17 Compare Kant, ibid., second section.
18 In a sense, this is the consequence of Aristotle's attack on Plato. See Aristotle, *On the Soul (De Anima)*, trans. S. A. Smith, in *The Complete Works of Aristotle (The Revised Oxford Translation)*, Vol. 1, ed. Jonathan Barnes (Princeton: Princeton University Press, 1984), Pt. III.
19 See Aristotle, *Metaphysics*, trans. W. D. Ross, in *The Complete Works of Aristotle (The Revised Oxford Translation)*, Vol. 2, ed. Jonathan Barnes (Princeton: Princeton University Press, 1984), Bk. I, ch. 9.
20 I am not altogether willing to concede that analytic epistemologies *are not* disposed to strong objectivist presumptions. It's only that they are prepared

to yield on particular cognitions, so long as the right generic assurances are in place. The most blatant evidence of this may be found in Donald Davidson, "A Coherence Theory of Truth and Knowledge," in Ernest LePore (ed.) *Truth and Interpretation: Perspectives on the Philosophy of Donald Davidson* (Oxford: Basil Blackwell, 1986).

21 But see the preface to the second edition of Kant's first *Critique: Immanuel Kant's Critique of Pure Reason*, trans. (with corrections) Norman Kemp Smith (London: Macmillan, 1933).

22 See Alasdair MacIntyre, *After Virtue*, 2nd edn (Notre Dame: University of Notre Dame Press, 1984).

23 See Jürgen Habermas, "Discourse Ethics: Notes on a Program of Philosophical Justification," *Moral Consciousness and Communicative Action*, trans. Christian Lenhardt and Shierry Weber Nicholsen (Cambridge: MIT Press, 1990).

24 Karl-Otto Apel, "Is the Ethics of the Ideal Communication Community a Utopia? On the Relationship between Ethics, Utopia, and the Critique of Utopia," in Seyla Benhabib and Fred Dallmayr (eds) *The Communicative Ethics Controversy* (Cambridge: MIT Press, 1990), p. 41. I note that Alan Gewirth has defended (in an effort too early to have had any contact with Apel) what he calls "the supreme principle of morality" – "the principle of generic consistency" – which he takes to be both "formally" and "materially necessary" in binding all human agents and all action. Gewirth anticipates to some extent Apel's notion of "pragmatic contradiction," though he does not express his thesis in such terms. His account may well be the most ambitious effort to date to construct a moral theory solely on the basis of the self-legislating powers of reason. See Alan Gewirth, *Reason and Morality* (Chicago: University of Chicago Press, 1978). Gewirth is a kind of Kantian, of course; but he mutes the sense in which he is by claiming to "use 'reason' in a strict sense as comprising only the canons of deductive and inductive logic, including among the latter its basis in particular sense perceptions" (p. 27). But, of course, what Gewirth would then regard as "empirically ineluctable" presupposes that there *is* an inductive canon directed to nomological invariances. Yield on that presumption: you cannot fail to move in something like Apel's (even Habermas's) direction. See, particularly, ch. 3.

25 Apel, "Is the Ethics of the Ideal Communication Community a Utopia?," p. 41.

26 Ibid., p. 43.

27 See Karl-Otto Apel, "From Kant to Peirce: The Semiotical Transformation of Transcendental Logic," *Towards a Transformation of Philosophy*, trans. Glyn Adey and David Frisby (London: Routledge and Kegan Paul, 1980); also, *Charles S. Peirce: From Pragmatism to Pragmaticism*, trans. John Michael Krois (Amherst: University of Massachusetts Press, 1981), Pt. III.

28 Apel is close to releasing a new collection of his essays in which this adjustment is made clear. I have heard his read drafts of several parts of the new argument at two recent conferences: one conference, at St Petersburg in

Russian sponsored by the EIDOS organisation (August 1995), titled "New
Paradigms for Philosophy"; the other, at the annual Wittgenstein conference
in Kürchberg, Austria (August 1995), titled "Culture and Value." But I
cannot see that Apel escapes the fatal difficulty. On the contrary, the more
Apel concedes to historical experience, the weaker the argument for transcendental invariances, whether theoretical or practical. I take this to be the *pons*
of the entire post-Kantian tradition, already apparent in Dilthey and Cassirer.

29 For a general account of the coherence of historicizing reference and
predication to contexts of cultural practice – adjusted to issues rather
different from those that Apel has in mind – see Joseph Margolis, *Interpretation Radical But Not Unruly: The New Puzzle of the Arts and History*
(Berkeley: University of California Press, 1995), particularly ch. 4.

30 Apel, "Is the Ethics of the Ideal Communication Community a Utopia?,"
p. 46.

31 Ibid., p. 33.

32 MacIntyre, *After Virtue*, p. 2.

33 Ibid., p. 268.

34 Ibid., p. 269.

35 See Joseph Margolis, *The Flux of History and the Flux of Science* (Berkeley:
University of California Press, 1993).

36 See Joseph Margolis, *The Truth about Relativism* (Oxford: Basil Blackwell,
1991).

37 See, for instance, Karl R. Popper, "Normal Science and its Dangers," in Imre
Lakatos and Alan Musgrave (eds) *Criticism and the Growth of Knowledge*
(Cambridge: Cambridge University Press, 1970).

38 2nd edn enlarged (Chicago: University of Chicago Press, 1970). See, further,
Joseph Margolis, "The Meaning of Thomas Kuhn's 'Different Worlds'," in
Kostas Gavroglu *et al.* (eds) *Science, Mind and Art* (Dordrecht: Kluwer,
1995).

39 Kuhn, *The Structure of Scientific Revolutions*, pp. 94, 151. See, also,
Postscript. I have taken advantage of the economy of following John
Earman's selection of the relevant passages in *Structure*. See John Earman,
"Carnap, Kuhn, and the Philosophy of Scientific Methodology," in Paul
Horwich (ed.) *World Change: Thomas Kuhn and the Nature of Science*
(Cambridge: MIT Press, 1993).

40 Alasdair MacIntyre, *Whose Justice? Which Rationality?* (Notre Dame:
University of Notre Dame Press, 1988), pp. 352, 354.

41 Richard Bernstein, I should say, has very usefully tracked the difficulty in
both Kuhn and MacIntyre and also grasped the parallels between them. See
Richard J. Bernstein, *Beyond Objectivism and Relativism: Science, Hermeneutics, and Praxis* (Philadelphia: University of Pennsylvania Press, 1983);
and *The New Constellation: The Ethical–Political Horizons of Modernity/
Postmodernity* (Cambridge: MIT Press, 1991), ch. 3. In *Beyond Objectivism
and Relativism*, Bernstein is inexplicably sanguine about recovering *objectivity* without yielding on historicity, but he nowhere explains his confidence.

In *The New Constellation*, he retreats further, I believe, to the role of reporting how the dilemma being traced has pervaded the Western world; he ventures no resolution of his own. I take this to be the slack message Bernstein offers in the line (ultimately from Hans-Georg Gadamer): "I agree with Gadamer that we belong to traditions before they belong to, and are appropriated by, us" (in Appendix, *The New Constellation*, p. 323). Further on Bernstein, see Joseph Margolis, *Pragmatism without Foundations: Reconciling Realism and Relativism* (Oxford: Basil Blackwell, 1986), ch. 3; and *The Truth about Relativism*.

42 MacIntyre, *Whose Justice? Which Rationality?*, pp. 402–3.
43 Ibid., p. 393.
44 MacIntyre, *After Virtue*, p. 188.
45 Ibid., pp. 187–8.
46 Ibid., p. 196.
47 See Kuhn, *The Structure of Scientific Revolutions*, Postscript.
48 See, further, Joseph Margolis, "Donald Davidson's Philosophical Strategies," in Carol C. Gould and Robert S. Cohen (eds) *Artifacts, Representations and Social Practice* (Dordrecht: Kluwer, 1994).
49 See Donald Davidson, "On the Very Idea of a Conceptual Scheme," *Inquiries into Truth and Interpretation* (Oxford: Clarendon, 1984).
50 MacIntyre, *Whose Justice? Which Rationality?*, p. 388.
51 Ibid., p. 385.
52 The last of these constraints conforms with the relativistic logic sketched in *The Truth about Relativism*. See, also, Margolis, *Interpretation Radical But Not Unruly*.
53 See MacIntyre, *After Virtue*, pp. 188–9.
54 See Ronald Dworkin, "Pornography, Feminism, and Liberty," *New York Review of Books*, August 18, 1991; and Catherine A. MacKinnon, *Only Words* (Cambridge: Harvard University Press, 1993).
55 Catherine A. MacKinnon, *Toward a Feminist Theory of the State* (Cambridge: Harvard University Press, 1989), pp. 162–3. The quoted phrase at the end of the passage is from Madeleine Gagnon, "Body I," in Elaine Marks and Isabelle de Courtivron (eds) *New French Feminisms* (Amherst: University of Massachusetts Press, 1980), cited by MacKinnon. The first phrase quoted is from Lawrence Tribe, "Constitution as Point of View," mimeograph (Harvard Law School, 1982), cited by MacKinnon.
56 MacKinnon, *Toward a Feminist Theory of the State*, p. 202n30.
57 Ibid., p. 3.
58 W. V. Quine, *Pursuit of Truth*, revd edn (Cambridge: Harvard University Press, 1992), p. 1.
59 Ibid., pp. 70–1.
60 The most egregious recent example that I know of appears in Davidson, "A Coherence Theory of Truth and Knowledge." Its further application, both in epistemology and moral philosophy, appears in Richard Rorty, *Contingency, Irony, and Solidarity* (Cambridge: Cambridge University Press, 1989). Rorty,

as is often true, states very clearly how he means to proceed, where his own mentors tend to be indirect. Thus, with regard to moral and epistemological matters, Rorty announces very plainly: "Conforming to my own precepts, I am not going to offer arguments against the vocabulary I want to replace. Instead, I am going to try to make the vocabulary I favor look attractive by showing how it may be used to describe a variety of topics" (p. 9). What I am suggesting is that the existential strategy would oblige Rorty (and Davidson and Quine and Rawls and the rest) to answer in their own terms but still in a dialectically relevant way. As far as I have been able to judge, none of them ever answers that challenge responsibly. In short, very slyly, they each gather to themselves the advantages of "First Philosophy" without taking up any of the required labor. I much prefer Aristotle's forthrightness.

61 Roberto Mangabeira Unger, *Social Theory: Its Situation and its Task* (Cambridge: Cambridge University Press, 1987), p. 1.

62 See, further, Unger, ibid., chs 1, 7, 8. Predictably, the liberal rejoinder to Unger's challenge and to that of other "Critical Legal Studies" voices, fastens on recovering the concept of "the rule of law" but neglects altogether to come to terms with the moderate historicism Unger favors. See, for instance, Andrew Altman, *Critical Legal Studies: A Liberal Critique* (Princeton: Princeton University Press, 1990). For a standard specimen of "naturalistic" moral theory – in fact, for a form of what is now called "moral realism" – see Peter Railton, "Moral Realism," *Philosophical Review*, XCV (1986). I shall come to the moral realists later, but Railton's paper is distinctive in that, although he appears to be aware of the difficulties I am adducing, he himself opts in a telltale way for a form of "supervenience." The importance of this will become clear in time. For the moment, I am merely signalling the fact that existential theories raise the prospect that moral norms and values and moral truths and legitimation may not be able to be "naturalized." Of course, Kant, as an adequationist, would deny the adequacy of naturalism. But Rawls *is* a naturalist, albeit a diminished Kantian.

63 MacKinnon, *Toward a Feminist Theory of the State*, pp. 237, 241, 249.

64 Ibid., p. 120ff.

65 Bernstein, *The New Constellation*, p. 8.

66 Ibid., p. 64.

67 This is the nerve of Bernstein's earlier treatment of the issue before us. See Bernstein, *Beyond Objectivism and Relativism*, p. 8.

68 Bernstein, *The New Constellation*, p. 63.

69 Ibid., pp. 63–4. See, also, MacIntyre, *Whose Justice? Which Rationality?*, chs 18, 20.

70 The matter at issue is the point of the profound controversy surrounding Kripke's well-known discussion of Wittgenstein's notion of "following a rule." See Saul A. Kripke, *Wittgenstein on Rules and Private Language: An Elementary Exposition* (Cambridge: Harvard University Press, 1982).

71 See Ludwig Wittgenstein, *Philosophical Investigations*, trans. G. E. M. Anscombe (New York: Macmillan, 1953).

72 Hans-Georg Gadamer, *Truth and Method*, trans. from 2nd edn Garrett Barden and John Cumming (New York: Seabury Press, 1975), p. 271; see, also, p. 573.

73 See Margolis, *The Truth about Relativism*.

74 I explore the notion of progressivism, particularly in the sciences, in my *The Flux of History and the Flux of Science*, chs 3–4.

75 Bernstein, *The New Constellation*, p. 327. The remark appears in the Appendix: "Pragmatism, Pluralism, and the Healing of Wounds," which was Bernstein's presidential address presented to the American Philosophical Association (Eastern Division), in 1988, and which must count as his most considered answer to the problem of defining the "third way."

76 Just recently, a well-informed American associate of Habermas's has "explained" to me that Habermas does indeed now view his moral theory as something akin to a "pascalian bet," that is, as *not* philosophically grounded in the way he has previously supposed. My informant would probably not wish me to reveal his name, and I find it rather difficult to believe Habermas would give up the contest so easily. But it hardly matters.

77 *Collected Papers of Charles Sanders Peirce*, eds Charles Hartshorne and Paul Weiss (Cambridge: Harvard University Press, 1931), 1.173. I have explored Peirce's notion at greater length in my "Peirce's Fallibilism," forthcoming in a volume devoted to Peirce's work edited by C. J. Delaney.

78 Putnam has come to acknowledge it partially – as far as science is concerned but not, curiously, in moral matters. See Hilary Putnam, *The Many Faces of Realism* (La Salle: Open Court, 1987), Lectures II, particularly p. 28. For a sense of Putnam's relatively undeveloped views on the corresponding moral matters, see Lecture III and "A Reconsideration of Deweyan Democracy," in his *Renewing Philosophy* (Cambridge: Harvard University Press, 1992).

79 *Collected Papers of Charles Sanders Peirce*, 5.494. See, also, 5.311; and 6.7–34 ("The Architecture of Theories").

80 *Collected Papers of Charles Sanders Peirce*, ed. Arthur W. Burks (Cambridge: Harvard University Press, 1968), 8.12. Hausman observes very neatly: "Peirce looked to the future, to a fallibilistically knowable foundation – an evolving ground that is foundational as an ideal limit." See Carl R. Hausman, *Charles S. Peirce's Evolutionary Philosophy* (Cambridge: Cambridge University Press, 1993), p. 197.

Chapter 2: Moral Philosophy in Four Tiers

1 For a sample of moral realism, see Geoffrey Sayre-McCord (ed.) *Essays in Moral Realism* (Ithaca: Cornell University Press, 1988).

2 Thomas Nagel, *The View from Nowhere* (New York: Oxford University Press, 1986), p. 138.

3 Mackie, *Ethics: Inventinq Right and Wrong* (Harmondsworth: Penguin Books, 1977)) p. 15.

4 Ibid., p. 15.

5 Ibid., p. 16.

6 Ibid., pp. 16–17. For a sense of the moral realist's recovery of the similarity in reasoning about science and morality, see Richard N. Boyd, "How to be a Moral Realist," in Sayre-McCord, *Essays on Moral Realism.*

7 Mackie, *Ethics*, pp. 48, 18.

8 Ibid., p. 22.

9 Ibid., pp. 26–7.

10 Ibid., pp. 27, 29.

11 Ibid., p. 38.

12 See below, chapter 4.

13 See further, the argument in Mark Platts, "Moral Reality and the End of Desire," in Mark Platts (ed.) *Reference, Truth and Reality: Essays on the Philosophy of Language* (London: Routledge and Kegan Paul, 1980).

14 Nagel, *The View from Nowhere*, p. 3.

15 Ibid., pp. 138–9.

16 As in John Rawls, *A Theory of Justice* (Cambridge: Harvard University Press, 1970).

17 Nagel, *The View from Nowhere*, p. 140.

18 Ibid., p. 142.

19 Ibid., p. 145.

20 Ibid., p. 144.

21 Ibid., p. 144.

22 Ibid., p. 146.

23 Ibid., p. 159.

24 Ibid., p. 158.

25 Ibid., p. 159.

26 Ibid., pp. 5, 7.

27 The clearest evidence of these uncertainties appears in David Wiggins, "Truth, and Truth as Predicated of Moral Judgments," *Needs, Values, Truth*, 2nd ed (Oxford: Basil Blackwell, 1991). The passage cited is from "Postscript," in the same volume, p. 356.

28 David Wiggins, "Truth, Invention, and the Meaning of Life," *Needs, Values, Truth*, 2nd edn (Oxford: Basil Blackwell, 1991), p. 88.

29 Wiggins, "Truth, Invention, and the Meaning of Life," pp. 104–5. The citations from Aristotle and Bentham are given by Wiggins.

30 Ibid., p. 107.

31 Ibid., p. 106.

32 See Richard Taylor, *Good and Evil* (New York: Macmillan, 1970).

33 Wiggins's paper, possibly somewhat altered, is reprinted in Sayre-McCord, *Essays on Moral Realism.*

34 Wiggins, "Truth, Invention, and the Meaning of Life," pp. 122–3.

35 Ibid., p. 126. Wiggins cites Aristotle's line.

36 See David Wiggins, "Postscript," *Needs, Values. Truth*, pp. 354–6.

37 I take Davidson and Kim to have fundamentally misunderstood Moore.

Moore holds that "non-natural" properties *depend* on natural properties; but he does not hold and (in context) he would undoubtedly deny that specific "non-natural" predications (there are other forms of supervenience Davidson and Kim claim) are necessarily *entailed* by specific natural predications: there is said to be a one-on-one correlation that holds in a modally necessary way. Moore's holism clearly goes against supervenience; but in any case Moore nowhere espouses the doctrine. See *The Philosophy of G. E. Moore*, ed. Paul Arthur Schilpp (Chicago: Open Court, 1942), p. 488. See, also, Donald Davidson, "Mental Events," *Essays on Actions and Events* (Oxford: Clarendon Press, 1980) and Jaegwon Kim, *Supervenience and Mind: Selected Philosophical Essays* (Cambridge: Cambridge University Press, 1993). I examine Davidson's and Kim's views in greater detail in "A Biopsy of Recent American Philosophy," *Philosophical Forum*, XXVI (1995). The Moorian argument is pressed by Simon Blackburn, "Moral Realism," *Essays in Quasi-Realism* (New York: Oxford University Press, 1993) and, further, in "Supervenience Revisited," in the same volume.

38 Wiggins, "Postscript," pp. 354–5.

39 Ibid., p. 354.

40 Ibid.

41 Wiggins, "Truth, Invention, and the Meaning of Life," pp. 95–6; see p. 126.

42 Ibid., p. 99.

43 I have, in *Values and Conduct* (Oxford: Clarendon, 1971), shown that "ought" is often not a copula but a predicate (or, also a predicate) reasonably rendered by "oughtful." This is conveniently in accord with Wiggins's continuum but is opposed to his strong disjunction between evaluative and directive discourse.

44 Wiggins, "Truth, Invention, and the Meaning of Life," p. 132. I have italicized the word, "contributed." I should perhaps explain that Charles Taylor is also committed to a "Hegelianized" account of the realism of moral values. Taylor is not, in my opinion, a theorist of the third-tier sort – and not, therefore, a "moral realist" in the sense given. Like MacIntyre, although not in agreement with MacIntyre, Taylor is a second-tier thinker. Still, he addresses a question rather like Wiggins's question about "the meaning of life" (more in the sense of a worthwhile life than of bare threshold "meaning"); and he is a realist in a sense akin to that in which Lovibond is a realist (but without a similar sense of overcoming the legitimate puzzles third-tier thinkers mean to confront). My own assessment of Taylor is that, although I cannot quite believe he means to subscribe to the strong realism he affirms, I cannot think that he does not know what he actually says! See Charles Taylor, *Sources of the Self: The Making of the Modern Identity* (Cambridge: Harvard University Press, 1989), pp. 28–9:. We lose our "identity," Taylor maintains, if we lose our "nature"; and we lose our "nature" if we lose our sense of the objective "horizon" or historical "framework" in which we acquire our personal (*a fortiori*, our moral) identity. I cannot agree with Taylor, because the thesis linking "identity"

and "moral orientation" (1) cannot be shown to be morally necessary; (2) threatens or produces logical and ontological paradox; (3) confuses "nature" and "history"; (4) conveys the false impression that we are or can be quite clear about the objectively valid moral values we are committed to; and (5) risks our (ontological) "identity" on the uncertainties of moral objectivity. At this late date, all that is much too much to take for granted.

45 Wiggins, "Truth, Invention, and the Meaning of Life," pp. 133–4. Wiggins himself has italicized "confer."

46 See Platts, "Moral Reality and the End of Desire."

47 See John McDowell, "Values and Secondary Qualities," in Ted Honderich (ed.) *Morality and Objectivity* (London: Routledge and Kegan Paul, 1985).

48 See Peter Railton, "Moral Realism," *Philosophical Review*, XCV (1986).

49 Sabina Lovibond, *Realism and Imagination in Ethics* (Minneapolis: University of Minnesota Press, 1983). See G. W. F. Hegel, *Philosophy of Right*, trans. T. M. Knox (Oxford: Clarendon, 1952).

50 I have pursued the issue in many places, most recently in *The Flux of History and the Flux of Science* (Berkeley: University of California Press, 1993) and *Interpretation Radical but Not Unruly* (Berkeley: University of California Press, 1995).

Chapter 3: Reasonableness and Moral Optimism

1 John Rawls, *Political Liberalism* (New York: Columbia University Press, 1991), p. 61n.

2 Cited in Susan Mendus, *Toleration and the Limits of Liberalism* (Atlantic Highlands: Humanities, 1989), p. 7; mentioned by Rawls.

3 Rawls, *Political Liberalism*, p. 61; italics added.

4 John Rawls, *A Theory of Justice* (Cambridge: Harvard University Press, 1970).

5 Rawls, *Political Liberalism*, pp. xv–xvi.

6 Ibid., p. 11.

7 Ibid., p. 10.

8 Ibid., p. 243 n32; italics added.

9 See Richard Hare, *Freedom and Reason* (Oxford: Clarendon, 1963), Ch. 2, for instance at pp. 12-13.

10 See W. V. Quine, "Epistemology Naturalized," *Ontological Relativity and Other Essays* (New York: Columbia University Press, 1959).

11 See Jürgen Habermas, "Discourse Ethics: Notes on a Program of Philosophical Justification," *Moral Consciousness and Communicative Action*, trans. Christian Lenhardt and Shierry Weber Nicholsen (Cambridge: MIT Press, 1990). For a utilitarian example, see Peter Railton, "Moral Realism," *Philosophical Review*, XCV (1986).

12 Rawls, *Political Liberalism*, p. 54.

13 Rawls, *Political Liberalism*, p. xviii.

14 Rawls, *Political Liberalism*, p. 54.
15 See J. L. Mackie, *Ethics: Inventing Right and Wrong* (Harmondsworth: Penguin, 1977).
16 See Richard Rorty, *Contingency. Irony, and Solidarity* (Cambridge: Cambridge University Press, 1989) and "The Primacy of Democracy in Philosophy," in Robert Vaughan (ed.) *The Virginia State of Religious Freedom Two Hundred Years After* (Madison: University of Wisconsin Press, 1988).
17 Rawls, *Political Liberalism*, p. 55.
18 Isaiah Berlin, "The Pursuit of the Ideal," *The Crooked Timber of Humanity* (New York: Knopf, 1991); cited in Rawls, *Political Liberalism*, p. 197 n.32.
19 Rawls, *Political Liberalism*, p. 57.
20 See Mackie, *Ethics*, ch. 1.
21 See, on relativism in general, Joseph Margolis, *The Truth about Relativism* (Oxford: Basil Blackwell, 1991) and *The Flux of History and the Flux of Science* (Berkeley: University of California Press, 1993); also, more amply with respect to the relation between argument and rhetoric, "Philosophy in the 'New' Rhetoric, Rhetoric in the 'New' Philosophy," in Steven Mailloux (ed.) *Rhetoric, Sophistry, Pragmatism* (Cambridge: Cambridge University Press, 1995).
22 See Margolis, *The Truth about Relativism*; also, "Plain Talk about Interpretation on a Relativistic Model," *Journal of Aesthetics and Art Criticism*, LIII (1995).
23 See Wesley C. Salmon, *Scientific Explanation and the Causal Structure of the World* (Princeton: Princeton University Press, 1984); also, Margolis, *The Flux of History and the Flux of Science*, pp. 84–90.
24 Peirce's view is not easy to capture. The limit of "the long run" is indeed not actual; but it is also the object of a rational "hope" that accords with a full interpretation of the data of science that construes it as actually regulative. See *Selected Papers of Charles Sanders Peirce*, ed. Charles Hartshorne and Paul Weiss (Cambridge: Harvard University Press, 1934–5) 5.430, 6.610.
25 See Ian Hacking, *Representing and Intervening: Introductory Topics in the Philosophy of Natural Science* (Cambridge: Cambridge University Press, 1983) and Arthur Fine, *The Shaky Game: Einstein, Realism, and the Quantum Theory* (Chicago: University of Chicago Press, 1986).
26 Rawls, *Political Liberalism*, p. 62.
27 See Habermas, *Moral Consciousness and Communicative Action*, p. 198 – in the context of "Discourse Ethics" and "Moral Consciousness and Communicative Action."
28 See Habermas, "Discourse Ethics," §ii.
29 Aristotle, *Metaphysics*, trans. W. D. Ross, Book Gamma, in *The Complete Works of Aristotle (The Revised Oxford Translation)*, ed. Jonathan Barnes (Princeton: Princeton University Press, 1984), Vol. 2.
30 See W. V. Quine, "Two Dogmas of Empiricism," *From a Logical Point of View* (Cambridge: Harvard University Press, 1953).

31 See John Stachel, "Comments on 'Some Logical Problems Suggested by Some Empirical Theories' by Professor Dalla Chiara," in Robert S. Cohen and Marx W. Wartofsky (eds) *Language, Logic and Method* (Dordrecht: D. Reidel, 1983); and Hilary Putnam, "What is Mathematical Truth?" and "The Logic of Quantum Mechanics," *Philosophical Papers*, Vol. 1 (Cambridge: Cambridge University Press, 1975).

32 Rawls, *A Theory of Justice*, pp. 42–3; §26.

33 Rawls, *Political Liberalism*, pp. xv, xxx.

34 Rawls, *A Theory of Justice*, pp. 49-50; *Political Liberalism*, pp. 9–10.

35 For a general overview of this aspect of Marx's conception, see Joseph Margolis, "Praxis and Meaning: Marx's Species Being and Aristotle's Political Animal" in George E. McCarthy (ed.) *Marx and Aristotle: Nineteenth-century German Social Theory and Classical Antiquity* (Savage, Md.: Rowman and Littlefield, 1992). See also Karel Kosík, *Dialectics of the Concrete: A Study of Problems of Man and World*, trans. Karel Kovanda and James Schmidt (Dordrecht: D. Reidel, 1976).

36 See, for instance, *False Necessity – Anti-Necessitarian Social Theory in the Service of Radical Democracy* (Part I of *Politics. A Work in Constructive Social Theory*) (Cambridge: Cambridge University Press, 1987), ch. 1.

37 Rawls, *Political Liberalism*, pp. 90–4.

38 See ch. 4.

39 See Bernard Williams, *Shame and Necessity* (Berkeley: University of California Press, 1993); "Moral Standards and the Distinguishing Mark of Man," *Morality: An Introduction to Ethics* (New York: Harper and Row, 1972); *Ethics and the Limits of Philosophy* (Cambridge: Harvard University Press, 1985), ch. 4.

40 See Karl-Otto Apel, "The Transformation of Transcendental Philosophy," *Understanding and Explanation: A Transcendental-Pragmatic Perspective*, trans. Georgia Warnke (Cambridge: MIT Press, 1984) and "Is the Ethics of the Ideal Communication Community a Utopia? On the Relationship between Ethics, Utopia, and the Critique of Utopia," trans. in Seyla Benhabib and Fred Dallmayr (eds) *The Communicative Ethics Controversy* (Cambridge: MIT Press, 1990).

41 See Thomas S. Kuhn, *The Structure of Scientific Revolutions*, 2nd edn enlarged (Chicago: University of Chicago Press, 1970); Imre Lakatos, "Falsification and the Methodology of Scientific Research Programmes," *Philosophical Papers*, Vol. 1, eds John Worrell and Gregory Currie (Cambridge: Cambridge University Press, 1978); and Arthur Fine, *The Shaky Game*. For a sense of Peirce's influence on Popper, see Karl R. Popper, "Of Clouds and Clocks," *Objective Knowledge: An Evolutionary Approach* (Oxford: Clarendon, 1972).

42 See Hilary Putnam, *The Many Faces of Realism* (La Salle: Open Court, 1987), Lecture II.

43 See Carl Page, *Philosophical Historicism and the Betrayal of First Philosophy* (University Park: Pennsylvania State University Press, 1995), especially ch 2.

44 See Donald Davidson, "Mental Events," *Essays on Actions and Events* (Oxford: Clarendon, 1980); also, Alvin I. Goldman, *Liaisons: Philosophy Meets the Cognitive and Social Sciences* (Cambridge: MIT Press, 1992).

45 See my *The Flux of History and the Flux of Science*, ch. 4. See, also, Joseph Margolis, *Pragmatism without Foundations; Reconciling Realism and Relativism* (Oxford: Basil Blackwell, 1986), ch. 2.

46 Putnam, *The Many Faces of Realism*, Lecture III, pp. 53–4.

47 Ibid., pp. 48–9.

48 See Donald Davidson, "A Coherence Theory of Truth and Knowledge" and Richard Rorty, "Pragmatism, Davidson and Truth," in Ernest LePore (ed.) *Truth and Interpretation: Perspectives on the Philosophy of Donald Davidson* (Oxford: Basil Blackwell, 1986). I have examined Davidson's and Rorty's naturalisms in "A Biopsy of Recent American Philosophy," *Philosophical Forum*, XXVI (1995).

49 Putnam, *The Many Faces of Realism*, Lecture III, p. 42.

50 See Immanuel Kant, *Groundinq for the Metaphysics of Morals*, trans. James W. Ellington, in *Immanuel Kant: Ethical Philosophy* (Indianapolis: Hackett Publishing , 1983), Third Section; and Immanuel Kant, *Lectures on Ethics*, trans. Louis Infeld (Indianapolis: Hackett Publishing, 1963), "The Supreme Principle of Morality."

51 Hilary Putnam, *Reason. Truth and History* (Cambridge: Cambridge University Press, 1981), p. 124.

52 Ibid., p. 216.

53 See Richard Rorty, "Putnam and the Relativist Menace," *Journal of Philosophy*, XC (1993).

54 See Hilary Putnam, *Realism with a Human Face*, ed. James Conant (Cambridge: Harvard University Press, 1990).

55 Putnam, *The Many Faces of Realism*, pp. 53–6.

56 Lecture III, p. 52.

57 See, for instance, Putnam, *The Many Faces of Realism*, Lecture I, p. 17. See, also, W. V. Quine, *Pursuit of Truth*, revd edn (Cambridge: Harvard University Press, 1992), pp. 32–3; and *Word and Obiect* (Cambridge: MIT Press, 1960), §§15–16.

58 See Quine, *Pursuit of Truth*, ch. 1.

59 Hilary Putnam, *Philosophical Papers*, Vol. 3 (Cambridge: Cambridge University Press, 1983): Introduction, pp. xvi–xvii. See, also, in the same volume, "Models and Reality" and "Reference and Truth."

60. Putnam, "Reference and Truth," p. 85.

61 Putnam, *Reason, Truth and History*, pp. 73–4.

62 For a sense of Putnam's former confidence, when he shared certain views of science with Richard Boyd regarding reference and explanation, see Hilary Putnam, *Meaning and the Moral Sciences* (London: Routledge and Kegan Paul, 1978): The John Locke Lectures, 1976, Lecture II, where he explains what he means by "convergence," particularly at pp. 21–5. He has given up this view. Accordingly, he is entitled to adjust his view of "convergence";

but he has not satisfactorily recovered any viable such sense, and it now looks impossible to do.

63 Putnam, *The Many Faces of Realism*, Lecture I, p. 8.
64 Ibid., Lecture I, pp. 17–18.
65 Ibid., Lecture I, p. 20.
66 Ibid., Lecture II, p. 28; see also p. 26.
67 Ibid., Lecture II, pp. 44–5. Compare, here, Richard Rorty, "Science as Solidarity," *Philosophical Papers*, Vol. 1 (Cambridge: Cambridge University Press, 1991) and "Habermas and Lyotard on Postmodernity," *Philosophical Papers*, Vol. 2 (Cambridge: Cambridge University Press, 1991).
68 Karl-Otto Apel, "The *a priori* of the Communication Community and the Foundations of Ethics: The Problem of a Rational Foundation of Ethics in a Scientific Age," *Towards a Transformation of Philosophy*, trans. Glyn Adey and David Frisby (London: Routledge and Kegan Paul, 1980), pp. 266, 268.
69 On this matter, see Michel Foucault's notion of the "historical *a priori*," in *The Order of Things: An Archaeoloqy of the Human Sciences*, trans. (New York: Vintage, 1970), ch. 10.
70 Hans Albert, *Treatise on Critical Reason*, trans. Mary Varney Rorty (Princeton: Princeton University Press, 1985), pp. xvi, 13.
71 Ibid., pp. xvi, 13–14; see also p. 48.
72 Ibid., p. 18.
73 Habermas, "Discourse Ethics," pp. 78–9.
74 See Albert, *Treatise on Critical Reason*, p. 19.
75 As a matter of fact, Habermas himself admits the point, in defending his own procedure, which requires a "maieutic" strategy in moving from "knowing how" to "knowing that" (that is, legitimatively). I shall come to the passage in a moment. See Habermas, "Discourse Ethics," p. 97.
76 See A. J. Watt, "Transcendental Arguments and Moral Principles," *Philosophical Quarterly*, XXV (1975) and R. S. Peters, *Ethics and Education* (London: Allen and Unwin, 1974). Both are favorably cited by Habermas.
77 Habermas, "Discourse Ethics," p. 82.
78 Watt, "Transcendental Arguments and Moral Principles," p. 40.
79 Habermas, "Discourse Ethics," pp. 98–9; see also pp. 95–6.
80 Ibid., p. 97; italics added.
81 Habermas, "Discourse Ethics," pp. 96–7.
82 Habermas, "Discourse Ethics," p. 88. See also Jürgen Habermas, "What is Universal Pragmatics?" *Communication and the Evolution of Society*, trans. Thomas McCarthy (Boston: Beacon, 1979).
83 See Karl-Otto Apel, "The Problem of Philosophical Foundations in Light of a Transcendental Pragmatics of Language," modified, translation (by Karl Richard Pavlovic) also modified, in *After Philosophy*, eds Kenneth Baynes, James Bohman, and Thomas McCarthy (Cambridge: MIT Press, 1987), particularly pp. 280–1.
84 See Robert Alexy, "A Theory of Practical Discourse," in Seyla Benhabib and

Fred Dallmayr (eds) *The Communicative Ethics Controversy* (Cambridge: MIT Press, 1990).

85 Habermas, "Discourse Ethics," p. 88.

86 See, further, Joseph Margolis, "The Passing of Peirce's Realism," *Transactions of the Charles S. Peirce Society*, XXIX (1993).

87 Habermas, "Discourse Ethics," p. 88.

88 Ibid., p. 89.

89 Ibid., pp. 86–9.

90 Alexy, "A Theory of Practical Discourse," pp. 174–5. (I have abbreviated (5.2.1) and (5.2.2)).

Chapter 4: A Reckoning of Sorts on Moral Philosophy

1 I have explored the issue in many places – in ways that have proved progressively more radical. See, for instance, Joseph Margolis, *The Flux of History and the Flux of Science* (Berkeley: University of California Press, 1993), ch. 7; *Texts without Referents: Reconciling the Natural and Human Sciences* (Oxford: Basil Blackwell, 1989), ch. 8; and *Culture and Cultural Entities: Toward a New Unity of Science* (Dordrecht: D. Reidel, 1984), ch. 1.

2 Minneapolis: University of Minnesota Press, 1983.

3 Hilary Putnam, "Beyond Historicism," *Philosophical Papers*, Vol. 3 (Cambridge: Cambridge University Press, 1993), pp. 287–8.

4 For a sense of just how impoverished Putnam believes relativism to be – in effect, an impression of just how impoverished Putnam's conception of relativism is – see Hilary Putnam, "Materialism and Relativism," *Renewing Philosophy* (Cambridge: Harvard University Press, 1992).

5 See chapter 1.

6 See chapter 3.

7 See Joseph Margolis, *The Truth about Relativism* (Oxford: Basil Blackwell, 1991).

8 Rorty, I think, defeats Putnam's argument quite effectively in a recent paper, although the weakness of Putnam's claim has been known for some time and although Rorty himself has nothing further to offer of a more constructive nature. See Richard Rorty, "Putnam and the Relativist Menace," *Journal of Philosophy*, XC (1993).

9 Ludwig Wittgenstein, *Philosophical Investigations*, trans. G. E. M. Anscombe (New York: Macmillan, 1953), §§201–2. See, further, Saul A. Kripke, *Wittgenstein on Rules and Private Language: An Elementary Exposition* (Cambridge: Harvard University Press, 1982), particularly "The Wittgensteinian Paradox."

10 This is my sense of the most conservative reading of Wittgenstein's notion. See Newton Garver, "Naturalism and Transcedentality: The Case of 'Form of Life'," in Souren Teghrarian (ed.) *Wittgenstein and Contemporary*

Philosophv (Bristol: Thoemmes Press, 1994). I fancy I see a different theme in Newton Garver and Seung-Chong Lee, *Derrida and Wittgenstein* (Philadelphia: Temple University Press, 1994), at pp. 88–9.

11 Alasdair MacIntyre, *After Virtue*, 2nd ed (Notre Dame: University of Notre Dame Press, 1984), pp. 288–9.

12 Alasdair MacIntyre, *Whose Justice? Which Rationality?* (Notre Dame: University of Notre Dame Press, 1988), p. 4.

13 See chapter 5.

14 David Hume, *A Treatise of Human Nature*, ed. L. A. Selby-Bigge (Oxford: Clarendon, 1888), p. 273. (You must read this in the context of the entire – extraordinary – text of the concluding section of Book I.) See, further, Annette C. Baier, *A Progress of Sentiments: Reflections on Hume's Treatise* (Cambridge: Harvard University Press, 1991).

15 See, in particular, G. W. F. Hegel, *Hegel's Philosophy of Right*, trans. (corrected) T.M. Knox (Oxford: Clarendon, 1945), and Friedrich Nietzsche, "On the Uses and Disadvantages of History for Life," *Untimely Meditations*, trans. R. J. Hollingdale (Cambridge: Cambridge University Press, 1983). See also Karl Löwith, *From Hegel to Nietzsche: The Revolution in Nineteenth-Century Thought*, trans. David E. Green (New York: Columbia University Press, 1991).

16 Aristotle, *Nicomachean Ethics*, trans. W. D. Ross, revised by J. O. Urmson, in *The Complete Works of Aristotle (The Revised Oxford Translation)*, Vol. 2, ed. Jonathan Barnes (Princeton: Princeton University Press, 1984), 1094a. See also A. J. P. Kenny, *The Aristotelian Ethics* (Oxford: Clarendon, 1978).

17 Aristotle, *Metaphysics*, trans. W. D. Ross, in *The Complete Works of Aristotle, (This revised Oxford Translation)*, ed. Jonathan Barnes, Vol. 1 (Princeton University Press, 1984), 1011a–b.

18 Aristotle, *Nicomachean Ethics*, 1007b.

19 Ibid., 1007a–b.

20 See Nāgārjuna, *The Philosophy of the Middle Way*, trans. David J. Kalupahana (Albany: SUNY Press, 1986).

21 Aristotle, *Nicomachean Ethics*, 1011b.

22 Ibid., 1012a.

23 Ibid., 1094a.

24 See Aristotle, *Posterior Analytics*, trans. Jonathan Barnes, *The Complete Works of Aristotle*, Vol. 1, Bk. I.

25 Immanuel Kant, *Foundations of the Metaphysics of Morals*, trans. Lewis White Beck, [slightly revised from the version that appeared in *Kant's Concept of Practical Reason and Other Writings in Moral Philosophy* (Chicago: University of Chicago Press, 1949)] (New York: Liberal Arts Press, 1959), p. 6 (p. 390: Akadamie edition).

26 Bernard Williams, *Ethics and the Limits of Philosophy* (Cambridge: Harvard University Press, 1985) pp. 62–3. See the rest of ch. 4.

27 Ibid., p. 64.

28 See Ibid., pp. 66–7. Nevertheless, I don't think Williams's objections get to

the heart of the matter, because (contrary to what Williams says) there is reason to think Kant would never treat moral or practical reasoning as "first-personal"; and because, in spite of that, assuming reason to be "pure," it must be shared by "all rational beings" (not merely human agents). See Kant, *Foundations of the Metaphysics of Morals*, p. 24 (p. 408: Akademie edition).

29 Kant, *Foundations of the Metaphysics of Morals*, p. 16 (p. 400: Akademie edition).

30 Ibid., p. 4 (p. 588: Akademie edition).

31 Ibid., pp.28–9 (pp. 411–12: Akademie edition).

32 Ibid., pp. 31, 33 (pp. 414, 416: Akademie edition).

33 Ibid., p. 39 (p. 421: Akademie edition).

34 Ibid., p. 36 (p. 418: Akademie edition). This formulation Kant offers against the possible pretensions of the "imperatives of prudence." I am applying it, against Kant's own intention, against moral imperatives.

35 *Immanuel Kant's Critique of Pure Reason*, trans. (corr.) Norman Kemp Smith (London: Macmillan, 1933), pp. 26–7. The letter to Herz appears in *Immanuel Kants Werke*, herausg. Ernst Cassirer: Band IX (*Briefe von und an Kant*. Erster Teil, 1744-1789) (Berlin: Bruno Cassirer, 1918).

36 See Edmund Husserl, *Cartesian Meditations: An Introduction to Phenomenology*, trans. Dorion Cairns (The Hague: Martinus Nijhoff, 1960), particularly the Fifth Meditation; and Eugen Fink, *Sixth Cartesian Meditation: The Idea of a Transcendental Theory of Method*, trans. Ronald Bruzina (Bloomington: Indiana University Press, 1993). Bruzina affords a very clear sense of Fink's concern about Husserl's "system" in his "Translator's Introduction"; see, particularly, pp. xxxvi–lxix.

37 For a phenomenological assessment of Kant's moral philosophy, see the brief account by Robert Sokolowski, *Moral Action*: A *Phenomenological Study* (Bloomington: Indiana University Press, 1985), Appendix D.

38 See Michel Foucault, *The Order of Things An Archaeology of the Human Sciences*, trans. (New York: Vintage, 1970), ch. 10.

39 *Immanuel Kant's Critique of Pure Reason*, p. 33.

40 See Joseph Margolis, *Historied Thought. Constructed World: A Conceptual Primer at the Turn of the Millennium* (Berkeley: University of California Press, 1995).

41 See W. V. Quine, *Word and Object* (Cambridge: MIT Press, 1960), §§37–8.

42 For a sustained discussion of the difference between Marx's and Aristotle's account, see Joseph Margolis, "Praxis and Meaning: Marx's Species Being and Aristotle's Political Animal," in George F. McCarthy (ed.) *Marx and Aristotle: Nineteenth-Century German Social Thought and Classical Antiquity* (Savage, MD: Roman and Littlefield, 1992).

43 Michael J. Sandel, *Liberalism and the Limits of Justice* (Cambridge: Cambridge University Press, 1982), p. 179.

44 For the briefest sense of Hegel's distinction, compare, in *Hegel's Philosophy of Right*, §§108–9 and §§142–57. See also Allen W. Wood, *Hegel's Ethical*

Thought (Cambridge: Cambridge University Press, 1990), particularly chs 7 and 11.

45 MacIntyre, *Whose Justice? Which Rationality?*, p. 4.

46 See Sandel, *Liberalism and the Limits of Justice*, pp. 175–8.

47 See Margolis, *Culture and Cultural Entities*, ch. 1; and *Interpretation Radical But Not Unruly* (Berkeley: University of California Press, 1995), chapter 7.

48 See, for instance, Margolis, *The Truth about Relativism*.

49 Mark Platts, "Moral Reality and the End of Desire," in Mark Platts (ed.) *Reference. Truth and Reality: Essays on the Philosophy of Language* (London: Routledge and Kegan Paul, 1980), p. 69.

50 See Michael Dummett, *Truth and Other Enigmas* (Cambridge: Harvard University Press, 1978), Preface, chs 1, 10.

51 Platts, "Moral Reality and the End of Desire."

52 See John McDowell, "Values and Secondary Qualities," in Ted Honderich (ed.) *Morality and Objectivity* (London: Routledge and Kegan Paul, 1985).

53 Donald Davidson, "A Coherence Theory of Truth and Knowledge," in Ernest LePore (ed.) *Truth and Interpretation: Perspectives on the Philosophy of Donald Davidson* (Oxford: Basil Blackwell, 1986), p. 314. Further on Davidson, see Joseph Margolis, "Donald Davidson's Philosophical Strategies," in Carol C. Gould and Robert S. Cohen (eds) *Artifacts, Representations and Social Practice* (Dordrecht: Kluwer, 1994).

54 See Sydney Shoemaker, *Self-Knowledge and Self-Identity* (Ithaca: Cornell University Press, 1963), ch. 6.

55 Lovibond, *Realism and Imagination in Ethics*, (Minneapolis: University of Minnesota Press, 1983), p. 1.

56 Ludwig Wittgenstein, *Tractatus Logico-Philosophicus.*, trans. and corr. D. F. Pears and B. F. McGuinness, (London: Routledge and Kegan Paul 1961), 6.41, 6.42, 6.421.

57 Ludwig Wittgenstein, "Lecture on Ethics," *Philosophical Review*, LXXVII (1965), p. 7.

58 This appears in "Notes on Talks with Wittgenstein" provided by Friedrich Waismann and published after Wittgenstein's "Lecture" in the same number of *Philosophical Review*, p. 15.

59 Wittgenstein, "Lecture on Ethics," p. 11.

60 Rush Rhees, "Some Developments in Wittgenstein's View of Ethics," which follows the "Lecture on Ethics" in the same volume of *Philosophical Review*, pp. 23–4.

61 Platts, "Moral Reality and the End of Desire," p. 81.

62 Platts, "Moral Reality and the End of Desire." See also, Mark de Bretton Platts, "Moral Reality," *Ways of Meaning: An Introduction to a Philosophy of Language* (London: Routledge and Kegan Paul, 1979).

63 Ludwig Wittgenstein, *On Certainty*, trans. Denis Paul and G. E. M. Anscombe, ed. G. E. M. Anscombe and G. H. von Wright (New York: Harper and Row, 1969), §281.

64 Lovibond, *Realism and Imagination in Ethics*, pp. 154, 158.

65 See Charles Taylor, "Philosophy and Its History," in Richard Rorty, J. P. Schneewind, and Quentin Skinner (eds) *Philosophy in History: Essays on the Historiography of Philosophy* (Cambridge: Cambridge University Press, 1984).
66 Lovibond, *Realism and Imagination in Ethics*, pp. 63–4.
67 Ibid., p. 63.
68 Ibid., §§41–3.
69 Ibid., p. 71.
70 See W. V. Quine, *Word and Object*, pp. 5–8; mentioned by Lovibond.
71 See ibid., pp. 68–79.
72 On Davidson's use of Tarski, see Margolis, "Donald Davidson's Philosophical Strategies."
73 Platts, "Moral Reality and the End of Desire," p. 70.
74 See, further, Platts, ibid.
75 Lovibond, *Realism and Imaaination in Ethics*, p. 148.
76 Ludwig Wittgenstein, *Remarks on the Foundations of Mathematics*, 3rd edn, trans. G. E. M. Anscombe, ed G. H. von Wright, R. Rhees, G.E. M. Anscombe (Oxford: Basil Blackwell, 1978), VI, §23.
77 There is, of course, every reason to believe that Hume held such a view. See David Hume, *A Treatise of Human Nature*, ed. L. A. Selby-Bigge (Oxford: Clarendon, 1888), Bk. III, especially Pt. 1, §11 and Pt. 2, §1. See Lovibond, *Realism and Imagination in Ethics*.
78 Lovibond, *Realism and Imagination in Ethics*, pp. 79–80.
79 Ibid., p. 85.

Chapter 5: Life without Principles

1 See P. F. Strawson, "Ethical Intuitionism," *Philosophy*, XXIV (1949).
2 Hume is "difficult" and, of course, supremely interesting. I feel I must take a moment to explain my dismissing Hume from the rank that Aristotle and Kant achieve among first-tier thinkers. Hume is a "naturalist" about morality, in the straightforward sense in which he is primarily concerned to explain how moral judgment arises from our "impressions" and "ideas," among which the sentiment of *sympathy* may well be the most important (for Hume). Accordingly, I find section ll (Bk II, Pt l) of Hume's *Treatise* to afford the quickest grasp of his general moral theory.

There are two decisive constraints Hume imposes on the account he offers. One is inevitably muted in his enthusiasm for moral reflection, namely, his inability to trace the idea of "self" or "person" to "any one impression" (p. 251) – consequently, his inability to ensure its constancy and constant structure through cultural divergence. Hume has nowhere given a satisfactory account of our "idea" of self. In a fair sense, therefore, his entire moral theory is hostage to this weakness.

My own view, remember, is that the self is an artifact of constructive social processes (enculturation), historicized in accord with the variable practices of this society and that. But Hume, of course, speaks directly of the nature of persons or selves – in particular, of the "passions" on which moral systems depend – as, effectively, humanly invariant. This conforms with the pivotal importance Hume assigns the "simple and uniform impressions" (the "direct passions") of *pride* and *humility* in his moral system. As he says: "pride and humility, tho' directly contrary, have yet the same OBJECT. This object is self, or that succession of related ideas and impressions, of which we have an intimate memory and consciousness. Here the view always fixes when we are actuated by either of these passions. Accordingly as our idea of ourself is more or less advantageous, we feel either of these opposite affections, and are elated by pride, or dejected with humility. Whatever other objects may be comprehended by the mind, they are always conceiv'd with a view to ourselves; otherwise they would never be able to excite these passions" (p. 277).

Here, you find both the general sense in which Hume sketches the constant nature of human beings relevant for moral judgment and the centrality of the idea of self. But Hume nowhere (1) ensures the numerical identity or constancy of self or (2) the constancy of what belongs to human nature. For all the *Treatise's* charm, therefore, I cannot see how Hume can be considered a moral philosopher of the same rank as Aristotle or Kant. (I am entirely willing to concede that he is at least as perceptive about human nature as Aristotle and that he is usually more perceptive than Kant.)

The second constraint arises in regard to Hume's analysis of *sympathy* and is explicit. The context of his account is, as always, that of "the combat of passion and reason" (p. 413), which leads to the famous dictum: "*first*, that reason alone can never be a motive to any action of the will; and *secondly*, that it can never oppose passion in the direction of the will" (p. 413). (That is: "reason is, and ought only to be the slave of the passions" (p. 415).) Once you have this in mind and the corollary – namely that "a passion is an original existence, or . . . modification of existence, and contains not any representative quality, which renders it a copy of any other existence or modification" (p. 415) – you can appreciate the central importance (for Hume) of "sympathy."

Sympathy is usually termed a passion but, technically, it is (for Hume) the process or the effect of "an evident conversion of an idea into an impression. This conversion arises from the relation of objects to oneself. Ourself is always intimately present to us. Let us compare all those circumstances [Hume goes on], and we shall find, that sympathy is exactly correspondent in the operations of our understanding; and even contains something more surprising and extraordinary" (p. 320). Hume then integrates his entire theory (or provides the essential clue for doing so): "We may observe," he continues, "that no person is ever prais'd by another for any quality, which would not, if real, produce, of itself, a pride in the person possest of it." Hence, "nothing is more natural than for us to embrace the opinions of others in this particular [viewing oneself 'in the same light, in which he appears to his admirer']; both from *sympathy*, which renders all their sentiments intimately present to us; and from *reasoning*, which makes us regard their judgment, as a kind of argument for what they affirm. These two principles of authority and sympathy [then] influence almost all our opinions" (pp. 300–21).

The important point is, first, that Hume's conceptual apparatus makes no sense if the concept of self or person is not rightly secured from paradox (which, of course, it is not) and, second, that there is no argument in Hume (and in a fair sense there cannot be) to show that human nature and existence *are* invariant in morally relevant respects. It is for this double reason that I "demote" Hume. But Hume, in his deficit, is every bit as perceptive as Aristotle and Kant in their failed efforts at legitimation. *I cannot see how Hume can be recovered in his own terms.* All references, here, are to David Hume, *A Treatise of Human Nature*, ed. L. A. Selby-Bigge (Oxford: Clarendon, 1888).

3 See Richard Rorty, *Philososhy and the Mirror of Nature* (Princeton: Princeton University Press, 1979); *Contingency, Irony and Solidarity* (Cambridge: Cambridge University Press, 1989).

4 See Jean-François Lyotard, *The Postmodern Condition: A Report on Knowledae*, trans. Geoff Bennington and Brian Massumi (Minneapolis: University of Minnesota Press, 1984).

5 Sabina Lovibond, *Realism and Imagination in Ethics* (Minneapolis: University of Minnesota Press, 1983), p. 85.

6 It is not at all easy to isolate Dewey's "Hegelian" tendencies except in the abstract. For an appreciation, see Elizabeth Flower and Murray G. Murphey, *A History of Philosophy in America*, Vol. 2 (New York: G. P. Putnam, 1977), ch. 14. Perhaps a fair impression can be got from John Dewey, *Reconstruction in Philosophy*, enlarged edn (Boston: Beacon Press, 1957). See also Richard J. Bernstein, *Praxis and Action; Contemporary Philosophies of Human Activity* (Philadelphia: University of Pennsylvania Press, 1971). A very recent book confirms my sense that there is almost nothing that is robustly Hegelian in Dewey. James Campbell has located the following remark of Dewey's (from Dewey's *Individualism Old and New*), in his *Understanding John Dewey: Nature and Cooperative Intelligence* (La Salle: Open Court, 1995), p. 12: "Gradually I came to realize that what the principles [of thinking] actually stood for could be better understood and stated when completely emancipated from Hegelian garb" – that is, cast more in accord with the Darwinian model. I think this pretty well means that none of the early pragmatists really made anything of history in any sense strongly akin to what Hegel favored. That is interesting in itself, because one often hears it said that the pragmatists – Dewey at least – espoused a kind of historicism. I see no evidence of that, and I think Campbell has caught the essential point.

7 See Michel Foucault, "Nietzsche, Genealogy, History," *Lanauage,*

Counter-Memory. Practice: Selected Essays and Interviews, ed. Donald F. Bouchard, trans. Donald F. Bouchard and Sherry Simon (Ithaca: Cornell University Press, 1977); also, Mark Poster, *Foucault. Marxism and History: Mode of Production versus Mode of Information* (London: Polity Press, 1984).

8 G. W. F. Hegel, *Natural Law*, trans. T. M. Knox (Philadelphia: University of Pennsylvania Press, 1975), pp. 77–8.

9 See Jürgen Habermas, "Discourse Ethics: Notes on a Program of Philosophical Justification," *Moral Consciousness and Communicative Action*, trans. Christian Lenhardt and Shierry Weber Nicholsen (Cambridge: MIT Press, 1990), pp. 43–4; italics in the original.

10 Ibid., pp. 65–6.

11 Jean-François Lyotard, *The Differend: Phrases in Dispute*, trans. Georges van den Abbeele (Minneapolis: University of Minnesota Press, 1988), §12.

12 See Zygmunt Bauman, *Postmodern Ethics* (Oxford: Basil Blackwell, 1993), particularly Introduction; and *Life in Fragments: Essays in Postmodern Morality* (Oxford: Basil Blackwell, 1995), particularly Introduction. See also David Theo Goldberg, *Racist Culture: Philosophy and the Politics of Meaning* (Oxford: Basil Blackwell, 1993).

13 See the discussion of this in Joseph Margolis, *Interpretation Radical But Not Unrulv* (Berkeley: University of California Prec 1995), ch. 2.

14 On the formal relationship between universalism and historicism, see Joseph Margolis, *Pragmatism without Foundations Reconciling Realism and Relativism* (Oxford: Basil Blackwell, 1986).

15 Hans-Georg Gadamer, *Truth and Method*, trans. from 2nd edn Garrett Barden and John Cumming (New York: Seabury Press, 1975), pp. 244–5.

16 Ibid., pp. 246, 247.

17 Ibid., p. 250.

18 Ibid., p. 251; see also p. 249.

19 Ibid., p. 253.

20 Jürgen Habermas, "Morality and Ethical Life: Does Hegel's Critique of Kant Apply to Discourse Ethics?" *Moral Consciousness and Communicative Action*, p. 208, in the context of the entire essay. Elsewhere ("Discourse Ethics"), Habermas says: "Because morality is always embedded in what Hegel called ethical life (*Sittlichkeit*), discourse ethics is always subject to limitations, though not limitations that can devalue its crucial function or strengthen the skeptic in his role as an advocate of a counter-enlightenment" (p. 99).

21 Hans-Georg Gadamer, "The Universality of the Hermeneutical Problem," *Philosophical Hermeneutics*, trans. and ed. David E. Linge (Berkeley: University of California Press, 1976), p. 7.

22 Jürgen Habermas, *On the Logic of the Social Sciences*, trans. Shierry Weber Nicholsen and Jerry A. Stark (Cambridge: MIT Press, 1988), p. 144.

23 For a sustained discussion of Davidson's theories, see Joseph Margolis,

"Donald Davidson's Philosophical Strategies," in Carol C. Gould and Robert S. Cohen (eds) *Artifacts, Representations and Social Practice* (Dordrecht: Kluwer, 1994).

24 Donald Davidson, "On the Very Idea of a Conceptual Scheme," *Inquiries into Truth and Interpretation* (Oxford: Clarendon, 1984), p. 190.

25 See Ian Hacking, *Why Does Language Matter to Philosophy?* (Cambridge: Cambridge University Press, 1975), ch. 12, and "Language, Truth and Reason," in Martin Hollis and Steven Lukes (eds) *Rationality and Relativism* (Cambridge: MIT Press, 1982).

26 Alasdair MacIntyre, *Whose Justice? Which Rationality?* (Notre Dame: University of Notre Dame Press, 1988), pp. 169, 172.

27 Ibid., p. 172.

28 Ibid., p. 175.

29 Ibid., pp. 9–10.

30 Ibid., p. 9, read in the context of p. 10.

31 The counterargument I am resisting here is, of course, a classic ploy. You will find it trotted out most recently by Carl Page, *Philosophical Historicism and the Betrayal of First Philosophy* (University Park: Pennsylvania State University Press, 1995). Page directs it against my own advocacy of historicism (ch. 2), but he fails to grasp the possibility that the denial of a modal invariance is not itself the affirmation of another. There is reason to believe that the oversight is essential to all the philosophical strategies of the "Straussians" (the followers of Leo Strauss). See, further, Margolis, *Interpretation Radical But Not Unruly*, ch. 2.

32 Alasdair MacIntyre, *After Virtue*, 2nd edn (Notre Dame: University of Notre Dame Press, 1984), p. ix.

33 Ibid., p. x.

34 Ibid., p. ix.

35 Ibid., p. 278.

36 See Martha Nussbaum's review of Alasdair MacIntyre, *Whose Justice? Which Rationality?*, *New York Review of Books*, December 7, 1989.

37 MacIntyre, *After Virtue*. p. 203.

38 Ibid., p. 225.

39 Ibid.

40 Stuart Hampshire, *Thought and Action* (London: Chatto and Windus, 1959), p. 223.

41 See Zeno Vendler, "The Grammar of Goodness," *Linguistics in Philosophy* (Ithaca: Cornell University Press, 1967).

42 See William Connolly, "Beyond Good and Evil: The Ethical Sensibility of Michel Foucault," *Political Theory*, XXI (1993).

43 MacIntyre, After Virtue, p. 187.

44 Ibid., pp. 188–9

45 Ibid., p. 190.

46 Ibid., p. 191; italics in the original text.

47 There is a useful summary given in Annette C. Baier, *A Progress of*

Sentiments: Reflections On Hume's Treatise (Cambridge: Harvard University Press, 1991), ch. 9.

48 I show the full connection among the concepts of historicism, *praxis*, the artifactual nature of selves, the analysis of reference and predication along historicized lines, and the viability of relativism in my *Historied Thought. Constructed World: A Conceptual Primer at the Turn of the Millennium* (Berkeley: University of California Press, 1995); also, in my *Interpretation Radical But Not Unruly*.

49 See G. E. L. Owen, "'Tithenai ta phainomena'," *Logic, Science, and Dialectic: Collected Papers in Greek Philosophy*, ed. Martha Nussbaum (Ithaca: Cornell University Press, 1986).

50 Martha C. Nussbaum, *The Fragility of Goodness: Luck and Ethics in Greek Tragedy and Philosophy* (Cambridge: Cambridge University Press, 1986), pp. 245–6.

51 See Aristotle, *Nicomachean Ethics* (1142a), a passage Nussbaum translates in *The Fraaility of Goodness*, p. 305.

52 Nussbaum, *The Fragility of Goodness*, p. 302; see also pp. 303–5.

53 Ibid., p. 305; compare Aristotle. *Nicomachean Ethics* (1142a23), which she cites.

54 The term is due to Charles Sanders Peirce, who plays an almost unique role in American philosophy in attempting to clarify the logic of general predicates. I agree with Peirce's judgment that there must be "real generals" but I disagree fundamentally with his analysis of how that comes about. See, further, Joseph Margolis, "The Passing of Peirce's Realism," *Transactions of the Charles S. Peirce Society*, XXIX (1993).

55 See P. F. Pears, "Universals," *Philosophical Quarterly*, I (1951).

56 See, further, Renford Bambrough, "Universals and Family Resemblances," *Proceedings of the Aristotelian Society*, IX (1960–1).

57 For the full argument, see Margolis, *Historied Thought, Constructed World*. I take this to be the right elaboration of Wittgenstein's essential contribution. It is also related to Peirce's semiosis. But Peirce never quite abandons the doctrine of universals. See, also, my "The Passing of Peirce's Realism."

58 Nussbaum, *The Fragility of Goodness*, p. 304.

59 See, for an interesting comparison, Bas C. Van Fraassen, *Laws and Symmetry* (Oxford: Clarendon, 1989).

60 Aristotle, *Nicomachean Ethics*, 1137b. The translation is given by Nussbaum, in *The Fragility of Goodness*, p. 301.

61 Martha C. Nussbaum, "The Discernment of Perception: An Aristotelian Conception of Private and Public Rationality," *Love's Knowledge: Essays on Philosophy and Literature* (New York: Oxford University Press, 1990), p. 85.

62 Nussbaum, *Love's Knowledge*, p. 85.

63 Cited from Hilary Putnam, "Taking Rules Seriously: A Response to Martha Nussbaum," *New Literary History*, XV (1983), in Nussbaum, *Love's Knowledge*, p. 93. See also "Flawed Crystals: James's *The Golden Bowl* and

Literature as Moral Philosophy," *Love's Knowledge*, which offers an improved version of the thesis Putnam commented on.

64 Nussbaum, *Love's Knowledge*, pp. 94–5.

65 Karl-Otto Apel, "The *a priori* of the Communication Community and the Foundations of Ethics: The Problem of a Rational Foundation of Ethics in a Scientific Age," *Towards a Transformation of Philosophy*, trans. Glyn Adey and David Frisby (London: Routledge and Kegan Paul, 1980), pp. 280–1. Compare Robert Nozick, *Anarchy, State, and Utopia* (New York: Basic Books, 1974), pp. 157–158; also, Alan Donagan, *The Theory of Morality* (Chicago: University of Chicago Press, 1977), pp. 65–6.

66 See Wesley C. Salmon, *Scientific Explanation and the Causal Structure of the World* (Princeton: Princeton University Press, 1984), ch. 9.

67 Ibid., p. 18; italics in original.

68 Ibid., p. 16.

69 Ibid.

70 See ibid., pp. 18, 19.

71 See, however, Joseph Margolis, *The Flux of History and the Flux of Science* (Berkeley: University of California Press, 1993), ch. 4.

72 I give a full account of the general problem in my *The Truth about Relativism* (Oxford: Basil Blackwell, 1991) and an application, in interpretive contexts, in *Interpretation Radical But Not Unruly*. Ronald Dworkin considers the similarity between interpretation in literature and interpretation in constitutional law. He takes a very strong line (in "hard cases") even against pluralism; but this may have more to do with his view of the institution. In literary cases, he considers relenting; but again he views this more in terms of the nature of the "institution" then of the logic of interpretation. See Ronald Dworkin, *A Matter of Principle* (Cambridge: Harvard University Press, 1985), chs. 5–6.

73 I draw this from a recent paper of mine, "Plain Talk about Interpretation on a Relativistic Model," *Journal of Aesthetics and Art Criticism*, LIII (1995).

74 You will find a noticeably slack account of principles in Robert Nozick, *The Nature of Rationality* (Princeton: Princeton University Press, 1993), ch. 1. The reason is plain: valid principles presuppose a valid account of rationality; but if rationality is itself artifactually variable from one historical society to another, then principles cannot, logically, be modally necessary. This is why decision theory cannot but be contingent – however valuable. The general enthusiasm for decision theory often does not concede the point.

Epilogue: A Second-best Morality

1 Plato, *Statesman*, trans. J. B. Skemp, in *Plato: The Collected Dialogues*, ed. Edith Hamilton and Huntingdon Cairns (Princeton: Princeton University Press, 1961).

2 This is not the place to offer a specimen theory. But see, further, Joseph

Margolis, *Historied Thought, Constructed World: A Conceptual Primer at the Turn of the Millennium* (Berkeley: University of California Press, 1995).

3 I should like to mention the work of a friend of mine, Henry Hiz, along related lines. I have heard Hiz speak about *summum malum* in a formal presentation at the Greater Philadelphia Philosophy Consortium (I think it was in 1989), at the University of Pennsylvania. Hiz, I believe, regarded *summum malum* as a kind of fundamental moral intuition. I construe it in an altogether different way. But our sympathies converge, and I am glad to be able to draw attention to his fresh discussion of the idea. Hiz was very strongly impressed by the Nazi invasion of Poland and its meaning. I have no knowledge of Hiz's more recent work on the matter.

Bibliography

Albert, Hans. *Treatise on Critical Reason,* trans. Mary Varney Rorty (Princeton: Princeton University Press, 1985).

Alexy, Robert. "A Theory of Practical Discourse," in Seyla Benhabib and Fred Dallmayr (eds), *The Communicative Ethics Controversy* (Cambridge: MIT Press, 1990).

Altman, Andrew. *Critical Legal Studies: A Liberal Critique* (Princeton: Princeton University Press, 1990).

Apel, Karl-Otto. "From Kant to Peirce: The Semiotical Transformation of Transcendental Logic," *Towards a Transformation of Philosophy,* trans. Glyn Adey and David Frisby (London: Routledge and Kegan Paul, 1980).

Apel, Karl-Otto. "The *a priori* of the Communication Community and the Foundations of Ethics: The Problem of a Rational Foundation of Ethics in a Scientific Age," *Towards a Transformation of Philosophy,* trans. Glyn Adey and David Frisby (London: Routledge and Kegan Paul, 1980).

Apel, Karl-Otto. *Charles S. Peirce: From Pragmatism to Pragmaticism,* trans. John Michael Krois (Amherst: University of Massachusetts Press, 1981).

Apel, Karl-Otto. The Transformation of Transcendental Philosophy," *Understanding and Explanation: A Transcendental-Pragmatic Perspective,* trans. Georgia Warnke (Cambridge: MIT Press, 1984).

Apel, Karl-Otto. "The Problem of Philosophical Foundations in Light of a Transcendental Pragmatics of Language" (modified), trans. Karl

Richard Pavlovic (modified), in *After Philosophy*, eds Kenneth Baynes, James Bohman, and Thomas McCarthy (Cambridge: MIT Press, 1987).

Apel, Karl-Otto. "Is the Ethics of the Ideal Communication Community a Utopia? On the Relationship between Ethics, Utopia, and the Critique of Utopia," in Seyla Benhabib and Fred Dallmayr (eds), *The Communicative Ethics Controversy* (Cambridge, Mass.: MIT Press, 1990).

Aristotle. *Metaphysics*, trans. W. D. Ross, in *The Complete Works of Aristotle (The Revised Oxford Translation)*, Vol. 2, ed. Jonathan Barnes (Princeton: Princeton University Press, 1984).

Aristotle. *On the Soul (De Anima)*, trans. S. A. Smith, in *The Complete Works of Aristotle (The Revised Oxford Translation)*, Vol. 1, ed. Jonathan Barnes (Princeton: Princeton University Press, 1984).

Aristotle. *Nicomachean Ethics*, trans. W. D. Ross (revised J. O. Urmson), in *The Complete Works of Aristotle (The Revised Oxford Translation)*, Vol. 2, ed. Jonathan Barnes (Princeton: Princeton University Press, 1984).

Aristotle. *Posterior Analytics*, trans. Jonathan Barnes, in *The Complete Works of Aristotle (The Revised Oxford Translation)*, Vol. 1, ed. Jonathan Barnes (Princeton: Princeton University Press, 1984).

Ayer, A. J. *Russell and Moore: The Analytical Heritage* (Cambridge, Mass.: Harvard University Press, 1971).

Baier, Annette C. *A Progress of Sentiments: Reflections on Hume's Treatise* (Cambridge, Mass. Harvard University Press, 1991).

Bambrough, Renford. "Universals and Family Resemblances," *Proceedings of the Aristotelian Society*, IX (1960–1).

Bauman, Zygmunt. *Postmodern Ethics* (Oxford: Basil Blackwell, 1993).

Bauman, Zygmunt. *Life in Fragments: Essays in Postmodern Morality* (Oxford: Basil Blackwell, 1995).

Berlin, Isaiah. "The Pursuit of the Ideal," *The Crooked Timber of Humanity* (New York: Knopf, 1991).

Bernstein, Richard J. *Praxis and Action: Contemporary Philosophies of Human Activity* (Philadelphia: University of Pennsylvania Press, 1971).

Bernstein, Richard J. *Beyond Objectivism and Relativism: Science, Hermeneutics, and Praxis* (Philadelphia: University of Pennsylvania Press, 1983).

Bernstein, Richard J. *The New Constellation: The Ethical Political Horizons of Modernity/Postmodernity* (Cambridge. MIT Press, 1991).

Blackburn, Simon. *Essays in Quasi-Realism* (New York: Oxford University Press, 1993).

Boyd, Richard N. "How to be a Moral Realist," in Geoffrey Sayre-McCord (ed.), *Essays n Moral Realism* (Ithaca: Cornell University Press, 1988).

Campbell, James. *Understanding John Dewey: Nature and Cooperative Intelligence* (La Salle: Open Court, 1995).

Connolly, William. "Beyond Good and Evil: The Ethical Sensibility of Michel Foucault," *Political Theory*, XXI (1993).

Davidson, Donald. "Mental Events," *Essays on Actions and Events* (Oxford: Clarendon, 1980).

Davidson, Donald. "On the Very Idea of a Conceptual Scheme," *Inquiries into Truth and Interpretation* (Oxford: Clarendon, 1984).

Davidson, Donald. "A Coherence Theory of Truth and Knowledge," in Ernest LePore (ed.), *Truth and Interpretation: Perspectives on the Philosophy of Donald Davidson* (Oxford: Basil Blackwell, 1986).

Dewey, John. *Reconstruction in Philosophy*, enlarged ed (Boston: Beacon Press, 1957).

Donagan, Alan. *The Theory of Morality* (Chicago: University of Chicago Press, 1979).

Dummett, Michael. *Truth and Other Enigmas* (Cambridge, Mass.: Harvard University Press, 1978).

Dworkin, Ronald. *A Matter of Principle* (Cambridge, Mass.: Harvard University Press, 1985).

Dworkin, Ronald. "Pornography, Feminism, and Liberty," *New York Review of Books*, August 18, 1991.

Earman, John. "Carnap, Kuhn, and the Philosophy of Scientific Methodology,' in Paul Horwich (ed.), *World Change: Thomas Kuhn and the Nature of Science* (Cambridge, Mass.: MIT Press, 1993).

Feyerabend, Paul. *Against Method* (London: Verso, 1975).

Fine, Arthur. *The Shaky Game: Einstein. Realism. and the Quantum Theory* (Chicago: University of Chicago Press, 1986).

Fink, Eugen. *Sixth Cartesian Meditation: The Idea of a Transcendental Theory of Method*, trans. Ronald Bruzina (Bloomington: Indiana University Press, 1993).

Flower, Elizabeth and Murray G. Murphey. *A History of Philosophy in America*, Vol. 2 (New York: G. P. Putnam, 1977).

Foucault, Michel. *The Order of Things*, trans. (New York: Vintage, 1970).

Foucault, Michel. *The Archaeology of Knowledge*, trans. A. M. Sheridan Smith (New York: Harper and Row, 1972).

Foucault, Michel. "Nietzsche, Genealogy, History," *Language, Counter-Memory, Practice: Selected Essays and Interviews*, ed. Donald F.

Bouchard, trans. Donald F. Bouchard and Sherry Simon (Ithaca: Cornell University Press, 1977).

Gadamer, Hans-Georg. *Truth and Method*, trans. from 2nd edn Garrett Barden and John Cumming (New York: Seabury Press, 1975).

Gadamer, Hans-Georg. "The Universality of the Hermeneutical Problem," *Philosophical Hermeneutics*, trans. and ed. David E. Linge (Berkeley: University of California Press, 1976)

Gagnon, Madeleine. "Body I," in Elaine Marks and Isabelle de Courtivron (eds), *New French Feminisms* (Amherst: University of Massachusetts Press, 1980).

Garver, Newton. "Naturalism and Transcendentality: The Case of 'Form of Life'," in Souren Teghrarian (ed), *Wittgenstein and Contemporary Philosophy* (Bristol: Thoemmes Press, 1994).

Garver, Newton and Seung-Chong Lee. *Derrida and Wittgenstein* (Philadelphia: Temple University Press, 1994)

Gewirth, Alan. *Reason and Morality* (Chicago: University of Chicago Press, 1978).

Goldberg, David Theo. *Racist Culture: Philosophy and the Politics of Meaning* (Oxford: Basil Blackwell, 1993).

Goldman, Alvin I. *Liaisons: Philosophy Meets the Cognitive and Social Sciences* (Cambridge, Mass.: MIT Press, 1992).

Habermas, Jürgen. "What is Universal Pragmatics?" *Communication and the Evolution of Society*, trans. Thomas McCarthy (Boston: Beacon, 1979).

Habermas, Jürgen. *On the Logic of the Social Sciences*, trans. Shierry Weber Nicholsen and Jerry A. Stark (Cambridge, Mass.: MIT Press, 1988).

Habermas, Jürgen. "Discourse Ethics: Notes on a Program of Philosophical Justification," *Moral Consciousness and Communicative Action*, trans. Christian Lenhardt and Shierry Weber Nicholsen (Cambridge, Mass.: MIT Press, 1990).

Habermas, Jürgen. "Moral Consciousness and Communicative Action," *Moral Consciousness and Communicative Action*, trans. Christian Lenhardt and Shierry Weber Nicholsen (Cambridge, MAss.: MIT Press, 1990).

Habermas, Jürgen. "Morality and Ethical Life: Does Hegel's Critique of Kant Apply to Discourse Ethics?" *Moral Consciousness and Communicative Action*, trans. Christian Lenhardt and Shierry Weber Nicholsen (Cambridge, Mass.: MIT Press, 1990) .

Hacking, Ian. *Why Does Language Matter to Philosophy?* (Cambridge: Cambridge University Press, 1975).

Hacking, Ian. "Language, Truth and Reason," in Martin Hollis and

Steven Lukes (eds), *Rationality and Relativism* (Cambridge, Mass.: MIT Press, 1982).

Hacking, Ian. *Representing and Intervening: Introductory Topics in the Philosophy of Natural Science* (Cambridge: Cambridge University Press, 1983).

Hacking, Ian. *Rewriting the Soul: Multiple Personality and the Science of Memory* (Princeton: Princeton University Press, 1995).

Hampshire, Stuart. *Thought and Action* (London: Chatto and Windus, 1959).

Haraway, Donna J. *Simians. Cyborgs and Women: The Reinvention of Nature* (New York: Routledge, 1991).

Hare, Richard M. *Freedom and Reason* (Oxford: Clarendon, 1963).

Hausman, Carl R. *Charles S. Peirce's Evolutionary Philosophy* (Cambridge: Cambridge University Press, 1993).

Hegel, G. W. F. *Philosophy of Right*, trans. T.M. Knox (Oxford: Clarendon, 1952).

Hegel, G. W. F. *Natural Law*, trans. T. M. Knox (Philadelphia: Univeristy of Pennsylvania Press, 1975).

Hume, David. *A Treatise of Human Nature*, ed. L. A. Selby-Bigge (Oxford: Clarendon, 1888).

Husserl, Edmund. *Cartesian Meditations: An Introduction to Phenomenology*, trans. Dorion Cairns (The Hague: Martinus Nijhoff, 1960).

Kant, Immanuel. *Immanuel Kants Werke*, herausg. Ernst Cassirer: Band IX (*Briefe von und an Kant*. Erster Teil, 1744-1789) (Berlin: Bruno Cassirer, 1918).

Kant, Immanuel . *Immanuel Kant's Critique of Pure Reason*, trans. (with corrections) Norman Kemp Smith (London: Macmillan, 1933).

Kant, Immanuel. *Kant's Concept of Practical Reason and Other Writings in Moral Philosophy*, trans. Lewis White Beck (Chicago: University of Chicago Press, 1949).

Kant, Immanuel. *Foundations of the Metaphysics of Morals*, trans. Lewis White Beck (New York: Liberal Arts Press, 1959).

Kant, Immanuel. *Lectures on Ethics*, trans. Louis Infeld (Indianapolis: Hackett Publishing, 1963).

Kant, Immanuel. *Grounding for the Metaphysics of Morals*, trans. James W. Ellington, in *Immanuel Kant: Ethical Philosophy* (Indianapolis: Hackett Publishing, 1983).

Kenny, A. J. P. *The Aristotelian Ethics* (Oxford: Clarendon, 1978).

Kim, Jaegwon. *Supervenience and Mind: Selected Philosophical Essays* (Cambridge: Cambridge University Press, 1993).

Kosík, Karel. *Dialectics of the Concrete: A Study on Problems of Man and World*, trans. Karel Kovanda and James Schmidt (Dordrecht: D. Reidel, 1976).

Kripke, Saul A. *Wittgenstein on Rules and Private Language: An Elementary Exposition* (Cambridge, Mass.: Harvard University Press, 1982).

Kuhn, Thomas S. *The Structure of Scientific Revolutions*, 2nd edn (Chicago: University of Chicago Press, 1970).

Lakatos, Imre. "Falsification and the Methodology of Scientific Research Programmes," *Philosophical Papers*, Vol. I (Cambridge: Cambridge University Presss 1978).

Latour, Bruno. *We have Never Been Modern*, trans. Catherine Porter (Cambridge, Mass.: Harvard University Press, 1993).

Lovibond, Sabina. *Realism and Imagination in Ethics* (Minneapolis: University of Minnesota Press, 1983).

Löwith, Karl. *From Hegel to Nietzsche: The Revolution in Nineteenth-Century Thought*, trans. David E. Green (New York: Columbia University Press, 1991).

Lyotard, Jean-François. *The Postmodern Condition: A Report on Knowledge*, trans. Geoff Bennington and Brian Massumi (Minneapolis: University of Minnesota Press, 1984).

Lyotard, Jean-François. *The Differend: Phrases in Dispute*, trans. Georges van den Abbeele (Minneapolis: University of Minnesota Press, 1988).

McDowell, John. "Values and Secondary Qualities," in Ted Honderich (ed.), *Morality and Objectivity* (London: Routledge and Kegan Paul, 1985).

MacIntyre, Alasdair. *After Virtue*, 2nd edn (Notre Dame: University of Notre Dame Press, 1984).

MacIntyre, Alasdair. *Whose Justice? Which Rationality?* (Notre Dame: University of Notre Dame Press, 1988).

Mackie, J. L. *Ethics: Inventing Right and Wrong* (Harmondsworth: Penguin, 1977).

MacKinnon, Catherine A. *Toward a Feminist Theory of the State* (Cambridge, Mass.: Harvard University Press, 1989).

MacKinnon, Catherine A. *Only Words* (Cambridge, Mass.: Harvard University Press, 1993).

Margolis, Joseph. *Values and Conduct* (Oxford: Clarendon, 1971).

Margolis, Joseph. *Culture and Cultural Entities: Toward a New Unity of Science* (Dordrecht: D. Reidel, 1984).

Margolis, Joseph. *Pragmatism without Foundations: Reconciling Realism and Relativism* (Oxford: Basil Blackwell, 1986).

Margolis, Joseph. *Texts without Referents: Reconciling the Natural and Human Sciences* (Oxford: Basil Blackwell, 1989).

Margolis, Joseph. *The Truth about Relativism* (Oxford: Basil Blackwell, 1991).

Margolis, Joseph. "Praxis and Meaning: Marx's Species Being and Aristotle's Political Animal," in George F. McCarthy (ed.), *Marx and Aristotle: Nineteenth-Century German Social Thought and Classical Antiquity* (Savage, MD: Rowman and Littlefield, 1992).

Margolis, Joseph. *The Flux of History and the Flux of Science* (Berkeley: University of California Press, 1993).

Margolis, Joseph. The Passing of Peirce's Realism," *Transactions of the Charles S. Peirce Society*, XXIX (1993).

Margolis, Joseph. "Donald Davidson's Philosophical Strategies," in Carol C. Gould and Robert S. Cohen (eds), *Artifacts, Representations and Social Practice* (Dordrecht: Kluwer, 1994).

Margolis, Joseph. "A Biopsy of Recent American Philosophy," *Philosophical Forum*, XXVI (1995).

Margolis, Joseph. "The Meaning of Thomas Kuhn's 'Different Worlds'," in Kostas Gavroglu et al. (eds), *Science. Mind and Art* (Dordrecht: Kluwer, 1995).

Margolis, Joseph. *Historied Thought, Constructed World: A Conceptual Primer at the Turn of the Millennium* (Berkeley: University of California Press, 1995).

Margolis, Joseph. *Interpretation Radical But Not Unruly: The New Problem of the Arts and History* (Berkeley: University of California Press, 1995).

Margolis, Joseph. "Philosophy in the 'New' Rhetoric, Rhetoric in the 'New' Philosophy," in Steven Mailloux (ed.), *Rhetoric, Sophistry, Pragmatism* (Cambridge: Cambridge University Press, 1995).

Margolis, Joseph. "Plain Talk about Interpretation on a Relativistic Model," *Journal of Aesthetics and Art Criticism*, LIII (1995).

Mendus, Susan. *Toleration and the Limits of Liberalism* (Atlantic Highlands: Humanities, 1989).

Nāgārjuna. *The Philosophy of the Middle Way*, trans. David J. Kalupahana (Albany: SUNY Press, 1986).

Nagel, Thomas. *The View from Nowhere* (New York: Oxford University Press, 1986).

Nietzsche, Friedrich. "On the Uses and Disadvantages of History for Life," *Untimely Meditations*, trans. R J. Hollingdale (Cambridge: Cambridge University Press, 1983).

Nozick, Robert. *Anarchy. State and Utopia* (New York: Basic Books, 1974).

Nozick, Robert. *The Nature of Rationality* (Princeton: Princeton University Press, 1993).

Nussbaum, Martha C. *The Fragility of Goodness: Luck and Ethics in Greek Tragedy and Philosophy* (Cambridge: Cambridge Universitv Press, 1986).

Nussbaum, Martha C.. Review of Alasdair MacIntyre, *Whose Justice? Which Rationality? New York Review of Books*, December 7, 1989.

Nussbaum, Martha C. "The Discernment of Perception: An Aristotelian Conception of Private and Public Rationality," *Love's Knowledge: Essays on Philosophy and Literature* (New York: Oxford University Press, 1990).

Nussbaum, Martha C. "Flawed Crystals: James's *The Golden Bowl* and Literature as Moral Philosophy," *Love's Knowledge: Essays on Philosophy and Literature* (New York: Oxford University Press, 1990).

Owen, G. E. L. "'Tithenai ta phainomena'," *Logic, Science, and Dialectic: Collected Papers in Greek Philosophy*, ed. Martha Nussbaum (Ithaca: Cornell University Press, 1986).

Page, Carl. *Philosophical Historicism and the Betrayal of First Philosophy* (University Park: Pennsylvania State Press, 1995).

Pears, P. F. "Universals," *Philosophical Quarterly*, I (1951).

Peirce, Charles S. *Collected Papers of Charles Sanders Peirce*, 8 vols, eds Charles Hartshorne, Paul Weiss, and Arthur W. Burks (Cambridge, Mass.: Harvard University Press, 1931–58).

Peters, R. S. *Ethics and Education* (London: Allen and Unwin, 1974).

Plato, *Statesman*, trans. J. B. Skemp, in *Plato: The Collected Dialogues*, ed. Edith Hamilton and Huntingdon Cairns (Princeton: Princeton University Press, 1961).

Platts, Mark de Bretton. "Moral Reality," *Ways of Meaning: An Introduction to a Philosophy of Language* (London: Routledge and Kegan Paul, 1979).

Platts, Mark. "Moral Reality and the End of Desire," in Mark Platts (ed.), *Reference, Truth and Reality: Essays on the Philosophy of Language* (London: Routledge and Kegan Paul, 1980).

Popper, Karl R. "Normal Science and Its Dangers," in Imre Lakatos and Alan Musgrave (eds), *Criticism and the Growth of Knowledge* (Cambridge: Cambridge University Press, 1970).

Popper, Karl R. "Of Clouds and Clocks," *Objective Knowledge: An Evolutionary Approach* (Oxford: Clarendon, 1972).

Poster, Mark. *Foucault, Marxism and History: Mode of Production versus Mode of Information* (London: Polity Press, 1984).

Putnam, Hilary. The Logic of Quantum Mechanics," *Philosophical Papers*, Vol. 1 (Cambridge: Cambridge University Press, 1975).

Putnam, Hilary. "What is Mathematical Truth?" *Philosophical Papers*, Vol. 1 (Cambridge: Cambridge University Press, 1975).

Putnam, Hilary. *Meaning and the Moral Sciences* (London: Routledge and Kegan Paul, 1978).

Putnam, Hilary. *Reason, Truth and History* (Cambridge: Cambridge University Press, 1981).

Putnam, Hilary. "Models and Reality," *Philosophical Papers*, Vol. 3 (Cambridge: Cambridge University Press, 1983).

Putnam, Hilary. "Reference and Truth," *Philosophical Papers*, Vol. 3 (Cambridge: Cambridge University Press, 1983).

Putnam, Hilary. "Taking Rules Seriously: A Response to Martha Nussbaum," *New Literary History*, XV (1983).

Putnam, Hilary. *The Many Faces of Realism* (La Salle: Open Court, 1987).

Putnam, Hilary. *Realism with a Human Face*, ed. James Conant (Cambridge, Mass.: Harvard University Press, 1990).

Putnam, Hilary. "Materialism and Relativism," *Renewing Philosophy* (Cambridge, Mass.: Harvard University Press, 1992).

Putnam, Hilary. "A Reconstruction of Deweyan Democracy," *Renewing Philosophy* (Cambridge, Mass.: Harvard University Press, 1992).

Putnam, Hilary. "Beyond Historicism," *Philosophical Papers*, Vol. 3 (Cambridge: Cambridge University Press, 1983).

Quine, W. V. "Two Dogmas of Empiricism," *From a Logical Point of View* (Cambridge, Mass.: Harvard University Press, 1953).

Quine, W. V. *Word and Object* (Cambridge, Mass.: MIT Press, 1960).

Quine, W. V. "Epistemology Naturalized," *Ontological Relativity and Other Essays* (New York: Columbia University Press, 1969).

Quine, W. V. *Pursuit of Truth*, revd edn (Cambridge, Mass.: Harvard University Press, 1992).

Railton, Peter. "Moral Realism," *Philosophical Review*, (1986).

Rawls, John. *A Theory of Justice* (Cambridge: Harvard University Press, 1970).

Rawls, John. *Political Liberalism* (New York: Columbia University Press, 1991).

Rhees, Rush. "Some Developments in Wittgenstein's View of Ethics," *Philosophical Review*, LXXVII (1965).

Rorty, Richard. *Philosophy and the Mirror of Nature* (Princeton: Princeton University Press, 1979).

Rorty, Richard. "Pragmatism, Davidson and Truth," in Ernest LePore (ed.), *Truth and Interpretation: Perspectives on the Philosophy of Donald Davidson* (Oxford: Basil Blackwell, 1986).

Rorty, Richard. The Primacy of Democracy in Philosophy," in Robert Vaughan (ed.), *The Virginia State of Religious Freedom Two Hundred Years After* (Madison: University of Wisconsin Press, 1988).

Rorty, Richard. "Private Irony and Liberal Hope," *Contingency, Irony, and Solidarity* (Cambridge: Cambridge University Press, 1989)

Rorty, Richard. "Habermas and Lyotard on Postmodernity," *Philosophical Papers*, Vol. 2 (Cambridge: Cambridge University Press, 1991).

Rorty, Richard. "Science as Solidarity," *Philosophical Papers*, Vol. 1 (Cambridge: Cambridge University Press, 1991).

Rorty, Richard. "Putnam and the Relativist Menace," *Journal of Philosophy*, XC (1993).

Rylton, Peter. *Russell, Idealism and the Emergence of Analytic Philosophy* (Oxford: Clarendon, 1990).

Salmon, Wesley C. *Scientific Explanation and the Causal Structure of the World* (Princeton: Princeton University Press, 1984).

Sandel, Michael J. *Liberalism and the Limits of Justice* (Cambridge: Cambridge University Press, 1982).

Sayre-McCord, Geoffrey (ed.). *Essays on Moral Realism* (Ithaca: Cornell University Press, 1988).

Schilpp, Paul Arthur (ed.). *The Philosophy of G. E. Moore* (Chicago: Open Court, 1942).

Shoemaker, Sydney. *Self-Knowledge and Self-Identity* (Ithaca: Cornell University Press, 1963).

Sokolowski, Robert. *Moral Action: A Phenomenological Study* (Bloomington: Indiana University Press, 1985).

Stachel, John. "Comments on 'Some Logical Problems Suggested by Some Empirical Theories' by Professor Dalla Chiara," in Robert S. Cohen and Marx W. Wartofsky (eds), *Language, Logic. and Method* (Dordrecht: D. Reidel, 1983).

Strawson, P. F. "Ethical Intuitionism," *Philosophy*, XXIV (1949).

Taylor, Charles. "Philosophy and its History," in Richard Rorty, J. P. Schneewind, and Quentin Skinner (eds), *Philosophy in History: Essays on the Historiography of Philosophy* (Cambridge: Cambridge University Press, 1984).

Taylor, Charles. *Sources of the Self: The Making of the Modern Identity* (Cambridge, Mass.: Harvard University Press, 1989).

Taylor, Richard. *Good and Evil* (New York: Macmillan, 1970).

Toulmin, Stephen E. *Cosmopolis: The Hidden Agenda of Modernism* (New York: Free Press, 1990).

Tribe, Lawrence. "Constitution as Point of View," mimeograph (Harvard Law School, 1982).

Unger, Roberto Mangabeira. *Social Theory: Its Situation and its Task* (Cambridge: Cambridge University Press, 1987).

Unger, Roberto Mangabeira. *False Necessity – Anti-Necessitarian Social Theory in the Service of Radical Democracy (Part I of Politics: A Work in Constructive Social Theory)* (Cambridge: Cambridge University Press, 1987).

Van Fraassen, Bas C. *Laws and Symmetry* (Oxford: Clarendon, 1989).

Vendler, Zeno, "The Grammar of Goodness," *Linguistics in Philosophy* (Ithaca: Cornell University Press, 1967).

Waismann, Friedrich, "Notes on Talks with Wittgenstein," *Philosophical Review*, LXXVII (1965).

Watt, A. J. "Transcendental Arguments and Moral Principles," Philosophical Quarterly, XXV (1975).

Wiggins, David. "Postscript," *Needs, Values, Truth*, 2nd edn (Oxford: Basil Blackwell, 1991).

Wiggins, David. "Truth, Invention, and the Meaning of Life," *Needs, Values, Truth*, 2nd edn (Oxford: Basil Blackwell, 1991) .

Wiggins, David. "Truth, and Truth Predicted of Moral Judgements," *Needs, Values, Truth,* 2nd edn. (Oxford: Basil Blackwell, 1991).

Williams, Bernard. "Moral Standards and the Distinguishing Mark of Man," *Morality: An Introduction to Ethics* (New York: Harper and Row, 1972).

Williams, Bernard. *Ethics and the Limits of Philosophy* (Cambridge, Mass.: Harvard University Press, 1985).

Williams, Bernard. *Shame and Necessity* (Berkeley: University of California Press, 1993).

Wittgenstein, Ludwig. *Philosophical Investigations*, trans. G. E. M. Anscombe (New York: Macmillan, 1953).

Wittgenstein, Ludwig. *Tractatus Logico-Philosophicus*, trans. (with corrections) D. C. Pears and B. F. McGuinness (London: Routledge and Kegan Paul, 1961).

Wittgenstein, Ludwig. "Lecture on Ethics," *Philosophical Review*, LXXVII (1965).

Wittgenstein, Ludwig. *Remarks on the Foundations of Mathematics*, 3rd edn, trans. G. E. M. Anscombe, ed. G. H. von Wright, R. Rhees, G. E. M. Anscombe (Oxford: Basil Blackwell, 1978).

Wood, Allen W. *Hegel's Ethical Thought* (Cambridge: Cambridge University Press, 1990).

Index

Index